MATCH OF THE DAY FOOTBALL ALMANAC

Six Decades of Trophies, Tournaments, and Timeless Moments

Nick Constable

BBC
BOOKS

1

BBC Books, an imprint of Ebury Publishing
Penguin Random House UK
One Embassy Gardens, 8 Viaduct Gdns,
Nine Elms, London SW11 7BW

BBC Books is part of the Penguin Random House group of companies
whose addresses can be found at global.penguinrandomhouse.com

Penguin
Random House
UK

Main text by Nick Constable
Foreword © Gary Lineker 2024
Copyright © BBC Books 2024

Illustrations: Shutterstock

First published by BBC Books in 2024

BBC Books would like to thank Phil Bigwood, Paul Armstrong, Richard Armstrong
and Sam Finkelstein for their help in creating this book.

www.penguin.co.uk

A CIP catalogue record for this book is available from the British Library

ISBN 9781785949166

Commissioning Editor: Phoebe Lindsley
Editorial Assistant: Celine Nyssens
Design: seagulls.net
Production: Antony Heller

Printed and bound in Great Britain by Clays Ltd, Elcograf S.p.A.

The authorised representative in the EEA is Penguin Random House Ireland,
Morrison Chambers, 32 Nassau Street, Dublin D02 YH68.

Penguin Random House is committed to a sustainable future for our business, our readers
and our planet. This book is made from Forest Stewardship Council® certified paper.

CONTENTS

FOREWORD
BY GARY LINEKER

At 3:00pm on 22 August 1964, a 21-year-old centre forward, Phil Chisnall, kicked off for Liverpool against Arsenal. He knew *Match of the Day* cameras were present and that for the first time he would be able to watch an hour of recorded action later. But he could not possibly have known that, with one touch of a football, he would launch a sporting and broadcasting icon. No other sports programme has embraced the nation's psyche so definitively, and while the term 'national treasure' is often bandied about, it is a title deservedly applied to MOTD.

I was only three when that Anfield game was aired, and like at least two generations of football fans I have grown up with the show. It is a rite of passage in which memories rarely fade. That first Saturday night on the sofa when you were deemed old enough to stay up and watch; the agonising temptation to listen to full-time results in advance; your heroes strutting their stuff in your own front room; and the following morning in the park as you re-enacted that screamer of a goal. Even today, with TV channels awash with live football, there is something about MOTD that continues to draw fans back every weekend.

The reasons may seem straightforward. Goals and controversies are big attractions in themselves. But the formula has survived for 60 years for the best part as a result of the passion, commitment and attention to detail of all involved – from the commentators and outside broadcast teams to the editors, technicians, set designers and those of us in front of the camera who strive to provide added value in the form of analysis, talking points and – of course – a touch of humour.

I have had the great fortune of presenting MOTD for 25 years, dearly loving every minute I have been on-air. The shape of each year has been marked by the footballing season, from dramatic debuts in August to thrilling title races and relegation battles the following spring. This book looks back and tells the story of *Match of the Day* – which is the story of football, really – through the highs and lows of each month in the football season.

It has not always been plain sailing. Take the rise of social media in recent times, where goals are available instantly, conveniently on your phone. Some might have said that the era of MOTD was over. Yet, the show goes on, and *Match of the Day* has quite rightly remained at the heart of our footballing week – created by football fans, for football fans. I hope this is because our audience feels, rightly, that it belongs to them. You get a hint of that with the disgruntled feedback we receive if someone's team is on last – AGAIN – or if Alan has dismissed a crucial penalty decision as 'soft'. Everyone likes to hear praise for their club's performance and there is nothing like watching top players win. But, even when your side loses, we try to offer fair criticism, an arm around the shoulder and a smidgeon of hope when all looks lost. At least there is always next weekend!

So, happy sixtieth, MOTD. Always changing, always the same.

TEAM NAME ABBREVIATIONS

ARS	Arsenal
AVA	Aston Villa
AWM/MKD*	AFC Wimbledon/Milton Keynes Dons
BBR	Blackburn Rovers
BDC	Bradford City
BOL	Bolton Wanderers
BOU	AFC Bournemouth
BSC	Bristol City
BUR	Burnley
CDF	Cardiff City
CHA	Charlton Athletic
CHE	Chelsea
CRY	Crystal Palace
CVC	Coventry City
DRB	Derby County
EVE	Everton
FUL	Fulham
IPS	Ipswich Town
LEE	Leeds United
LEI	Leicester City
LIV	Liverpool
LUT	Luton Town
MCI	Manchester City
MID	Middlesbrough
MUN	Manchester United
NEW	Newcastle United
NOR	Norwich City
NTG	Nottingham Forest
OAT	Oldham Athletic
PTM	Portsmouth
QPR	Queens Park Rangers
RDG	Reading
SHU	Sheffield United
SOU	Southampton
SUN	Sunderland
SWA	Swansea City
TOT	Tottenham Hotspur
WAT	Watford
WBA	West Bromwich Albion
WHU	West Ham United
WIG	Wigan Athletic
WLV	Wolverhampton Wanderers

* Wimbledon FC moved grounds and officially became Milton Keynes Dons in 2004. AFC Wimbledon was founded by supporters in 2002 to save a Wimbledon-based club.

AUGUST:
DEBUT DAYS

It's late summer. Deprived of league games for three months, the loyal fan has taken solace in febrile media gossip about who's signing who, who's splashing the cash and whether that wantaway star striker really does wantaway or simply has an agent who does. Now, finally, it's the opening day of the new season: a time to cast aside the disappointments (there are always disappointments) of last season, forget the eyeball-popping season ticket bill, snap on the lucky underpants and head for the game with a choice chant on the lips and a rock-hard pie in the hand.

In those final hours before kick-off there's a genuine feeling of anticipation and hope, much of which rests on the success of the summer signings. A decent debut lifts both fans and players while giving the reassuring impression that the manager has a masterplan on the road to glory. Whereas a dog of a debut – especially where the player has signed for top dollar – is immediately filed under 'disappointments'.

So, we kick off August with a team's worth of dream debuts. If that sounds too positive, fear not. Glass-half-empty fans will be getting their fix through a horror debuts XI straight afterwards. Whatever your football psyche though, there's only one place to start: Selhurst Park, 1992, the opening day of the new Premier League and the debut of *MOTD*'s very own Alan Shearer for Blackburn Rovers.

THE DREAM DEBUT XI

1 15 August 1992: Crystal Palace 3-3 Blackburn Rovers (Alan Shearer)

Shearer came into this game following a summer of intense newspaper speculation about his future club. Southampton had placed a £3.4 million price tag on him and while that might seem loose change in comparison to today's market, at the time it broke the English transfer record and was enough to see off interest from Sir Alex Ferguson at Manchester United. Palace fans were therefore desperate to see Shearer fluff one, while the Rovers contingent were unsure why chairman Jack Walker had pulled quite so much from out of the back of his sofa. There was also added pressure for Blackburn – this was their first game back in the top-flight after a 26-year absence.

Things started well for the Riversiders when their other new signing – winger Stuart Ripley – cancelled out Mark Bright's early goal with a flicked header. Palace took the lead again through a cracking volley from future England manager Gareth Southgate, but then on 67 minutes Shearer unleashed a viciously dipping half-volley from 20 yards out. *MOTD* commentator Tony Gubba takes up the story:

> Fantastic goal from Alan Shearer. That's what the
> money was for and that's the sort of goal to ease the
> pressures of that £3.4 million price tag. A goal out of
> nothing. After 67 minutes Palace are stunned. Both the
> Blackburn new boys have now scored on their debuts.

And then:

> Can he do it again? Oh, he can. Two in the space of
> 15 minutes. Right out of the top drawer. He kisses the
> shirt and it may well have been a shirt of a different
> colour but the other clubs thought £3.4 million was
> too much to pay and that's what they've missed.

Palace's equaliser in the dying seconds can hardly have
dampened the mood on the trek back up the M1. Shearer
ended his first season with 16 league goals, despite serious
injury, and went on to net an astonishing 34 in 43 games
to help Rovers take the title in 1995. He remains the record
Premier League scorer, with 260 goals, which suggests
£3.4 million was not bad business for Blackburn.

That Selhurst Park match was not even Shearer's first top-
flight dream debut. In 1988 he was a promising Southampton
youth team player, spotted four years earlier while playing for
Wallsend Boys Club, Newcastle. He'd come on as a sub for
Saints' first team a couple of times but on the morning of
9 April wasn't expecting to make his full debut against sixth-
placed visitors Arsenal. Then, as he tucked into a pre-match
meal, manager Chris Nicholl suddenly appeared alongside
with the words: 'You're playing. You're in.' Not a bad
decision. With the game five minutes old, Shearer nodded
in the opener, added a second header after 20 minutes and

completed his hat-trick on 49 minutes from inside the six-yard box. Aged 17 years and 240 days, it was the goal which broke Jimmy Greaves' record – also set on debut in 1961 – as the youngest player to score an English top-flight hat-trick.

2 20 August 1994: Sheffield Wednesday 3-4 Tottenham Hotspur (Jürgen Klinsmann)

Jürgen Klinsmann joined Spurs from Monaco for £2 million in the summer of 1994, reportedly lured to the club during a 'cappuccino offensive' aboard club chairman Alan Sugar's yacht in Monte Carlo harbour. It was a controversial signing – not because Klinsmann's abilities as a world-class striker were in any doubt – rather that he could be somewhat theatrical in the tackle. English fans well remembered the moment in the turgid Italia '90 World Cup final when Argentina's Pedro Monzón scythed him down in an admittedly dreadful studs-up tackle. Jürgen responded by leaping into the air to perform what ice skaters might recognise as a half-decent quad-throw Salchow, his face contorted in agony, ensuring the ref clocked that it was a bad 'un. Monzón rightly received a red card – the first player to be sent off in a World Cup final – and Germany went on to win 1-0 thanks to a dodgy 85th minute penalty. Perhaps unfairly, critics suggested Klinsmann should have got an Oscar with his winners' medal.

Fast forward to Hillsborough and Jürgen – already unimaginatively dubbed The Diver by the tabloids – walked out to the sight of Wednesday fans brandishing diving scorecards. Unfazed, he tormented a parlous home defence before sealing the points with an 82nd-minute bullet header. Good goal that it was, the real takeaway was the celebration. Klinsmann and his teammates launched themselves into a mass dive, earning a laugh from even the most disillusioned of Owls fans. The striker went on to bag a season's tally of 21 league goals.

3 17 August 1996: Middlesbrough 3-3 Liverpool (Fabrizio Ravanelli)

Oh, to be a Boro fan in the mid-1990s. After years as the unfashionable neighbours of Newcastle and Sunderland, they were treated to an all-birthdays-come-at-once spending spree that brought magicians like Juninho and fellow Brazilians Branco and Emerson to the Riverside. The biggest gift of all, however, was one Fabrizio Ravanelli, who arrived on a £7 million transfer from Juventus to face a formidable Liverpool side who would go on to lead the table for much of the season. If the striker known as White Feather (on account of his bleached hairdo) felt over-awed by the occasion it didn't show. He bagged a memorable hat-trick to win instant hero status on the Tees and give the Sunday papers' back page subs the easiest headline they'd ever written: 'The Italian Job'.

4 19 August 2000: Coventry City 1-3 Middlesbrough (Alen Bokšić)

Croatian superstar Alen Bokšić should have joined Ravanelli in the Premier League debut hat-trick Hall of Fame. He nodded in unchallenged which would have doubled the Riversiders' early lead against Coventry. However, to the bewilderment of both sets of players, referee Barry Knight ruled his effort out for foul play. In the end it mattered little. The former Lazio idol went on to net a brace inside two minutes and provided the assist for his fellow debutant Joseph-Désiré Job to head in another.

It all pointed to £2.5 million well spent, although Boro manager Bryan Robson seemed tetchy about Bokšić's contract, reportedly worth £63,000 per week. In one interview he insisted his new star's remuneration was far more modest, and had been fixed long before rival clubs even knew the player was up for grabs. 'The wages quoted are a total nonsense,' said Robson. 'I got to hear about this long before anyone else and that's why we acted quickly and decisively. Talk of £63,000 a week is utter rubbish.' Put another way, Bokšić's teammates should back off seeking a pay rise.

5 28 August 2000: Crystal Palace 2-3 Nottingham Forest (Barry Roche)

If there's pressure facing an expensive striker on debut, pity the rookie goalie – even a rookie goalie that didn't cost a penny. So respect to 18-year-old Irishman Barry Roche, signed by Forest player-manager David Platt on a free from Leeds, who was minding his own business warming the bench as this game ticked towards stoppage time, with the visitors hanging on to a 2-3 lead. Then veteran first-choice keeper Dave Beasant upended Palace's Chinese international defender Fan Zhiyi with an agricultural tackle in the Forest penalty area, simultaneously producing a mass punch-up, a red card for himself and a penalty to the Eagles. Platt immediately substituted forward Jack Lester and beckoned Barry into action.

At first, it didn't feel like a dream debut. Barry's first task was to pick the ball out of the net following winger Julian Gray's spot kick. But referee Ray Olivier had spotted a Palace player encroaching and ordered the kick retaken. Gray went for the opposite corner but this time Barry guessed right. He saved the penalty with his first touch in top-flight football, handed his manager two points and sent the Forest faithful home in ecstasy. Pressure? What pressure? His feat is still revered by goalkeeping stats nerds alongside that of Birmingham City's Tony Coton who in 1980, then aged 19, began his professional career by saving a Sunderland penalty awarded on 54 seconds – his first touch of the game.

6 14 August 2010: Wigan Athletic 0-4 Blackpool (Marlon Harewood)

Football fans love an odds-defying story. The plucky underdog, the dark horse – you can build idioms of improbability through any number of animal metaphors. For Blackpool, who had just emerged blinking into the glare of a Premier League season after scrabbling up through the Championship play-offs, even turning up with a full team on the opening day looked a little iffy. A menagerie of half-crippled animals would, metaphorically speaking, barely have done justice to the speed with which they were written off on day one of the 2010–11 season. And yet, at least for a glorious hour or so that day, the Tangerines became outright leaders of the English footballing pyramid for the first time since 10 December 1955.

The task which faced manager Ian Holloway put the woes voiced by many a Premier League manager into perspective. Essentially, Blackpool were broke. The club had committed to building a new stand, and Holloway's attempt to woo big names on the promise of below-par wages, bracing sea air and a trip up the Blackpool Tower was futile to say the least. Three days before kick-off, he had only 15 eligible players and was resorting to a flurry of last-ditch deals in the hope that throwing together a coachload of complete strangers would do the job. The one plus was that 30-year-old Marlon Harewood, a proven top-flight striker with both Nottingham Forest and West Ham, had joined on a temporary deal early in August and was in talks to sign a permanent contract. When those talks broke down with a week to go, Holloway's Tangerine Dream *(editor's note: this pun barely works and only for fans of 1970s' German electronic music)* looked doomed. However, Harewood and agent Phil Sproson reopened negotiations, and the player signed a two-year deal 72 hours before Blackpool's trip down the M6 to Wigan Athletic.

The Latics were themselves no strangers to an also-ran tag, but neither could they be considered an easy opening fixture. 2010–11 was their sixth consecutive start in the Premier League and the previous season's manager, Roberto Martínez, had guided them to wins over Chelsea, Liverpool and Arsenal. No one was throwing money at an away win for the visitors, which was just as well for the bookies because Blackpool put Wigan to the sword. The visitors were 3-0 up at half-time thanks to an opener from Gary Taylor-Fletcher and two from star debutant Harewood, putting the game out of reach long before Alex Baptiste added a fourth with his cross-cum-shot. Blackpool sat proudly top of the league on goal difference until Chelsea spoilt the party with a 6-0 annihilation of West Bromwich Albion in the late kick-off. Sadly it couldn't last. The following week Holloway's side lost 6-0 away at Arsenal and were later relegated along with West Ham and Birmingham.

7 15 August 2011: Manchester City 4-0 Swansea City (Sergio Agüero)

Where to begin with this one? A dream debut bettered only by a dream season climax (more of which in our **May** chapter) delivered by a player rightly considered one of the greatest strikers ever to grace an English football pitch. Agüero signed for Manchester City from Atlético Madrid for a club record fee of around £38 million and went on to bag the most goals for a non-English player in Premier League history. Those 184 league goals in 275 appearances over ten years also made him the competition's fifth-highest scorer of all time.

The Argentine's tally began in the 68th minute of this game as he tapped in unmarked at the far post nine minutes after coming on as a substitute. Three minutes later he neatly chipped onrushing Swans' keeper Michel Vorm, before balletically flicking the ball back for David Silva to add a third. He then rounded off a jaw-dropping 32 minutes with a stunning 25-yard strike, fair warning to defending champions Manchester United that he was coming for them.

8 18 August 2012: Fulham 5-0 Norwich (Mladen Petrić)

Petrić joined Fulham on a free summer transfer from Hamburg, linking up with his former boss at the German club, Martin Jol. The Croatian was a familiar face, having knocked England out of the 2008 Euro qualifiers with a cracking 25-yard winning goal at 'New Wembley', England's first competitive defeat there. His arrival at Craven Cottage generated much excitement among Cottagers fans who well remembered the striker's brilliant free kick for Hamburg which consigned their team to a 2-1 defeat in the 2009–10 Europa League semi-final second leg. Sure enough, just 41 minutes into his debut, he was off the mark with a header.

Petrić netted his second – an admittedly fortunate deflected shot – nine minutes after the break and then delivered a perfect flicked pass for Swedish winger Alexander Kačaniklić to convert for Fulham's fourth. A minute later he was substituted to a standing ovation from the home support, now convinced that here was a striker to make them serious top-half contenders. But dream debuts raise expectations higher than the average fan's already unfeasibly high ones. Petrić netted only three more goals in 23 Premier League appearances and at the end of the 2012–13 season was shuffled off to West Ham. Fulham finished 12th.

9 18 August 2012: Queens Park Rangers 0-5 Swansea City (Michu)

Sometimes a good debut is hard-fought; sometimes it is literally hand-delivered. So it was for Michu who, within eight minutes of taking the field for the Swans, saw his eminently stoppable shot palmed into the bottom corner by Rangers' keeper Rob Green (see Nightmare Debut XI below). The £2 million Spanish striker then hit the bar before curling an exquisite left-foot effort into the top corner of Green's goal early in the second half.

At which point QPR moved seamlessly into self-destruct mode as Nathan Dyer netted twice in quick succession and Scott Sinclair completed the rout. But this win – Swansea's first

ever at Loftus Road in 20 attempts – was deservedly credited
to Michu, whose inspirational performance assured him of
instant hero status among the away fans. It was also a stylish
way to get into the good books of Michael Laudrup in his
debut game as Swansea manager. Michu went on to score
18 league goals in 35 appearances to help his side achieve a
respectable ninth-place finish.

10 14 August 2016: Arsenal 3-4 Liverpool (Sadio Mané)

So, you've joined Liverpool from Southampton for £34 million,
making you the most expensive African player in history.
You've gone straight into the first team for a tough opening
day match at the Emirates Stadium against an Arsenal side
which finished runners-up the previous season. The pressure
is on. You need your teammates to settle the nerves. Which is
precisely what they do ... eventually.

Half an hour in, things hadn't looked promising for the Reds.
Having just missed a penalty, Theo Walcott put the Gunners
in front on 31 minutes and it took a superb free kick from
Philippe Coutinho to bring the visitors back into the game.
But the second half was a very different story. With Mané's
explosive pace putting the heebie-jeebies into a second-string
Arsenal back four, there was too much space for Coutinho
and Adam Lallana, both of whom scored. The Senegalese
then showed defenders Nacho Monreal and Calum Chambers
why they were right to worry, cutting the home defence apart
before dispatching the ball deliciously into keeper Petr Čech's
top right-hand corner. It was just as well he did – Arsenal
pulled back two inside 12 minutes – but Liverpool held on.

Mané's debut sparked the Kop's love affair with their winger, who would score 13 league goals in his first season and was named the club's Player of the Season despite being sidelined with injuries late in the campaign. Anfield echoed to the tune of Abba's 1976 classic 'Money, Money, Money' and the adapted lyrics:

> *Mané, Mané, Mané,*
> *Sadio Mané,*
> *Plays for Liverpool ...*
> *Ah ha aah aah,*
> *All the things he can do.*
> *We have Sadio Mané,*
> *He plays for Liverpool.*

See what they did there?

11 13 August 2017: Manchester United 4-0 West Ham United (Romelu Lukaku)

Lukaku joined Manchester United from Everton in July 2017 the day after Wayne Rooney moved in the opposite direction back to his boyhood club. For United the acquisition of a proven, powerful striker was worth every penny of the £75 million price tag if it meant clawing back ground on the other five members of the so-called Big Six – Chelsea, Tottenham, Manchester City, Liverpool and Arsenal. At 0.48 goals per game over his five previous seasons with West Brom and Everton, Lukaku's stats were right up there with some of United's greatest. His record eclipsed both Wayne Rooney (0.42) and Andrew Cole (0.45) and was comparable to Robin van Persie's total Premier League average of 0.51.

This season opener at Old Trafford wasn't the trickiest but, nonetheless, chances still had to be finished. Lukaku delivered with aplomb on his debut, showing class in his link-up play and formidable physical presence in the West Ham penalty area. His first goal had him sprinting on to a Marcus Rashford pass to smash in a rising drive off the post while his second, a glancing header on 52 minutes, effectively ended the contest. He missed out on a hat-trick thanks only to Pablo Zabaleta's last ditch block, while Anthony Martial and Paul Pogba each added a goal in the final minutes. 'When you play for Manchester United, you have a job to do and mine is to score goals,' Lukaku told his post-match interviewer. 'It is promising.'

Indeed it was. Lukaku hit 27 goals in all competitions that season, helping United to a runner-up spot in the league and an FA Cup final (which they lost 1-0 to Chelsea). Unfortunately, the 2018–19 season was comparatively underwhelming for the Belgian international who managed just 15 goals in all competitions. Yet stats never quite tell the whole story. United struggled throughout the first half of the season and José Mourinho, who had brought Lukaku to Old Trafford, was sacked in December after posting just seven wins in 17 league games. He was succeeded by Ole Gunnar Solskjær who had a clear preference for Rashford up front. In July 2019 Lukaku was transferred to Inter Milan for a reported £67 million and over the next two seasons it was business as usual, with a Serie A goals-per-game average of 0.65.

THE NIGHTMARE DEBUT XI

Sincere apologies to players for whom the following events have been filed away in a dusty corner of their consciousness, in an ominous-looking box marked 'DO NOT OPEN'. But, for the rest of us, red cards, penalty shockers and goalkeeping blunders are all part of the game's fascination. It's worth issuing a disclaimer that not all these incidents were necessarily the debutant's fault and that the majority of the players in question shrugged them off to become hugely important figures for their clubs.

1 26 August 1995: Queens Park Rangers 1-0 Manchester City (Michael Brown)

Michael Brown was a nervous, super-keen 18-year-old midfielder fresh out of City's academy when new manager Alan Ball gave him a league debut in this game as a 68th-minute substitute. It didn't go well. Inside 12 minutes he was back in the dressing room, having received a straight red card from ref Paul Danson for pulling Andy Impey's shirt when the QPR winger was through on goal. Brown felt he was 'extremely unlucky' because 'the referee thought I was the last man but the video showed Alan Kernaghan was covering anyway.'

If only Video Assistant Referees had been around – assuming Brown was right he'd have stayed on the field, as VARs can overturn wrongly-awarded straight reds. Whatever, it mattered little in the long term. Three years later he was named player of the year at Manchester City and went on to help Sheffield United reach two cup semi-finals and a Championship play-off final, while at Portsmouth he featured in the 2010 FA Cup final. Neither did it really matter to Manchester City, who were in financial meltdown (how times change) and beyond dire anyway, losing eight and drawing three of their first 11 games. They were relegated on goal difference, and although Ball stayed in post he quit three games into the 1996–97 Division One campaign.

2 10 August 1997: Tottenham Hotspur 0-2 Manchester United (Teddy Sheringham)

No one can doubt Teddy Sheringham's prowess as a predatory goal-scorer. His career included 75 goals for Tottenham in 166 league appearances and 31 for United in 104. Neither could anyone doubt his prowess at joyfully winding up opposition fans opining unkindly about him. Even so, making your United league debut at White Hart Lane on the opening day of the season, just weeks after securing a move to Old Trafford on the basis that you felt Spurs 'lacked ambition', was always going to be challenging. So delicious was the prospect for fans, *Match of the Day* producers and sports reporters generally that you half-wondered whether the Premier League's 'random' fixture generator had been got at.

After enduring an hour's worth of choice banter from the very home fans who once hero-worshipped him, Sheringham was gifted the chance of revenge. An attempted clearance by Spurs' left-back Justin Edinburgh struck the defender's hand as he slipped over. The ref pointed to the spot and up stepped Teddy to a predictably loud chorus of boos and whistles. The ball hit the post and bounced back into play but, forgetting Law 14 (which in such circumstances prevents the penalty taker from touching it again until someone else has) Sheringham had another go and ballooned it over the bar. 'Oh, Teddy Teddy,' sang the jubilant masses. It could have been far worse for the

debutant had the Red Devils not secured a win. But they did
– first through an 82nd minute Nicky Butt effort and, before
Sheringham had stopped celebrating, a Ramon Vega own goal.

3 15 August 1998: Newcastle United 0-0 Charlton Athletic (Richard Rufus)

This turned out to be Kenny Dalglish's penultimate game as
Newcastle manager – he was sacked 12 days later despite
signing £13 million worth of talent during the close season –
and in many ways it summed up Newcastle's problem. They
were up against a Charlton side who had only just squeezed
through the First Division play-offs thanks to a last-gasp
goal from Richard Rufus. Yet the Toon's refashioned lineup
huffed and puffed for over an hour against ten-man Charlton,
who saw Rufus given his marching orders by referee Dermot
Gallagher for elbowing Nikos Dabizas as the visitors prepared
to defend a corner. Newcastle, incidentally, didn't get a penalty
as the ball was not 'live'.

This may not have been Rufus' first outing for Charlton but
it was his debut appearance in the Premier League, and for a
player who had fought so hard to secure his club that berth
it must have felt horribly harsh. In the 85th minute of that
Wembley play-off final he had scored the first league goal of
his senior career to force extra time. That allowed Charlton to
eventually beat Sunderland 7-6 on penalties.

4 23 August 2003: Bolton Wanderers 2-2 Blackburn Rovers (Steven Reid)

Any debut in this Lancashire hotpot of a derby is always going
to be edgy and so it was for 20-year-old Irish international

midfielder Steven Reid. He was sent on as 76th-minute substitute by Rovers manager Graeme Souness as the visitors – anonymous in the first half – pressed for an equaliser. But as testosterone levels rose in the final minutes it all got a bit unnecessary and Reid's late challenge on Stelios Giannakopoulos 12 minutes later earned him a straight red and seemingly the end of Blackburn's hopes of a point.

Fortunately for Reid, Bolton had taken their frustrating habit of conceding late goals into the new season and Dwight Yorke – who had already missed two good chances to equalise – made no mistake with an injury time header to save his teammate's blushes. Reid went on to make 19 appearances in the 2003–04 season and over the following six years became a stalwart of Rovers' central midfield.

5 20 August 2006: Chelsea 3-0 Manchester City (Bernardo Corradi)

Manchester City fans might want to skip this one, if only to avoid the memory of a dismal season. For everyone else it's sufficient to note that they scored only ten goals at home in the league (a home goal difference of minus six) and none at all after the seismic shock of beating Everton 2-1 at Eastlands on New Year's Day 2007. Then there was striker Bernardo Corradi, just arrived from Valencia. He secured his first yellow card on debut after 49 minutes (tackling Paulo Ferreira from behind) and his second 13 minutes later (a reckless lunge at Michael Essien). Essien didn't react well – childishly grabbing the Italian's hair – but that couldn't save Corradi from manager Stuart Pearce's laser stare as he trooped off. Pearce had just brought on two attackers in the shape of Paul Dickov and Stephen Ireland to try and claw back a 2-0 deficit.

Later Corradi reasoned to the *Manchester Evening News* that Essien must have liked his hair, and promised to cut off a lock to give the Ghanaian when Chelsea visited Eastlands for the return fixture. City fans would perhaps have preferred him to exact revenge by scoring but, with hindsight, that was always a false hope. In December Corradi was again sent off for two yellows after diving theatrically during a 3-1 defeat in the Manchester derby. Pearce told the press afterwards:

> Bernardo went down a little bit too easily and I am not like the other 19 managers, who would sit here and give you a load of cock and bull about it. I would prefer him to stay on his feet and I intend to speak to him about it this week. Hopefully then, he will stay on his feet.

Whatever Pearce said to his player – and it may not have been precisely those words – it didn't kick-start Corradi's City career. After 29 league appearances his end-of-season report read: red cards, 2; goals, 3.

6 15 August 2010: Liverpool 1-1 Arsenal (Joe Cole)

The first of a two-for-one offer on August red card debuts. Joe Cole was Roy Hodgson's first signing for Liverpool and his move on a free transfer from Chelsea had been trailed as a major coup for the Reds, providing much-needed midfield creativity and innovation. Even so, his reported £90,000-a-week wage needed some justifying. Club captain

Steven Gerrard duly obliged, comparing the 28-year-old's technical ability with Lionel Messi, and for the first 44 minutes of this match all went reasonably OK. Then, perhaps conscious that he needed to stamp his authority on the game, Cole poleaxed Arsenal defender Laurent Koscielny with a dreadful tackle and both players left the fray – Cole courtesy of a red card and Koscielny courtesy of a stretcher. Koscielny did make it back for the second half, though not quite *all* of the second half.

7 15 August 2010: Liverpool 1-1 Arsenal (Laurent Koscielny)

The 24-year-old French defender was brought in by Arsène Wenger from Lorient for a reported £8.4 million, apparently to 'add height' and because the Gunners were short of centre-backs. Koscielny certainly looked a decent prospect – even after his Cole clattering – and might have been forgiven for thinking a debut win was on the cards against ten men. Yet within a minute of the restart the visitors were behind from a David N'Gog strike. Liverpool held on until the 89th minute when Marouane Chamakh bumped into Reds' keeper Pepe Reina, the ball bounced back off a post and Reina inadvertently chucked it into his own net. With five minutes of stoppage time it suddenly looked as though Arsenal were on for the proverbial smash-and-grab win. Then Koscielny mis-controlled, earning a 92nd-minute yellow card for taking down Dirk Kuyt, and followed up with a second, harsh, yellow three minutes later for handball. At least he didn't have to hang around alone for long in the dressing room.

8 13 August 2011: Newcastle United 0-0 Arsenal (Gervinho)

You'd have thought Gervinho would have had fair warning from his new North London teammates not to get wound up by Newcastle's Joey Barton. The previous season's corresponding fixture had seen Arsenal rocket into a 4-0 lead only to be pegged back to a 4-4 draw. The turnaround came when Abou Diaby reacted badly to a heavy Barton tackle and was sent off. Arsenal manager Arsène Wenger felt Barton was lucky to stay on the pitch; Toon manager Alan Pardew saw nothing wrong. Whatever, the lesson was clear. Don't let Joey get under your skin.

Unfortunately, Gervinho did exactly that in the 74th minute of this dull game after the Newcastle midfielder, suspecting the Ivorian of diving in an attempt to get a penalty, hoisted him by the scruff of the neck. Had Gervinho simply protested his innocence by deploying standard posture (arms outstretched, hands up, look of incredulity on face) it would probably have been Barton who took the rap. Instead he foolishly tapped his opponent across the face, got an immediate red card and had to spend the next three matches on the bench.

9 18 August 2012: Queens Park Rangers 0-5 Swansea City (Rob Green)

This is a little unfair on Rob Green, who has already had a mention on account of his 8th minute mistake in this game to gift Michu a place in the Dream Debut XI. It's also fair to say that when goalkeepers make a mistake it gets hung around their necks like a badge of shame. When strikers miss a nailed-on expected goal or defenders fail to do their job it's soon forgotten. So while Green certainly had a nightmare start at Loftus Road, it wasn't entirely his fault. Far from it. An analysis of the four other goals reveals Michu's second to be, as *MOTD* commentator Alistair Mann put it, an 'exquisite finish', a curling shot from 18 yards into the top corner which no goalie in the world could have been expected to save. The only question was how on earth Swansea's Wayne Routledge was allowed to waltz through the QPR defence unchallenged for 30 yards before laying on the assist.

The third, a counterattack from a charged down clearance in the Swansea half, saw Nathan Dyer emerge one-on-one against Green with four – count 'em – defenders either playing him onside or failing to mark him – while the fourth again saw Dyer one-on-one thanks to a parlous back four playing him onside. The fifth was defensively so embarrassing the Rangers Under-12s would have done a better job. Winger Scott Sinclair found himself on the edge of the box amidst four opponents apparently surprised to see him there. Another unstoppable finish. There should have been a sixth but an unmarked Danny Graham fluffed his shot from five yards with only Green to beat. 'My goodness,' concluded Alistair with glorious understatement, 'QPR are going to spend a lot of time watching this game back with their defensive coaches.' No doubt they did. But Rob Green was the least of their problems.

10 11 August 2023: Manchester City 3-0 Burnley (Anass Zaroury)

Moroccan international Anass Zaroury made his Premier League debut to the sound of a uniquely ambitious terraces chant from the visiting support. To the tune of 'Heartbeat', a 1950s Buddy Holly classic, the Turf Moor creatives divided themselves into separate choirs singing the intro alternately: *Anass Zaroury (Anass Zaroury) Anass Zaroury (Anass Zaroury)*, before joining in combo to continue: *Anass, Anass Zaroury runs down the wing for me … Anass Zaroury (Anass Zaroury)* etc. Try it. It works. At least, it works a whole lot better than Anass' ugly lunge from behind aimed at stopping City's Kyle Walker running down the wing for them. His scissor-leg tackle in stoppage time caught the England defender awkwardly and he hobbled off nursing a sore ankle. Zaroury appeared to have escaped with a yellow card. But a VAR intervention, with just seconds left on the clock, saw it upgraded to red by referee Craig Pawson. At least it allowed Burnley wits to try another Buddy tune: 'It Doesn't Matter Anymore'.

11 14 August 2023: Manchester United 1-0 Wolverhampton Wanderers (Mason Mount)

You'd have to be an unforgiving football fan to deny that Mason Mount is a skilful, honest and hard-working player. Trouble is, data analysis *is* unforgiving. And in this, his Old Trafford debut following a £60 million transfer from Chelsea, the stats were brutal. Mount's numbers read: goals, 0; assists, 0; chances created, 0; crosses, 0; tackles won, 0; aerial duels won, 0. Mason probably didn't clip the match reports for his scrapbook. But then it's unlikely his teammates bothered either. They scraped this win thanks to Raphaël Varane's close range header and were lucky to avoid a penalty in the final moments when goalkeeper André Onana ploughed into Saša Kalajdžić without making contact with the ball.

AND FINALLY ...

Nightmare debuts are not confined to the start of the season. In March 1996 Garry Flitcroft lasted a mere three minutes for Blackburn after his elbow mysteriously found its way into Everton striker Duncan Ferguson's face. Christian Negouai's first game for Manchester City on Boxing Day 2004 was also his last for the club after he was handed a straight red in the 83rd minute against Everton. His career was unfortunately blighted by injuries. Perhaps the most bizarre debut sending-off in Premier League history fell the way of poor Everton keeper Iain Turner in February 2006. After just nine minutes he was trudging back to the dressing room for handling the ball outside his penalty area – the result of a dodgy headed back pass from defender Alan Stubbs which prevented a clear goal-scoring opportunity. Finally, spare a thought for an 18-year-old kid making his international debut as a sub. He ran about like a scared rabbit for a little over 30 seconds, elbowed an opponent and saw straight red. Despite this setback, Lionel Messi went on to do OK.

SEPTEMBER: TRANSFER FEVER

August may be the month for debuts but September is when the main transfer window slams shut and fans start to discover what they've been landed with. Often, a bum deal is depressingly obvious – who can forget the case of Southampton's Ali Dia, chronicled later in this chapter – but sometimes even big-ticket players take time to settle. Take Thierry Henry's arrival at Arsenal from Italian giants Juventus in 1999 for a reported £11 million. Having mostly played on the wing, Henry was converted into a striker by Arsène Wenger who then had to resolutely back his star buy through an opening lean spell of just one goal in 12 games. But Arsène knows, as they still say in the red half of North London, and Thierry eventually began scoring for fun, amassing 228 goals in 377 Arsenal appearances.

Conversely, relative unknowns can be instant hits. Few Leicester City fans had ever heard of N'Golo Kanté when the Foxes signed him for £5.6 million from Caen in 2015.

Talk about a steal. Kanté played only one season for Claudio Ranieri but we all know what happened. Many pundits regard this as the greatest Premier League debut season ever, as evidenced by some of the Frenchman's 2015–16 overall stats (175 tackles and 156 interceptions, respectively 31 and 15 more than anyone else). Chelsea were suitably impressed, shelling out a hefty £32 million to bring him to Stamford Bridge.

Both Henry and Kanté were largely in control of where they plied their trade. But it wasn't always so. Not until 1963 – just as *Match of the Day* was preparing to beam into the nation's living rooms – did players start to break the stranglehold which clubs held on their careers. It followed a High Court ruling in the case of *Eastham v Newcastle United*, which saw a starring role for new Professional Footballers Association chairman Jimmy Hill, later a *MOTD* presenter whose long, bearded chin became synonymous with the show between 1973 and 1988. Hill was the catalyst for reform, but it was the 1995 Bosman ruling which became, literally, a game changer. The background to all this is worth a recap given that it redefined the transfer market and brought British fans the array of international talent now taken for granted on *MOTD*.

Back to George Eastham – a stylish inside forward who made 19 appearances for England. He spent four seasons with Newcastle until things turned sour in 1959, when he complained that his digs were a disgrace and the part-time job he'd been promised (clubs would arrange these for players to supplement their meagre pay packets) had never materialised. So when Eastham's contract ended he refused a new one and instead slapped in a transfer request. Newcastle responded by refusing to play him, pay him or move him on.

25

Mystifying as this may seem today, the Toon were within their rights. The Football Association had introduced professional player registrations in the late 19th century, leading to a 'retain and transfer' system which meant that, provided a football club held a player's registration papers, he couldn't play for anyone else. This was rolled out with the best of intentions – the FA had wanted to stop top players being lured away by an elite coterie of the wealthiest owners – but it meant unsettled players were left in limbo. Clubs could stop them moving to rivals in the hope of bringing them to heel and didn't have to pay wages if they were out of contract.

Exasperated, Eastham quit Tyneside and moved south to work as a cork salesman for an old family friend, Ernie Clay, a future chairman of Fulham. It was better paid than running the channels for Newcastle and he could stay fit by training with amateur clubs like Reigate and Redhill. Bizarrely, he even had a run-out with a TV All Stars XI alongside Tommy Steele and the comedy duo Mike and Bernie Winters. Such a frivolous spectacle did not go down well at Lancaster Gate, the FA's London HQ. 'The FA objected strongly to that,' Eastham later explained to the *Independent on Sunday*, 'so we told them what to do as well. I had no contact with Newcastle at all. The manager was Charlie Mitten and his attitude was: "If you don't play for us, you won't play for anybody."' The Magpies did eventually relent, accepting a £47,500 bid from Arsenal in 1960, but Eastham was determined not to let the matter lie.

Backed by Jimmy Hill, who persuaded the PFA to stump up £15,000 for legal fees, he sued for restraint of trade and unpaid wages. It was a big call for Hill who was taking on not only Newcastle but also the FA and Football League, both named as co-defendants. But it wasn't the first time he'd stood up to the football establishment. In January 1961, his last full season as a Fulham player, he'd instigated a successful players' revolt over pay caps. This ended the cosy club cartel which had forced stars like Stanley Matthews and Tom Finney to accept a maximum £20 per week. Hill famously greeted new Fulham recruit Rodney Marsh, a future England international who had just turned professional, with the words: 'Welcome aboard Rodney. We're going on strike.' Within a couple of months, their teammate Johnny Haynes was on £100 per week.

Hill had been warned by the Association's lawyers that the chances of getting the entire British transfer system flagged by the courts as unlawful was at best 50:50. Had the PFA lost, and been forced to pay costs, it could have broken the organisation. But Mr Justice Wilberforce ruled that the retain and transfer system *was* unreasonable and, in the legal jargon, *ultra vires* (literally meaning 'beyond the powers'). It meant any club trying to retain a player's registration forms against his will could in future open themselves to legal action.

'They [Newcastle] thought I'd give it up once the transfer went through,' recalled Eastham. 'But the PFA had spent a lot of money, just about all the funds they had, so I said I would see it through.' He described his courtroom questioning by Newcastle director William McKeag, a criminal lawyer by profession, as 'absolutely terrifying', adding that 'after he finished with me I thought I was the criminal'. The judgement certainly seemed like a victory for player power, but by September 1963 lawyers at the Football League were already hard at work unpicking it.

League secretary Alan Hardaker drafted a letter to clubs suggesting that Eastham had won only because of 'certain Football League regulations in relation to the retain-and-transfer system which were no longer in force.' *The Times* of October 3rd reported him as saying:

> 'I cannot tell you the details of our plans but I will say that they do not envisage freedom of contract for the players. By this I mean that they cannot leave a club at will after their contract is finished.' He continued: 'The retain and transfer system is fundamental to the league and must go on. What we have tried to do following the Eastham case is to evolve a scheme which is fair to club and player, which is not in restraint of trade, and which is legally valid.'

In short, an out-of-contract player – these days known as a 'free agent' – could move wherever he wanted. But only if the two clubs involved agreed transfer terms. And that seemed to be that. Until, 27 years later, a Belgian footballer called Jean-Marc Bosman decided there was unfinished business.

In 1990 Bosman, 25, was registered with Belgian club RFC Liège. His contract was running out and he wanted to accept an improved offer from the French second division side Dunkerque. The problem was that Liège wanted a £500,000 transfer fee which Dunkerque couldn't possibly meet. Result: stalemate. Bosman refused to play for Liège and, as he was no longer in the first team, Liège slashed his pay by 70%. So, backed by his legal team of Luc Misson and Jean-Louis Dupont, Bosman took Liège, the Royal Belgian Football Association and UEFA to the European Court of Justice. His case rested on the 1957 Treaty of Rome, which guaranteed free movement of labour within the European Union. Predictably, the football establishment fought back hard.

It took five years before judgement was finally handed down, and in that time Bosman became something of a pariah in European football. He was banned by the Belgian governing body for refusing to sign his low-wage contract, was shunned by most other clubs and managed to play only briefly for French sides Saint-Quentin and Saint-Denis along with the odd lower league side. In another life these would, arguably, have been the best years of his career, and his only consolation was that he won. On 15 December 1995 the ECJ ruled that the retain and transfer system was unlawful and that all EU footballers out of contract were entitled to a free transfer, provided this involved clubs within EU football associations. As Sir Alex Ferguson observed in his 2015 book *Leading*, 'all hell broke loose. Suddenly it was a free-for-all.'

The ruling gave players huge leverage to negotiate better deals and signing-on fees because any club courting them no longer had to pay previous employers a transfer fee. But it also brought unintended consequences. Football agents became the game's new kingmakers, pushing up wages or transfer fees (and therefore commission fees) for coveted players approaching the final year of their contracts. Fearing they could lose a prized asset for nothing, clubs often preferred to cash in. Despite receiving a compensation package worth £312,000, Bosman was equivocal about his courtroom legacy. He told the *Guardian*:

> Now the 25 or so richest clubs transfer players for astronomical sums and smaller clubs cannot afford to buy at those prices. So the 25 pull further and further

away from the rest, deepening the gap between big
and small. That was not the aim of the Bosman ruling.

There were other impacts, more visible to fans. Before the ECJ
judgement European clubs were restricted on the number of
foreign players they were permitted to employ – the so-called
'three-plus-two' rule, referring to three foreign signings plus
two foreign players who had graduated through the club's
academy. Neither could managers field more than three
foreigners in European competitions. The ECJ decided that
these UEFA rules were a further restraint of trade because they
prevented a truly free market from operating. Now clubs could
play as many foreigners as they wished, and in the Premier
League they didn't hang about. According to stats analyst
Opta, 1996–97, the first full season after Bosman, saw the
biggest drop in the proportion of minutes played by English
footballers between one Premier League season and the next –
a whopping 8.2%.

There was no better illustration of the trend than the calendar
year 1999. Early on it was revealed that Liverpool's Steve
McManaman had run down his contract and would be
leaving the club which had spotted and nurtured him to
join Real Madrid on a free transfer. This didn't land well at
Anfield where the celebrated winger – easily the most valuable
English player to take advantage of Bosman so far – found
himself working out his notice amid mass baiting from the
terraces. Then, on 27 February, Aston Villa manager John
Gregory presented a team sheet to referee Uriah Rennie which
listed an all-English starting XI for Villa's home game against
Coventry City. It may have been unremarkable at the time
but this was the last so-called 'Full English' served up in the

Premier League. (Middlesbrough fans will point out that their team for the trip to Fulham on the final day of the 2005–06 season contained 11 English players at the kick-off, although James Morrison was later found to be eligible for Scotland and won a Scottish cap two years later.)

May 1999 saw Manchester United achieve their historic Treble, beating Bayern Munich 2-1 at Barcelona's Camp Nou, with eight squad players who would have been deemed ineligible foreigners four years earlier. And ten months after that Villa-Coventry game, Chelsea manager Gianluca Vialli showed how times had changed by naming a starting XI comprising players of nine different nationalities, not a single one English, in a 1-2 Boxing Day win at Southampton.

By the dawn of the millennium the transfer market bandwagon had forced UEFA to implement a compulsory Europe-wide transfer window, something some national leagues had already adopted voluntarily. The chief executive, Gerhard Aigner, said it would 'stop the confusion that has followed Bosman' and prevent relegation-threatened clubs from poaching their rivals' players to, as he put it, 'survive the season'. Premier League chairmen were reportedly unhappy about the restriction but could do little to prevent it taking effect from the 2002–03 season. In England, aside from some tight exemptions, it meant no contracted player could switch clubs after midnight on 31 August (later pushed back to 11pm on 1 September to avoid August bank holidays) until the 'winter window' opened in January. Thanks to Bosman, free agents could move at any time. But if Premier League bosses thought this was the end of transfer shenanigans they would soon get a reality check. On transfer deadline day 2006,

West Ham United pulled off the transfer coup of the summer, signing Argentinian World Cup stars Carlos Tevez and Javier Mascherano from Brazilian giants Corinthians.

Question was, how did West Ham manage it? Tevez adopted an opaque approach on his website. The players had signed for an undisclosed fee. The transfers were permanent. All other details would be 'confidential'. It was never going to hold. Before Tevez had even made his 10 September debut, stories emerged that other Premier League clubs had rejected the duo's services over stipulations demanded by the third parties which owned their playing rights. Within months a League investigation established that while those rights had been passed to the Hammers, transfer fees had been trousered by the third party owners – namely Media Sports Investments, founded by the Iranian businessman Kia Joorabchian, and Just Sports Inc. West Ham were found to have broken Premier League regulations which banned third party ownership on the basis that it could materially influence the performance of teams.

It all got very messy. The Hammers avoided a points deduction but were slapped with a record £5.5 million fine. Mascherano was cleared to join Liverpool in the January transfer window, while Tevez was allowed to carry on playing and scored on the last day of the season to save his club from relegation. But that meant Sheffield United went down. The Blades later sued West Ham and eventually settled for £20 million. The following summer Tevez signed for Manchester United but only after Joorabchian paid a reported £2 million to West Ham to buy out his contract. Lord knows what George Eastham would have made of it all.

We could go on. We could look in detail at how Financial Fair Play is the latest spectre to haunt the transfer market. How Premier League clubs must conform to 'Profitability and Sustainability' rules permitting them to lose no more than £105 million in any consecutive three-year period. How some costs are worked out through 'amortisation' (dividing incoming players' transfer fees by the length of their contracts); how staff wages and agents commission payments are factored in; how the costs of women's teams, stadium infrastructure and youth academies can be set against FFP liabilities. We could even look at new UEFA spending rules which mean that by 2025–26 a club's total outlay on transfers and wages cannot exceed 70% of its total income. We could do this. But let's not.

TRANSFER SHOWSTOPPERS AND SHOCKERS

In 2022 Virgin Media O2 commissioned a national poll of football fans to gauge opinion on the best and worst signings or 'ins' by Premier League clubs. The results were as follows.

Best Value for Money Signings:

- Eric Cantona, 1992
  (£1m, Leeds United to Manchester United)

- Jamie Vardy, 2012
  (£1m, Fleetwood Town to Leicester City)

- Cristiano Ronaldo, 2003
  (£12m, Sporting Lisbon to Manchester United)

- Thierry Henry, 1999
  (£11m, Juventus to Arsenal)

- Mohamed Salah, 2017
  (£37m, Roma to Liverpool)

- Kenny Dalglish, 1977
  (£440k, Celtic to Liverpool)

- Dennis Bergkamp, 1995
  (£7.5m, Inter Milan to Arsenal)

- Alan Shearer, 1996
  (£15m, Blackburn Rovers to Newcastle United)

- Frank Lampard, 2001
  (£11m, West Ham United to Chelsea)

- Patrick Vieira, 1996
  (£3.5m, Milan to Arsenal)

Worst Value for Money Signings:

- Andy Carroll, 2011
  (£36m, Newcastle United to Liverpool)

- Fernando Torres, 2011
  (£52m, Liverpool to Chelsea)

- Ángel di María, 2014
  (£67m, Real Madrid to Manchester United)

- Danny Drinkwater, 2017
  (£34m, Leicester City to Chelsea)

- Alexis Sánchez, 2018
  (swap deal with Henrikh Mkhitaryan, Arsenal to
  Manchester United)

- Nicolas Pépé, 2019
  (£72m, Lille to Arsenal)

- Mario Balotelli, 2014
  (£18m, Milan to Liverpool)

- Donny van de Beek, 2020
  (£35m, Ajax to Manchester United)

- Michael Owen, 2005
  (£22m, Manchester United to Newcastle United)

- Rhian Brewster, 2019
  (£23m, Liverpool to Sheffield United)

It's impossible to objectively identify the best value for money acquisition. Much easier to build a case for the worst though. His name doesn't feature above, but that's probably just because most fans outside Southampton have long forgotten him. His entire Premier League playing career lasted 53 minutes. Step forward Ali Dia.

In November 1996 Dia was invited to train with Southampton on the back of an apparent gold-plated recommendation from FIFA World Player of the Year and Ballon d'Or winner George Weah. 'George' rang up to say that he'd played with Ali, his cousin, at Paris Saint-Germain, the lad was a Senegalese international and it would be worth Saints manager Graeme Souness, whose squad was bedevilled with injuries, giving him a trial. Souness was desperate. It was surely worth a go. Trouble was the caller, whoever he was, was not George Weah. Ali Dia was not a Senegalese international. He had already failed trials at Gillingham, Bournemouth and Rotherham. He was not anywhere close to being a Premier League footballer.

This became blindingly obvious to Southampton star Matt Le Tissier the day before the club's 23 November home game

against Leeds. Quoted later in the *Guardian*, he recalled:
'He joined in the five-a-side on the Friday morning, and was
introduced to us as a trialist. I remember at the time thinking:
"He's not very good. He's probably not going to make it."'
Oh, but he did. Souness named him on the subs bench for the
Leeds match and, in a twist well beyond irony, brought him on
for the injured Le Tissier after 32 minutes.

Le Tissier, among the most gifted players of his generation, was
aghast. 'He ran around the pitch like Bambi on ice,' he said.

> It was very, very embarrassing to watch. We were like:
> "What's this geezer doing? He's hopeless." Graeme
> named him as a sub and we couldn't believe it ... when I
> saw him warming up, I'm going: "Surely not?" ... He kind
> of took my place, but he didn't really have a position. He
> was just wandering everywhere. I don't think he realised
> what position he was supposed to be in.

Le Tissier described the mood in the dressing room after
Southampton's 2-0 defeat as 'pretty sombre', ensuring Dia's
performance wasn't discussed. 'I think on Monday morning it
was probably more of a topic. By then he was gone, never to
be seen again.'

Souness defended his decision on the basis he had no one else
to play up front and was forced to gamble. 'I sent him on today
having never seen him play Premiership football,' he said.

> But I do not have any strikers. Am I enjoying this?
> Do you enjoy a kick in the b******s? ... It just goes
> to show the state of things at the club at the moment
> that a player I have never even seen, let alone watched
> playing in a game, was able to play in the Premiership.

Later, after learning more about the hoax, he added:

> I don't feel I have been duped in the slightest ...
> because that's the way the world is these days. It cost
> us a couple of grand for two weeks wages. It has not
> broken our hearts – and we certainly don't feel hard
> done-by. He was an international player [later revealed
> to be untrue by the Senegalese football authorities] so
> we gave him a go, but he didn't impress and has now
> left the club.

SEVEN DEADLY INS: STARS WHO TRANSFERRED BETWEEN ARCH-ENEMIES

Little agitates the average fan more than a hero hotfooting off
to the opposition. And if that opposition also happens to be
a deadly rival – or any team that is particularly hated because,
well, it just *is* – then 'treachery' doesn't come close to an
adequate description. Yet over the last sixty years plenty of
players have taken the Walk of Shame. Here we recall some
of the most notorious.

Robin van Persie, 2012 (Arsenal to Manchester United)

Sprinkled through these pages you'll occasionally find
reference to the greatest Premier League title climax ever
(though importantly not the greatest English top-flight climax
ever, which was Liverpool v Arsenal, 1989 – see the **May**
chapter). The Premier League accolade goes to Manchester
City's final game of 2012 which ended 3-2 for City. Sergio
Agüero's last gasp winner on 13 May snatched the title from
Manchester United on goal difference and ended his club's

44-year wait to become champions again. How would Sir Alex Ferguson respond? How could he show players and fans that United were not about to lie down and be trampled? Easy. He signed Robin van Persie.

Securing the previous season's most prolific striker – Van Persie scored 30 league goals for Arsenal at an average of 0.81 per full-match appearance – was enough in itself. To take him from formidable rivals, see him reject overtures from still-gleeful champions Manchester City and know the kind of service he'd be getting from Wayne Rooney, must have given Sir Alex the kind of warm feeling which for months had been limited to a mouthful of his morning porridge.

And RVP duly delivered. He scored his first goal a week after joining the squad – a scintillating volley at home to Fulham – and in his third outing, on 2 September, bagged a hat-trick in United's 2-3 win at Southampton. His understanding with Rooney blossomed throughout the season, typified by his first-half hat-trick at Old Trafford on 22 April 2013. This 3-0 defeat of Aston Villa both secured United the title and produced arguably the greatest technical volley ever seen in the Premier League. Van Persie ran on to Rooney's long, high floated pass, meeting it on the edge of the penalty area with a vicious, dipping strike into the bottom left corner. *Match of the Day* viewers got to know that goal well because it featured in every opening title sequence the following season. RVP ended the campaign with 26 league goals from 35 full appearances. Sir Alex chose the aftermath of the game to announce his retirement.

So why did Arsenal sell him? The background to the £24 million transfer is curious – not least because, after years of open hostilities between Gunners manager Arsène

Wenger and Sir Alex it all seemed to go seamlessly. United's boss told the BBC he never thought he could sign RVP and made his move only after reading that the 29-year-old had rejected a new contract. He described negotiating with Wenger as 'amicable', adding:

> Arsène knew the boy wanted to leave. He knew he wanted to join us. That made it a bit easier but not in terms of trying to reduce the fee. He [Wenger] could run a poker school in Govan. He got a great price but we are also happy the matter is concluded. From the starting position when we first started negotiating, Arsène has done well.

Wenger was rather more reserved.

> I have regrets. We have lost a good player because of a simple reason. He only had one year left on his contract and he wanted to go. We lost a good player, a world-class player – I don't deny that.

It was Van Persie himself who lifted the lid. Speaking on Jake Humphrey's *High Performance Podcast*, he revealed he had started contract talks with Arsenal chief executive Ivan Gazidis during which RVP highlighted seven points to help the club improve. This is what happens when you're Premier League top scorer. You try to conduct your boss's performance review. 'In my opinion', said RVP,

> those seven points – they should [have started] dealing with those straightaway to compete with the best teams. It doesn't really matter what points they were. What matters is Ivan decided that he didn't agree on one single point. So taking that information on board,

Arsenal doesn't offer me a deal. They didn't agree with my views ... honest views of how the club should move forward. It was my period when I was the captain, top scorer. That's the period where I felt that my views would count.

He said he was grateful for his eight years at Arsenal and the way Wenger had made him a better player. But he concluded:

Ivan and me didn't really click, that can happen, but it's a big man world. There is a moment where you have to move on and sometimes at the top it can be ruthless, sometimes in your favour and sometimes against you.

Many Gunners fans were outraged that Van Persie had forsaken them for an old enemy, but in truth Arsenal were in gradual decline, far from the heady early heights of Wenger's 22-year reign. So too for Manchester United, for whom the post-Ferguson era would bring a decade of underachievement.

Carlos Tevez, 2009 (Manchester United to Manchester City)

When in 2008 Sheikh Mansour, the politician and scion of Abu Dhabi's Al Nahyan royal family, bought a £200 million majority stake in Manchester City, the standing joke went that he wasn't in it for the money but certainly *was* in it *with* the money. Recent estimates of the family's net wealth – £250 billion, give a billion or so – make the sheikh easily the richest football club owner in history. His investment in City over 16 years has been commensurately eye-watering: in the first two years alone he approved a reported £325 million on new signings.

The first of those was a declaration of intent. Brazilian winger Robinho arrived at the City of Manchester Stadium in a £32.5 million transfer, a marquee acquisition albeit one that never really delivered. The jaw-dropping coup came the following year as Tevez's two-year loan deal with United expired. His move sent two unmistakeable messages from the blue half of Manchester to the red. The first was that they were no longer the poor relations. They would be not so much rocking the boat as kicking the gunwales out of it, and the poaching of a prized Old Trafford asset from under Sir Alex Ferguson's nose was just the start. The other message was even less subtle – a large billboard poster deliberately positioned directly opposite the Manchester Arena on the border between the city of Salford, where United's support was concentrated, and its traditional boundary with Manchester. The brainchild of City's chief brand and marketing executive David Pullan, the poster showed Tevez in his new kit alongside the words 'Welcome to Manchester'. In other words, the *real* Manchester. Ouch! For a few weeks United fans hurled socks full of red paint at it to try and obliterate the blue. But it only seemed to emphasise how miffed they were.

Tevez had been admired at Old Trafford, appreciated for his hard work, versatility and skill on the ball. He'd scored for the first time away at Liverpool on 13 September and went on to add another four league goals that season, including one which helped secure a 2-0 home win in the Manchester derby of 10 May. However, that same day media reports suggested he was unsettled at the club, disgruntled that his loan move from West Ham had not become permanent and disappointed at being subbed regularly. His derby goal duly prompted chants of 'Fergie, Fergie sign him up', and sure enough after the next game at Wigan, in which Tevez came off the bench to score with a cheeky back-heel, Sir Alex announced that talks were underway.

United offered to pay the transfer option fee of £25.5 million and by June had a lucrative five-year contract on the table. But it was already too late. Former Old Trafford hero Mark Hughes, now City's manager (at least for another six months) quickly closed the deal and Tevez's people informed Sir Alex that he no longer wanted to play for the Red Devils. With the poster plastered in place, United's manager was in no mood for conciliatory words. 'It's City, isn't it?' he told the BBC.

> They're a small club with a small mentality. All they can talk about is Manchester United; they can't get away from it. They think taking Carlos Tevez away from Manchester United is a triumph. It is poor stuff.

He was wrong, though not entirely. By the 2010–11 season Tevez had become City's captain and talisman, scoring 20 goals in 31 league appearances. Yet his mercurial tendencies eventually worked against him. After a public spat with manager Roberto Mancini, in which the player allegedly refused to warm up when asked to come on as a substitute during a 2011 Champions League defeat at Bayern Munich, fans sided with Mancini. Tevez headed back to Argentina for a five-month sulk, for which he later apologised, but returned the following season to help clinch that 2011–12 Premier League title as City clawed back an eight-point United advantage over the final six games.

Ashley Cole, 2006 (Arsenal to Chelsea)

Few transfers in the annals of English football match the animosity which greeted Ashley Cole's move from London N7 to London SW6. The left-back had come through the Gunners academy to become a Highbury hero, regarded by neutrals as one of the finest defenders in the world. He'd won two Premier League titles with his boyhood club, including the 2003–04 Invincibles season which saw Arsenal undefeated, and three FA Cup wins, two of which were league-and-cup Doubles. So when Arsenal fans discovered that in January 2005 their England international had been in secret 'tapping up' talks with Chelsea manager José Mourinho, it felt like betrayal.

The background was that Cole had been offered a new contract at Highbury. But, at £55,000 per week, he believed it was nowhere near his true market value. Together with a couple of agents he met Mourinho and Chelsea chief executive Peter Kenyon at London's Royal Park Hotel, Lancaster Gate, for a 'chit-chat'. In his autobiography *My Defence* he dismissed any suggestion that this amounted to tapping up, writing:

> I can only speak about what was said and not said while I was in the room and in those 15–20 minutes the chit-chat never strayed anywhere near what could be considered an approach by Chelsea. Not once was there anything mentioned about figures, transfers, further meetings or even leaving Arsenal.

He claimed the Arsenal board had made him a scapegoat.

Unfortunately for Cole, Mourinho, Kenyon et al., the Lancaster Gate meeting wasn't quite as discreet as they had perhaps imagined. Arsenal's then vice-chairman David Dein later recounted how he'd taken a call from a reporter at the now-defunct *News of the World*, who said 'Your player Ashley Cole is being tapped up by Chelsea. I think you should come and see us.' He was presented with a signed statement said to be from a restaurant waiter – 'an Arsenal fan, the waiter, clearly' – and the story broke within hours. Dein told talkSPORT he regretted Arsenal hadn't done more to retain Cole but that construction of the new Emirates Stadium had meant money was tight: 'Tensions were raging about how we were going to finance the stadium,' he said. 'We were watching every penny. We didn't do enough to keep him, and I regret that with hindsight. Ashley, if you're listening, I'm sorry.' It was a view echoed by Arsène Wenger, who described the saga as 'a mistake ... a misunderstanding for a few thousand pounds.'

The Premier League launched an immediate inquiry and Cole was found guilty of making contact with Chelsea without telling Arsenal. He was fined £100,000 and Mourinho £200,000 though both penalties were reduced on appeal to £75,000. Chelsea took a £300,000 hit. But that wasn't the end of it. Cole agreed a one-year contract extension, although it was clear to fans that he was on borrowed time. Why else would he have been excluded from the new season's official team photograph? In July 2006 Dein announced that Arsenal were in 'civil talks' with Chelsea over a transfer deal and, after much horsetrading, a deal was struck in which Cole was bought for £5 million with unsettled Blues' defender William Gallas moving the other way. The deal went through in the early hours of 1 September after the transfer window had shut (at the time the deadline was midnight on 31 August) and required special Premier League dispensation.

It seemed like a decent compromise. Mourinho had been desperate to strengthen the left side of his defence while, in Gallas, Wenger had a high quality international centre-back who could not only partner Kolo Touré but also play at either full-back position if required. Surely everyone could move on? Not a chance. Chelsea released a statement in which they accused Gallas of threatening to make deliberate mistakes or score an own goal. 'Before the first game of the season against Manchester City,' it read,

> when only four defenders were available and John Terry was doubtful with an injury, he refused to play. He went on to threaten that if he was forced to play, or if he was disciplined and financially punished for his breach of the rules, that he could score an own goal or get himself sent off or make deliberate mistakes. Clearly this was a totally unacceptable situation for the manager, the team and the club.

Gallas angrily denied the claim. 'If people want to hide behind false accusations in order to give a reason for why I left so they can calm down the club's supporters then they can,' he said. 'All this is very, very petty on behalf of Chelsea.'

Gunners fans, meanwhile, made sure Ashley (who they rechristened 'Cashley') got the full pantomime villain treatment during the teams' first meeting of the season, a 1-1 draw at Stamford Bridge. As he took the field, the away end waved fake £20 notes emblazoned with his face. Cole went on to make 229 appearances for Chelsea in which he won a Champions League trophy, Premier League title and four FA Cups. Over the next four years Gallas made 101 appearances for Arsenal in which they won just one trophy, the 2014 FA Cup. He remained a controversial figure and was stripped of the captaincy in 2008 after publicly accusing younger players of lacking courage. Two years later he refused a new contract and left Arsenal as a free agent, this time signing for an even more hated rival in the form of Tottenham. Less of a fuss was made about that – perhaps Gunners fans were clean out of creative jibes – but, whatever, it provided a nice football trivia poser: name the only player in the modern game to turn out for Chelsea, Arsenal and Tottenham.

Sol Campbell, 2001 (Tottenham Hotspur to Arsenal)

Derby rivalry is one thing. It's part of the game, it reflects the passion of fans and it produces great atmospheres in the stadiums. But when that rivalry turns into pure vitriol aimed at a player who – let's face it – has simply moved jobs, it becomes unacceptable. The hostility 26-year-old Sol Campbell endured after he ran down his contract at Tottenham to leave on a Bosman-style free to Arsenal was off the scale.

Perhaps it was fuelled by his public statements that he intended to stay with Spurs and, once, that he would never play for Arsenal. Perhaps it was because, in his first 2001–02 season, he helped the Gunners clinch their second domestic double in four years by marshalling the second meanest defence in the league – just 36 goals against; Tottenham finished ninth on 53 goals against. Mostly though, from a Spurs perspective, here was a lad who had worked his way through the academy to become a feted fixture of the first team. He knew the football culture in North London, knew the importance of bragging rights. Yet still he'd been lured by the dark side. This was despite Tottenham reportedly offering him the most lucrative contract in the club's history.

Campbell's position was that he'd joined Arsenal to get Champions League experience, partly on the advice of England manager Sven-Göran Eriksson. But it must also have been partly on the line in his contract which read £60,000-a-week plus bonuses and a £2 million signing-on fee. Either way, his return to White Hart Lane for the first meeting between the sides – a 1-1 draw – saw him walk out to a sea of white banners and balloons bearing the single word 'Judas'. Not that the outpouring of abuse seemed to bother him. His first meaningful touch was a robust challenge which took out both Les Ferdinand and Gus Poyet.

Campbell's ordeal wasn't confined to stadiums. No longer could he enjoy a quiet day off in public for fear that an embittered Spurs fan would start on him. Arsène Wenger later admitted that, with hindsight, he wasn't sure he would have signed the player. 'The situation was really stressful for Sol,' said Wenger. 'He told me afterwards how severe it became. He couldn't go to certain places for dinner or walk freely in London because of the anger of the Tottenham fans.' Decades later, the legacy of that period still lingers with Campbell, who feels the criticism he took went 'way beyond football' and would never be tolerated today. 'People started encroaching on who you are, your personality, your family and things like that, which was bang out of order,' he told one interviewer. 'That was not right. You couldn't get away with it now. You'd get put inside or you'd get a criminal record.'

Eric Cantona, 1992 (Leeds United to Manchester United)

As the Premier League's 1992–93 debut got underway, Eric Cantona had been a Leeds United player for barely eight months. Yet for the Elland Road faithful, his assists and midfield wizardry had already secured him god-like status.

He'd been key to their title-winning run the previous season and now here he was scoring for fun. By the time the club began its European Cup campaign in Stuttgart on 16 September, the Frenchman's season goal tally already stood at 1.5 goals per game in all competitions – including two hat-tricks. What could possibly go wrong? Unfortunately for the Mighty Whites, an awful lot.

Unbeknown to those travelling fans, tension between their new cult hero and manager Howard Wilkinson was building. When Cantona, struggling with a hamstring niggle, misdirected a pass to gift Stuttgart their opening goal in what became a 3-0 win, Wilkinson was furious. Their relationship was fraying at the edges and, when Cantona was substituted after an uncharacteristically poor performance in a second round European Cup game away at Rangers, he stormed straight into the dressing room – an act Wilkinson regarded as disrespectful to teammates. Cantona was dropped for Leeds' next game against QPR, and then again after missing two chances in a League Cup defeat to Watford. These were signals of open warfare to a player with mercurial tendencies who didn't do steps back. Cantona refused to report for training and on 24 November faxed over a transfer request naming Manchester United, Liverpool or Arsenal as his preferred destinations. All three were key rivals in Leeds' defence of their title. But *of* the three, the most entrenched hostility among Whites fans was reserved for United. Selling to them would be a deal with the Devil. Worse, a Red Devil.

The following day, in one of those strange 'sliding doors' moments, United's chairman Martin Edwards was due to meet manager Alex Ferguson to discuss transfer targets. Accounts of what happened differ depending on which memoir you read but, in essence, Edwards was aware of the fallout between Cantona and Wilkinson and knew Ferguson had received glowing reports on the player from France manager Gérard Houllier. United's marquee close season signing, Dion Dublin, had broken a leg, while attempts to lure Alan Shearer, Matt Le Tissier and David Hirst to Old Trafford had all hit the buffers. Set against the way United had presented Leeds with the title the previous season – top with a game in hand on 16 April they had managed to lose three of their last four games – a goal scorer or creator was a must. Cantona was both.

The way Edwards tells it in his book *Red Glory*, Leeds chairman Bill Fotherby called him to ask about the availability of defender Denis Irwin. After insisting that Irwin wasn't for sale, Edwards saw an opportunity to pitch for Cantona. 'I had never had a conversation about Cantona with Alex,' he wrote,

> but had read that Howard Wilkinson and him didn't get on. So I blurted it out. I actually rang Alex at the training ground and told him. He said: "Too right I would have Cantona." So the next day I called Bill and said we would take Cantona off their hands. As though we were doing them a favour. We got him for £1m but Bill asked that we say it was £1.6m to appease the Leeds fans.

When Ferguson's assistant Brian Kidd discovered the bargain price tag he pondered whether Cantona had 'lost a leg or something'.

Ferguson later described the timing of the deal as 'weird, absolutely uncanny', and observed:

> If ever there was one player, anywhere in the world,
> that was made for Manchester United, it was
> Cantona. He swaggered in, stuck his chest out, raised
> his head and surveyed everything as though he were
> asking: "I'm Cantona. How big are you? Are you big
> enough for me?"

Although football stats are often interpreted to fit an argument, United's numbers pre- and post-Cantona are illuminating. At the point he signed they were all mid-table mediocrity, having won just six of their first 16 games. Suddenly they started to believe, winning 19 out of 26 to clinch the club's first title in 26 years.

His very presence on the pitch produced an astonishing turnaround. In 1992, the 37 games United played before his arrival produced 38 goals and 54 points. In the 37 games that followed they hit 77 goals and collected 88 points. They went on to win four of the next five Premier League titles, and would almost certainly have won a fifth had Cantona not had his foolish 'kung fu' moment at Crystal Palace and got himself banned for nine months (see **Fiery February**). His talents were perfectly summed up by *MOTD* commentator John Motson during United's January 1993 4-1 thrashing of Spurs, a game which Cantona controlled with all his arrogance and pomp. 'Every time he gets the ball the game wakes up', observed Motson. 'This man is playing a game of his own.' Leeds finished the season 17th, two points off the relegation places.

Denis Law, 1973 (Manchester United to Manchester City)

This was a transfer less controversial than it's sometimes portrayed. It also fed one of the great myths of English football history. In April 1974 Law's back-heel effort for City in the final moments of their 1-0 win over United was reported in the papers as the goal that relegated his old club. It didn't – other results meant the Red Devils were doomed anyway – but that would have spoiled the story.

Law first signed for Manchester City from Huddersfield in 1960 but stayed only a season before moving on to Torino. A year later the striker was signed by United manager Matt Busby for a club record £115,000, a continuation of the rebuilding process which followed the 1958 Munich disaster. Law proved his worth, scoring 29 goals in all competitions, including the opener in his side's 3-1 FA Cup final win over Leicester City. But, despite Bobby Charlton's presence in the side, United were poor overall and narrowly escaped relegation. It wasn't until 18 January 1964 – seven months before *MOTD* took to the airwaves – that things began to look a whole lot different. For the first time, United's starting lineup included Law, Charlton and some kid from Northern Ireland called George Best. Law, who was having a magnificent season, scored twice in a 4-1 away victory at West Bromwich Albion while the other two weighed in with a goal apiece. It was the first time the 'Holy Trinity' of Law, Best and Charlton had played together, and for United it was the turn of the tide. They finished second that season, won two of the next three titles, and in 1968 became the first English team to win the European Cup.

Yet by the end of the 1972–73 season they were once again in decline. Charlton was retiring and new manager Tommy Docherty was looking to rebuild. He allowed Law a free transfer in recognition of his long service and in July 1973 Manchester

City agreed terms. There was no Tevez-style rumpus attached to this. Law had once been a City player and rivalry between the red and blue halves of Manchester was largely good-natured. Indeed, fans from both clubs would often watch whoever was playing at home. The controversy only erupted with that 81st minute back-heel goal in the penultimate game of the 1973–74 season at Old Trafford. Law didn't celebrate and later admitted he'd been hoping for a 0-0 draw. He described the feeling as 'awful', believing he might have relegated a club he loved. However, a 0-0 draw would have been no good to United that day. Birmingham City's defeat of Norwich and West Ham's point against Liverpool meant they dropped to the second tier for the first time since 1938.

Phil Chisnall, 1964 (Manchester United to Liverpool)

Alright, this one wasn't really controversial. But it certainly *would* be today, and in any case it provides a nice link to our **October** chapter covering all things *Match of the Day*. That's because the first player to touch the ball in the very first programme – Liverpool v Arsenal, 22 August 1964 – was none other than Liverpool centre-forward Phil Chisnall. Still the last player to transfer directly between Manchester United and Liverpool, Chisnall was just 21 when he moved down the East Lancs Road to join Bill Shankly's newly crowned champions in April 1964. He'd done well at Old Trafford, and England Under-23s manager Alf Ramsey even described him as 'probably the best passer of a ball in the country'. But the second half of the 1963–64 season saw him failing to make United's starting lineups, and manager Matt Busby provisionally accepted a £25,000 offer from Shankly, a man with whom he had a close personal friendship ...

Years later, Chisnall told the *Liverpool Echo* how the move ensured he would 'become the answer to a quiz question'. He was never pressurised by Busby, who simply said it was 'up to him', and that although unusual, 'there wasn't a big deal made of it.' Chisnall added: 'After I signed, I went back and played for Liverpool against United at Old Trafford. I can't remember getting any stick – it wasn't like that back then.' His Liverpool career never ignited and he scored only twice in nine appearances before moving to Southend in 1967. But at least, thanks to that kick-off in 1964, he launched the most iconic sports programme in UK history.

OCTOBER:
MATCH OF THE DAY
MATTERS

For *Match of the Day*, 2 October is always a big anniversary. It's the date in 1965 that a Saturday night football highlights package finally secured its place in British culture, and the game's relationship with broadcasters entered its revolutionary phase. That 1964 season opener between Liverpool and Arsenal might have been *MOTD's* debut but the path ahead was perilous. The very notion of football on the box was viewed with suspicion and hostility by the Football League, the FA and a clique of the most powerful clubs. Neither could the show be portrayed as an instant ratings winner. It was launched on BBC2, a new channel operating on a higher-definition 625-line UHF radio wave system which meant directors were no longer restricted to close-up action, as the ball was clearly visible in wide-angle footage. But BBC2 was available only in the London area and many sets still operated only on the established

BBC Television Service 405-line frequency. Unsurprisingly, the estimated viewing figures were low – at 20,000, less than half the Anfield attendance. Nonetheless, technology was moving fast. New electronic cameras and videotape machines meant match footage could be wired to an off-site editing suite and quickly cut to fit pre-set time slots. Club chairmen realised the show would be rolled out nationally and asked themselves, why would fans pay gate money if they can follow their team at home in front of the fire?

Throughout the summer of 1965 the dispute between leading clubs and the BBC over televised games rumbled on. The Corporation thought *MOTD* was a great way to prepare outside broadcast and production crews for live coverage of the forthcoming 1966 World Cup. The chairmen had a different take. Still smarting from the increased wages bill resulting from Jimmy Hill's players' strike, and bitter at George Eastman's undermining of their hallowed transfer system (see **September**), they saw *MOTD* as a real threat to attendances. Fears were heightened still further when it was announced that the programme would move to BBC1 for the start of the 1965–66 season. The football authorities dug in. There would be no televised games until they said so. Two weeks before the season got underway the row reached the House of Commons. Albert Murray (Labour, Gravesend) asked Sports Minister Denis Howell whether he would reconsider his decision to give clubs staging World Cup matches a grant from the taxpayer. 'As long as there are long-term benefits which the Football Association will receive from a grant from public funds,' he said, 'would it not be in the interest of the public, particularly old-age pensioners, the sick and infirm, if they could enjoy the benefits of seeing football matches on television?' Howell responded that the televising of live games had 'an almost catastrophic effect on the gates.'

It seemed that *MOTD* might be strangled at birth. But eventually a deal was reached which required the BBC to keep its chosen game under wraps until the entire Saturday fixture programme was complete. Highlights would also be strictly limited to 45 minutes. So it was that on 2 October 1965 – with the new season already ten games old – *MOTD* was allowed to begin coverage in earnest, choosing West Bromwich Albion v Chelsea for the comeback. Viewers were greeted by commentator Frank Bough and his version of Received Pronunciation, that speech affectation of the British upper middle classes which defined BBC broadcasting for decades. It was no doubt supposed to make commentary clear; Frank sounded like he'd been kicked in the unmentionables. But at least it felt as though you were right there with him in the stands. One nearby fan was keen to deploy a football hand-rattle at every opportunity, drowning out some of Frank's commentary jewels like: 'Chelsea today have abandoned their royal blue and are playing in what you will see as white but is in fact the most delicious and jazzy canary yellow.' The game ended in a 1-2 win for the visitors, allowing Blues fans to sing their favourite ditty to the tune of 'Michael, Row the Boat Ashore', a recent hit for 'King of Skiffle' Lonnie Donegan: 'Chelsea's gonna win the League, hallelujah'. They finished fifth, ten points off the pace.

NO MORE FIFTY SHADES OF GREY: THE COLOUR TV REVOLUTION AND AN ICONIC THEME TUNE

With its future secure, *Match of the Day* moved on to the next big step-change – colour broadcasting. BBC2 was again the guinea pig in 1967, initially with four hours a week, showing the Wimbledon Tennis Championships in colour for the first time. BBC1 decided to join the party, and in October 1969 a small army of technicians was secretly dispatched to Anfield to prepare for the channel's first *MOTD* colour match between Liverpool and West Ham on 15 November. This was a huge challenge in itself. Clubs had no proper facilities for TV crews, so the boardroom had to be rewired as a makeshift studio. Liverpool secretary Peter Robinson described this as 'a mammoth task'. Meanwhile producer Alec Weeks was busy ramping up prepublicity by seeing how many times he could use the word 'colour' in interviews. 'We chose Liverpool for the first colour transmission because we wanted a colourful place,' he told the *Liverpool Echo*. 'There's nowhere as colourful as Anfield, both literally and in character, with the Kop and their comments. Football in colour is fantastic. Tonight the red and light blue on the green will stand out. Identification of the players is much easier – you can see the colour of their hair, even the blushes if someone is being bawled out.' The *Echo* also reported a scramble to get hold of colour sets, with frantic scenes at electrical retailers. 'Demand exceeds supply,' the newspaper warned. 'Everyone wants one.' Yet at around £250, plus a hike in the licence fee, not everyone got one. For many fans it was a case of tracking down friendly, well-heeled neighbours to catch the 35-minute highlights package with goals from Chris Lawler and Bobby Graham seeing the Reds home. Now *MOTD* just needed one final tweak. A new tune for the new look.

In 1970 producers began casting around for music to replace the original 1964 theme tune 'Drum Majorette', a military march written by former Welsh Guards band member Major Leslie Statham. Though distinctive and upbeat, it felt dated and had something of a *Pathé News* newsreel about it (1970 was, incidentally, the year *Pathé News* finally disappeared from cinemas). The brief from new *MOTD* editor Sam Leitch was simply to produce 'something good', and Barry Stoller, a 29-year-old composer from East London, tried his luck. He enlisted the help of two musicians, turned his basement into a basic home recording studio and set about the job. Though not a football fan, he knew it inspired passion and the drama of physical combat. He wanted a 'gladiatorial' feel.

> What came into my mind actually was the fanfare, those last few notes, they represent gladiators, footballers in the arena. They're the people, that's everything, and so from that moment I knew the piece had to be played completely by trumpets. When it was on for the first year I was really delighted. Then it came back for a second year – I was over the moon about that. Then five years, ten years – it's still there. It's the most instantly recognisable theme throughout the country and I'm really humbled by that. It's people. It's *Match of the Day*.

And woe betide any BBC executive who messes with it. But mess with it they did. When a new version was adopted it prompted an outpouring of fury among viewers. Presenter

Jimmy Hill responded on air: 'Now to reveal the subject that has provoked a lot of gentlemen, and even more ladies, to write pleading letters to the programme in recent weeks. It's simply this.' As the camera cut away, and the new theme played, Jimmy and co-presenter Bob Wilson shook their heads. 'Bob and I agree with most of you,' said Jimmy. 'We like the old music better.' Stoller's masterpiece was soon restored.

THE PRESENTERS

Of course, *Match of the Day* is not the only early-1960s programme to have reached its diamond anniversary. *Doctor Who*, launched in 1963, is also still going strong. But whereas there have been 15 different Doctors, there have only ever been five main *MOTD* presenters.

Kenneth Wolstenholme: 1964–1967

Wolstenholme launched *MOTD* to the sound of the Beatles' 'She Loves You' blaring from the Anfield PA system: 'Welcome to *Match of the Day*, the first of a weekly series coming to you every Saturday on BBC2. As you can hear we're in Beatleville ...' And he soon established himself as the show's main anchor and commentator. He possessed the crucial qualities of excellent timing and a love of language, while conveying the impression of a friendly uncle taking you to the game. At a time when technical glitches were a regular part of the job, Wolstenholme exuded calm, perhaps because he'd already experienced real jeopardy in the workplace, through being shot at on a daily basis. During the Second World War he served as an RAF bomber pilot and by the age of 23 had flown over 100 missions, a record which earned him the Distinguished Flying

Cross and Bar. The BBC hired him in 1948, whereupon he was thrust straight into the commentary hot seat at a Southern v Northern Counties football trial in Romford.

His commentary as Geoff Hurst's third goal sealed England's 1966 World Cup final victory – ' ... and here comes Hurst ... some people are on the pitch, they think it's all over ... it is now' – remains the UK's most recognisable piece of sports broadcasting. But he was not infallible. A few weeks earlier, in the FA Cup final, he'd suffered the commentator's curse by screaming 'It's Wednesday's Cup', as David Ford put away the Sheffield side's 57th minute second goal. Within two minutes Harry Catterick's Everton pulled one back and the Toffees went on to win 3-2. The following year Wolstenholme briefly co-presented *MOTD* with new kid on the block David Coleman, before handing over the anchor role.

His BBC contract specified that he would continue to cover the biggest games, but this was thrown into doubt when his name was missed off the *Radio Times* listing for the 1970 World Cup final in Mexico between Brazil and Italy. A stern phone call from his lawyer to BBC executives followed and Wolstenholme was duly handed the commentary mic. But only for the 90 minutes of football. Once the match ended, the favoured Coleman took over and described the scenes as Brazilian fans celebrated their side's 4-1 victory. Wolstenholme later confessed to feeling 'a bit miffed', code for 'furious'. He quit the Corporation the following year after covering the 1971 European Cup final at Wembley. For years he insisted his proudest moment was the launch of *Match of the Day*, but that changed after the 1993 memorial service in honour of England's World Cup-winning captain Bobby

Moore. The hushed congregation was played a recording of his commentary as Moore collected the Jules Rimet Trophy in front of an ecstatic Wembley crowd: 'It is only 12 inches high,' said Wolstenholme, 'it is solid gold … and it undeniably means England are champions of the world.'

David Coleman: 1967–1973

The personality gulf between Wolstenholme and Coleman can be captured in a single incident at the Mexico World Cup. Whereas the former was a strictly old school, hands-off football broadcaster, Coleman's hard-nosed background in news journalism meant he ached to be in the midst of a breaking story. When Bobby Moore was falsely accused of stealing a bracelet in Bogotá, Coleman joined the press pack at Mexico City International Airport to await his arrival. Spotting the England captain collecting his luggage, he pushed past security officials, placed an arm around Moore and shepherded him straight to a waiting BBC camera crew for an exclusive chat. His reporting skills would be severely tested two years later when he found himself covering the Black September attack at the Munich Olympics – at one point discovering that the terrorists were listening to his broadcast.

Coleman was already a consummate sports commentator and anchor when he arrived in the *MOTD* hot seat. He'd made his first BBC TV appearance in 1954 on a Saturday night programme called *Sports Special* and was spotted as a rising star by one of the Corporation's top executives, Paul Fox. By the late 1950s Coleman was presenting the flagship Saturday sports show *Grandstand,* smoothing over technical hitches and seamlessly flitting between outside broadcast units. His obsession with preparation was particularly apparent – no more so than when he manned the *Grandstand* teleprinter, bringing instant context to incoming football results: 'Third division again, Brighton 1, Watford 4: Brighton remain third from the bottom; Watford's first win in 11 matches.' His competitive streak was also legendary. When, in 1965, ITV launched *World of Sport* to challenge *Grandstand*'s domination, Coleman, a no-nonsense grammar school boy from Cheshire, pledged to 'blow the b******s out of the water'. ITV's Brian Moore recalled how his rival would sometimes greet him at major sporting events with the words: 'Oh, here he is, seeking an inferior audience again.' Moore took it well: 'You would curse yourself for not having a rejoinder ready but it was just his way of hyping himself up and trying to get one up on you. He was the last word in competitiveness.'

Coleman combined *MOTD* duties with his own show – *Sportsnight with Coleman* – while also retaining his position as the BBC's lead football commentator. Over the years his in-game gaffes were faithfully and gleefully published by the satirical magazine *Private Eye*, which named its 'Colemanballs' column after him. Lines included: 'Forest have now lost six matches without winning', and 'Don't tell those coming in the final result of that fantastic match, but let's just have another look at Italy's winning goal'. Coleman took the teasing in good part probably because, as Brian Moore put it, 'he knew he was the best and professionally, all said and done, we knew he had set the standard.' His concise yet passionate style endeared him to a generation of football fans, and his standard 'one-nil' to accompany an opening goal (always delivered with an air of the inevitable) became a trademark phrase, along with 'quite remarkable'. After leaving the *MOTD* presenting chair he continued to commentate on live matches for the BBC, his last being England's 3-1 win against Scotland in May 1979 for *International Match of the Day*.

Jimmy Hill: 1973–1988

The champagne corks must have been popping like machine-gun fire at Broadcasting House the day Jimmy Hill signed for *MOTD*. It wasn't just that he'd been poached from the programme's main rival, ITV's *The Big Match*. Hill was a massive name in terms of football experience, credibility and new thinking. Here was a former professional footballer, players' shop steward, coach, manager, club chairman, administrator, and television executive, who had influenced the modern English game more than any other individual through innovations that would stand the test of time. Hill, as chairman of Coventry City, pioneered development of the country's first all-seater stadium and proved instrumental in improving the quality of professional football as a spectacle. He persuaded the Football League to introduce three points for a win (instead of two), incentivising teams to attack more on the basis that the reward of two extra points for pushing hard in a game heading for a draw would outweigh the risk of losing it and surrendering a point. The idea was widely acknowledged as a success when launched in 1981 and was later adopted worldwide.

The following year another Hill innovation changed the way the game was played. He, like many who watched the 1980 FA Cup final, was appalled when West Ham's 17-year-old starlet Paul Allen went through for a clear goal-scoring opportunity only to be cynically brought down by Arsenal's Willie Young.

Match referee George Courtney could only book Young and award a free kick. Although West Ham eventually won 1-0, Allen was in tears as he collected his medal, knowing he would probably never get a better chance to score in the Cup final. Hill campaigned for such professional fouls, including deliberate handball, to be treated as red card offences, and was appointed by the Football League to lead a consultation. Although the International Football Association Board declined to change the Laws, the League instructed referees to interpret professional fouls as serious foul play, and therefore worthy of a red card, from the start of the 1982–83 season.

Once ensconced at *MOTD,* Hill built on the success he'd enjoyed as head of sport at London Weekend Television, where his introduction of match analysts had proved a huge hit. Within a year, his avuncular, fan-focused presenting skills pushed the programme's viewing figures to a record 12 million and made him a household name. He was also quick to adapt to changes forced upon the programme, such as the Football League's decision to give ITV the Saturday night highlights packages – dubbed by headline writers 'Snatch of the Day' – on alternate seasons between 1980 and 1983. *MOTD* switched to Sunday afternoons, which meant refocusing the brand. Hill's solution was 'pullover punditry', in which he and Bob Wilson swapped their formal shirts and ties for casual jumpers, hoping to tap into a post-roast relaxed atmosphere in the country's living rooms. His ability to shape televised football was summed up years later by commentator John Motson, with whom he worked closely for years. 'He was, in the truest sense, a visionary,' said Motson. 'He was an activist too. He had a remarkable ability not just to see the future but to make it happen.'

Des Lynam: 1988–1999

In early 1988 TV sport executives were locked in negotiations with the Football League over a new broadcast rights deal. The BBC and ITV tendered a joint bid in which they would share a highlights package and exclusive rights to some live games. Everything looked rosy until, in May 1988, new satellite channel British Sky Broadcasting lived up to its burgeoning reputation as television's Disruptor-in-Chief by slapping a ten-year, £9 million-per-season offer on the table. To top it, even as joint partner, the BBC would have had to blow a massive hole in its sport programming budget. ITV Sport's wily chairman Greg Dyke knew this and opted to go it alone, negotiating directly with the League himself. He won a four-year, £11 million-per-season deal, leaving *MOTD* with only the FA Cup and a few England games. The BBC responded by freshening up the programme with a new title – *Match of the Day: The Road to Wembley* – and a new, but familiar, face.

Des Lynam was already well known as the main presenter of *Grandstand* and had fronted major events such as the Grand National, Wimbledon and the Olympic Games. He had a proven history in sports journalism and his relaxed style was a winner with viewers. Tony Gubba would sometimes fill in on *Grandstand*, but there was no alternative show to offer Jimmy Hill, who the BBC did not want to lose. The solution was to move Hill sideways into an *MOTD* punditry role. Lynam was worried about how that might go down. 'I thought I'd better OK this with Jimmy,' he recalled later,

> because Jimmy was an old friend. I didn't want to
> upset the guy and I would have to work with him.
> He said: "I'm OK with it. I'd rather you did it than

somebody I don't like." So I did it and Jimmy became the leading pundit and we worked for years like that very successfully and happily. In fact doing it with him and [then Tottenham manager] Terry Venables were some of the highlights of the shows because they argued all the time. It wasn't stage-managed – they actually did see the opposite point of view about everything. But they were great friends of course.

As a partnership, Lynam and Hill's finest hour came on 15 April 1989, when it fell to them to bring the nation coverage of the Hillsborough Disaster. *MOTD* was in Sheffield to cover the Liverpool v Nottingham Forest FA Cup semi-final, abandoned after six minutes as the scale of the tragedy began to emerge. Ninety-seven Liverpool fans were crushed to death, unlawfully killed due to grossly negligent failures by the police and ambulance service according to verdicts recorded years later by a coroner's court. What happened is now clear. But these were the days before rolling news programmes and as *MOTD* went live, Lynam and Hill could rely only on crowd scenes, eyewitness accounts and hazy information from police and politicians. The full death toll was still being calculated.

'It's been a black day for football,' Lynam began.

On a sunny afternoon at Hillsborough, Sheffield, no fewer than 93 football supporters died in the most tragic accident for the sport ever in this country. Jimmy Hill and I were there and it becomes a sad duty tonight for those of us normally concerned with the lighter side of television reporting to deal with a sombre subject.

Scenes of the crush outside and inside the ground followed as Lynam described what happened, carefully emphasising that there was no violence – only impatience in areas of the ground where fans couldn't appreciate the severity of the problem. He ended with: 'This was to have been a sports programme, you will understand on a day of such momentous tragedy it would be inappropriate to show football action.' The final, haunting image was of Liverpool scarves tied to poles on the terraces as the first wreaths were laid at the Leppings Lane end.

Gary Lineker: 1999–

Given that Lineker is now the longest-serving *MOTD* main presenter (2024 is his 25th anniversary as well as the show's 60th), it's easy to forget that he was a world-class footballer. His acceleration and pace, spatial awareness, poacher's instinct and courage to get stuck in when the studs were flying led his former England manager Bobby Robson to conclude that he was 'simply the best finisher I've ever seen.' In spells with his boyhood club Leicester City, and later Everton and Tottenham, he scored a total of 192 league goals in 340 appearances – at various times featuring as top Division One scorer with each of them. He added a further 42 goals in 103 appearances during a three-year stint with Barcelona, becoming one of the most feared strikers in the world. No Englishman has scored more World Cup goals than Gary Lineker (six in 1986; four in 1990), and his total tally of 48 puts him behind only Wayne Rooney and Bobby Charlton in the list of retired England top scorers. Astonishingly, in more than 600 club and international appearances, he was never once booked. His footballing CV is impeccable. How would he do in front of the cameras?

When Lineker began guest-presenting *Match of the Day* in 1998 he took nothing for granted, replaying his early shows to get feedback from his editors. 'I told them to be brutal with me,' he said later. 'I just really wanted to learn.' He also took lessons from a voice coach to help get 'enthusiasm and light and shade into my voice.' It wasn't a long apprenticeship. In August 1999 Des Lynam resigned, wooed by ITV's ultimately successful pledge to acquire an exclusive Premier League highlights package for three seasons from 2001–02, and Lineker was appointed main presenter. It was a big opportunity and occasionally the nerves showed, something well understood by his predecessor. 'I knew he'd always wanted to [anchor *MOTD*]', said Lynam.

> [Paul] Gascoigne used to call him Des because he'd admitted wanting to be a sports presenter. He came into it, learnt the ropes, and I could see he was going to be good. But who is brilliant to start with? Did you see my first television appearances? I certainly wouldn't want to look back on them – I was frightened as a rabbit.

Former *MOTD* and ITV football commentator Clive Tyldesley remembers how the programme's editor in the early 1990s, Brian Barwick, would try to coach players-turned-presenters into a new mindset, telling them:

> 'We know that you know a lot about football. But your job now is to convey your knowledge to people who have never been there, never stood on a touchline, never taken a penalty in a big game. It's not just a simple question of us thinking you talk quite well, you used to be a footballer. You've got to embrace *our* industry.' That has been a difficult journey for some.

I'm sure it was for Jimmy, it certainly was for Bob Wilson and it was for Gary Lineker in the early days. To obtain sufficient broadcasting skills – a brand new skillset – in order to bring all that you did as a truly great footballer in Gary's case and actually look down that black hole [of the camera] and be as good a presenter ... that's a long, long journey.

THE PUNDITS

Dozens of great current and former players have sat in front of *Match of the Day*'s cameras as analysts over the years. There's not enough space here to do them all justice so we're focusing on perhaps the three best-known stalwarts – starting with the Prince of Punditry himself.

Alan Hansen: 1992–2014

The doyen of *Match of the Day* pundits, Alan Hansen came to the programme having won everything the English domestic game has to offer several times over. His 434 appearances in 14 years with Liverpool produced an honours haul of three European Cups, eight Division One titles, two FA Cups and three League Cups. As one of the greatest defenders in the English game, his insight offered a new dimension to *MOTD* when he joined the programme at the launch of the Premier League era in 1992. Whereas some pundits felt uneasy about criticising fellow pros, the Scot told it as he saw it. His trademark phrases – 'shockin' defendin'' and 'diabolical defendin'' – must have haunted many a back four, although he was also quick to praise goal-saving tackles or promising young defenders making their way in the game.

Slightly odd then, you might think, that his punditry career is best remembered for one throwaway phrase delivered on the evening of 19 August 1995 as he discussed with Des Lynam Manchester United's 3-1 defeat away at Aston Villa. Over the summer, United had lost three key players in Paul Ince, Mark Hughes and Andrei Kanchelskis and now had a few on the injury list. Alex Ferguson's starting lineup included six players aged 20 or under, among them Paul Scholes, Nicky Butt and the Neville brothers, with David Beckham coming on as sub halfway through. 'Well,' said Des, 'United were scarcely recognisable from the team we've seen over the last couple of seasons. What's going on do you feel?' Alan's reply began in measured tones. 'I think they've got problems,' he said. 'I wouldn't say they've got major problems. Obviously, three players have departed, the trick is always buy when you're strong, so he needs to buy players.' Then came the fateful phrase:

> You can't win anything with kids. You look at that lineup, Manchester United today, and Aston Villa at quarter-past-two, when they get the team sheet it's just going to give them a lift and it'll happen every time he plays the kids. He's got to buy players, simple as that.

Des pointed out that Ferguson's injury list included star players like Andrew Cole, Ryan Giggs, Eric Cantona and Steve Bruce, but Alan wasn't having it. 'It's not enough. The trick of winning the [Premier League] Championship is strength in depth. They just haven't got it.' United went on to win a Premier League and FA Cup Double and their fans were never going to let the Liverpool icon forget it.

The players, though, were more conciliatory. Looking back, keeper Peter Schmeichel suspects some of his younger teammates felt intimidated by the remark, even though their determination was undimmed. 'It wasn't like, "oh, he's said that, we'll go and try even harder" because you were at the try-very-hard club anyway,' he said.

> If you don't try hard at Manchester United you're not going to make it. [The 'kids' comment] made Alan Hansen [as a pundit] and it's kind of funny. But it was a special crop of kids. Alan wasn't to know – you're a few years on and you haven't seen them playing. But we knew at some point they were all going to come good. It just took everyone by surprise that it [happened] so early.

Paul Scholes agreed. 'At the time I probably thought he was right,' he said. 'But [his comment] acted as a kind of motivation throughout the season really and from that day onwards we improved and managed to prove him wrong.'

Hansen announced his retirement from *MOTD* in an interview with the *Daily Telegraph* in September 2013, in which he praised his main presenting colleagues as 'two of the best'. 'Des was the best, and is the best, because he was just an unbelievable presenter,' he said.

> I could say virtually anything to him and he would come back with a line. And his knowledge of football was far greater than anything I thought it would be. He really did know the game. When it comes to Gary, you will be three or four questions in but he already knows question five, six or seven because he is that good.

Ian Wright: 1997–2024

Arsenal legend Ian Wright was still playing for the Gunners when he made his debut appearance as a guest pundit in December 1997 alongside Trevor Brooking. His first words on being welcomed by Des were: 'This is my Graceland. *Match of the Day*, I love it, man.' Apart from a spell away from the programme between 2007 and 2015 he has been a punditry staple – particularly voluble on the subject of his beloved Arsenal, for whom he banged in an impressive 128 goals in 221 league appearances between 1991–98. Before that, he didn't do too badly at Crystal Palace either, with 90 in 225. Announcing his decision to step down from *MOTD* at the end of the 2023–24 season he wrote on Twitter/X:

> I feel very privileged to have had such an incredible run on the most iconic football show in the world … . Anyone that knows my story knows how much the show has meant to me since I was a young boy. *MOTD* is my Holy Grail. On my first ever show, I told Des Lynam, 'This is my Graceland'. It will always be my Graceland and I will always be watching.

Alan Shearer: 2006–2024

One extraordinary statistic sums up Shearer's playing career. For 31 years – since December 1993 to be precise – he has been the Premier League's all-time top scorer, with 260 goals. It's a record that seems unlikely to be broken any time soon, given that his nearest rival, Harry Kane, was 47 behind when he left Tottenham for Bayern Munich in 2023, and the only other active Premier League player in the top ten, Mohamed Salah, was over 100 behind at the start of 2024. Shearer, who had spells at Southampton, Blackburn and Newcastle, was voted FWA Player of the Year in 1994 and PFA Player of the Year in 1995. He came third in both the Ballon d'Or and FIFA World Player of the Year in 1996, and in 2004 was named by Pelé on FIFA's list of the 100 greatest living players. He scored 30 goals in 63 appearances for England and won the Golden Boot at Euro 96.

Shearer's playing experience and concise analysis has enlightened *MOTD* viewers since 2006 following his final season with Newcastle. Apart from a brief stint back at St James' Park as manager in 2009 – an ultimately futile bid to help his hometown club avoid relegation – he has been the programme's principal analyst. In an interview with the *Guardian* to celebrate the show's 50th birthday he admitted to being nervous in his early days: 'you can make an error on a football pitch but you can't on live TV because there's no going back.'

THE COMMENTATORS

John Motson

The Edgar Street stadium, Hereford, 5 February 1972. Rookie 26-year-old commentator John Motson is on trial for *Match of the Day*, assigned to cover the FA Cup third round replay between Hereford United and Newcastle United. It's a big night for the Southern League underdogs and an estimated 16,000 fans have turned up, not all of them inside the ground. The cameras focus on various unofficial berths such as trees and electricity pylons, and while anticipation is tangible the locals know a shock result is unlikely. First Division Newcastle, playing their prolific £180,000 striker Malcolm Macdonald, are hot favourites. Still, you never know. Especially on a quintessentially 1970s waterlogged pitch, as much mud as grass. In the later stages, cramp was going to be a factor for both sets of players.

In the 82nd minute the favourites looked home and dry thanks to a trademark Macdonald bullet header. Three minutes later, Motson's career was up and running:

> Radford – now Tudor's gone down for Newcastle
> – Radford again … Oh, what a goal! What a goal!
> Radford the scorer! Ronnie Radford! And the crowd,
> the crowd are invading the pitch! And now it will take
> some time to clear the field. What a tremendous shot
> by Ronnie Radford. No goalkeeper in the world would
> stop that.

On paper, the words don't look like a commentary classic. Yet Motson's passion for the moment, his boyish excitement, his love of football's unpredictability shone through to make this arguably the most famous piece of FA Cup commentary ever. Who remembers poor old Ricky George, the substitute who actually *won* the game for Hereford with a superb low drive in the 13th minute of extra time? But them's the breaks, as the saying goes; Radford walked off into cup history and 'Motty' into a glittering *MOTD* career. Fans loved him simply because he sounded like one of them. As the BBC's former head of sport, Jonathan Martin, later famously put it: 'John is talking from the terraces.' There's more on this remarkable match in the **January** chapter.

Motson joined the BBC as a Radio 2 sports presenter in 1968 after a journalistic apprenticeship at the *Barnet Press* and *Sheffield Morning Telegraph*. He pestered his way into *MOTD* and was given a season's trial, starting with a 0-0 draw in October 1971 between two mid-table sides, Liverpool and Chelsea. After his Hereford heroism he was trusted to handle higher profile matches, but his second big career break didn't come until 1977, when *MOTD's* lead commentator David Coleman pulled out of the Liverpool-Manchester United FA Cup final over a contractual dispute and Motson was thrust into the hot seat at short notice. His commitment to meticulous research – imprinted in his DNA – demanded that he count the number of steps the winning captain would climb to receive the trophy. It proved great prep, and he was proud of it. As he later recalled:

> Martin Buchan, the United captain, was preparing to go up and receive the Cup, [and] I said: "Isn't it appropriate that a man named Buchan should climb the 39 steps at Wembley to receive the Cup?", which recalled John Buchan, the novelist who wrote *The Thirty-Nine Steps*. A lot of people thought I'd scripted that but it was spontaneous.

In his time, Motson covered over 2,000 football matches – armed always with his colour-coded handwritten notes – including 10 World Cups, 10 European Championships and 29 FA Cup finals. Among his many memorable lines were: 'The Crazy Gang have beaten the Culture Club' (Wimbledon's defeat of Liverpool in the 1988 FA Cup final); 'Is it over? It is! It's dramatic, it's delightful, it's Denmark who are European champions' (Denmark's 2-0 win over Germany in the 1992 Euros); and, 'Here's Gascoigne. Oh brilliant! Oh yes! Oh yes!' (Paul Gascoigne's moment of genius in England's 2-0 defeat of Scotland at Euro 96).

Barry Davies

Just as John Motson had fame thrust upon him courtesy of Ronnie Radford's wonder goal, so Barry Davies' *MOTD* profile got a leg up through a simple twist of fate. For the 1969–70 season he'd been handed the programme's northern patch under a new format in which each region would get a supplementary game in addition to the main national one. On the morning of 9 August, the day of the big kick-off, he was in the Queens Hotel, Leeds, preparing for Leeds v Tottenham, when his producer rang summoning him to London *tout de suite*. Main match commentator Kenneth Wolstenholme had gone down with a bug, while next-in-line David Coleman was also feeling rough and had lost his voice. Davies 'barely had time to eat his cornflakes' before being shovelled into a fast car and driven to Selhurst Park for Crystal Palace v Manchester United. Although in later years he was criticised for lacking Motson's man-of-the-people approach to commentary, this was unfair. True, he generally preferred a spare style, but he knew his *MOTD* viewers as well as anyone at the BBC. When, in this game, a camera focused on the back of United's No.11, Davies instantly seized on Best's rockstar image. 'There's George Best,' said Barry, 'with the hair blending into the shirt. And on the front of that hair we'll find he's growing just a little bit of a beard. Either that or he didn't have time for a shave this morning.'

Although intrinsically linked to *MOTD*, Davies was a true all-rounder, taking the mic for a dizzying array of sports including tennis, gymnastics, cycling, athletics, badminton, ice hockey, skating, beach volleyball and rowing (he was the 'Voice of the Boat Race' for a decade until 2004). He was also the BBC's go-to guy for the Olympics, making one of his driest observations during the Men's Hockey final at Seoul '88 as GB's Imran Sherwani's third goal sunk Germany. 'Where were the Germans?' asked Barry. 'But, frankly, who cares?' For *MOTD* his most memorable line came during commentary of Manchester City's 1-2 home defeat to Derby in 1974. At the end of the previous season Francis Lee had left Maine Road in high dudgeon after manager Malcolm Allison signed Rodney Marsh from Queens Park Rangers. Convinced he was being sidelined, Lee forced a £100,000 transfer to Derby County, but continued to nurture the feeling that his old club had shafted him. Back at Maine Road on 28 December he reminded City chairman Peter Swales that the feeling hadn't gone away. 'Interesting,' suggested Barry, as Lee drove past four defenders on the edge of the City penalty area before unleashing a worldie into the top corner of Joe Corrigan's goal. Then: 'Very interesting ... oh, look at his face. Just look at his face.' Lee's grin was as wide as the Manchester Ship Canal. Derby went on to win the title by two points. Man City finished eighth.

During his *MOTD* career Davies covered 12 European Cup finals, including wins for Nottingham Forest and Liverpool, nine World Cups and seven European Championships. But he suffered under editors who couldn't decide whether he or Motson was their main man. Motson had been assigned all FA Cup finals between 1977–94 but then Davies suddenly came in from the cold – getting the 1994 World Cup final and both subsequent FA Cup finals. The flip-flopping never translated into animosity between the two but, after 35 years on the show, Davies called it a day in September 2004. In his autobiography *Interesting, Very Interesting* he writes of feeling 'downgraded': he'd been offered none of England's

2004 European Championship games and his latest contract extension specified that he'd be getting no live football commentaries – ruling him out of the 2006 World Cup. Ahead of his final commentary game between Manchester City and Arsenal he emphasised his decision was 'not a fit of pique', adding 'I wanted more than just doing a few minutes' commentating on the roster.' Then the really substantive point, echoing his whole broadcasting philosophy: 'There is too much talk from commentators nowadays. Dramatic moments in football speak for themselves.'

Gubba the Dubber

Today's *MOTD* commentator, the likes of Guy Mowbray, Steve Wilson, Conor McNamara, Simon Brotherton and Robyn Cowen, has to juggle technology unimaginable to the programme's first pundits. With around 30 cameras trained on a Premier League game, a TV match director in their ear highlighting fouls, flare-ups and offsides, a live feed to the VAR team and a range of monitors to, well, monitor, football commentary is now a multi-skilled business. It's a world away from the early days of the League, when instant videotape replays were a distant dream and commentators had to visualise how a replay might look and immediately deliver a matching description. Some were masters of the art. David Coleman, for instance, would pause in the aftermath of a goal, count to four, and deliver a concise summary of the lead-up and assist he was imagining, often ending in 'finishing of the very highest order'. But not everyone was a Coleman. In the post-match editing suite it could be difficult to link what was said – assuming something *was* said – to what actually happened. Many games didn't even have a commentator and so would need a familiar voice dubbed on later. Dark arts of the television trade were required. Enter Gubba the Dubber.

Tony Gubba joined the BBC as a Liverpool-based sports reporter and was quickly promoted – first to cover the 1972 Olympic Games, then the same year to the anchor role in *Sportsnight*. He became a stand-in presenter on *Grandstand* and from 1975 was a regular on *MOTD*, eventually overtaking Barry Davies as the UK's third longest-serving football commentator behind John Motson and ITV's Gerald Sinstadt. But with Motson and Davies as established operators, Gubba was rarely allocated a marquee fixture. Part of his job was to pull together brief highlights of second-string games – a role he relished according to his colleague Clive Tyldesley. 'When I arrived at the BBC in 1992 John and Barry were fully established as number one and two,' said Tyldesley.

> Tony was the number three commentator, and I was the young upstart coming to maybe challenge for that role. Tony was lovely to me from the beginning, and we became close friends. He also became Gubba the Dubber because whenever there were goals which had been filmed, but not commented on, it would be either Tony or I who would be called in to give them 15 seconds of authenticity. Tony got quite cheeky with these commentaries – almost as if he knew what was going to happen. "He might just try it from here, you never know", he'd say before somebody lashed one in from 30 yards. Tony was the wisest man after the event in British television . . . and we loved him for it.

As the number of televised TV matches has grown so has the roll call of *MOTD* commentators, each with their distinctive styles. Familiar voices include Guy Mowbray, who has commentated on more FA Cup finals and international tournament finals for the BBC than anyone bar Kenneth Wolstenholme and John Motson; Jonathan Pearce, who since joining *MOTD* in 2004 has covered five men's World Cups, four men's Euros, three women's World Cups and one women's Euros; and Steve Wilson, now a frontline *MOTD* commentator. Robyn Cowen, Vicki Sparks and Pearce are the only *MOTD* lead commentators to have covered England succeeding at an international tournament – the 2022 Euros – since Wolstenholme in 1966.

NOVEMBER:
A STEP TO VAR

When on 15 November 2018 the Premier League voted
to introduce Video Assistant Referees for the start of the
2019–20 season, football fans across the country were, you
might say, definitely onside. No more long debates about
whether a goal should have stood or a penalty been awarded.
VAR replays would make things clear to the ref in seconds,
and to viewers of *Match of the Day* in hours. And, while
the technology might take time to bed in, ultimately there
would be fewer refereeing errors and fairer results, allowing
everyone to focus on the action.

What wasn't to like? How long have you got?

Rare has been the Saturday night in which a VAR controversy
hasn't hogged the headlines. Students of Greek mythology
will be familiar with the story of Pandora's box, which is
presented by the gods to Pandora, the first mortal woman on
Earth, and contains some blessings but also many evils. She
is told not to open it but, curious about the contents, she lifts

the lid and out fly the evils to wreak chaos and misery across the world. The tale gave rise to the idiom 'opening Pandora's box', a phrase defined as 'any source of great and unexpected troubles' (*Chambers Dictionary*, 1998) or 'a present which seems valuable but which in reality is a curse' (*Brewer's Concise Dictionary of Phrase and Fable*, 1992). The fifth anniversary of that fateful Premier League decision on VAR coincided with games which showed precisely why it is a technological Pandora's box. We'll look at three key November 2023 fixtures – Newcastle v Arsenal, Tottenham v Chelsea and Wolves v Fulham – and throw in a couple of early-season shockers at Old Trafford and Tottenham Hotspur Stadium.

But first, here's a brief *MOTD* pocket guide on the basics of VAR as it operates in the Premier League.

What will VAR automatically review?

The awarding of goals or penalties, straight red cards (but not second yellows) and cases where the wrong player has been penalised (i.e. the referee mistakenly books or dismisses an innocent party). But the VAR won't intervene over a yellow card or any free kick outside the box unless the kick either involves a red card offence or leads directly to a goal or penalty.

How does it work?

The Premier League's VAR centre is based at Stockley Park, a business hub in West London, where each match is assigned a lead official who makes recommendations to the match referee on the outcome of any review. The lead is supported by an assistant, who continues to follow the live game while a check or review is in progress, and a technical operator who presents on-screen video evidence from the ball-tracking system Hawk-Eye to the lead official.

What's the difference between a check and a review?

The VAR will inform the referee if they want to check an incident. Most checks are over in seconds, and neither fans nor viewers will even be aware they've happened. But if, following a check, the lead official believes the referee has made a clear and obvious error, or missed a serious incident, then they'll ask the ref to stop play in a neutral area and move to a review. Standard practice is for the VAR to listen to the on-field referee's description of why they did or didn't take action. If the video evidence establishes that what *actually* happened isn't what the ref *thought* happened, then that's a clear and obvious error. The referee will hold a finger to an ear, indicating a delayed restart, and will be invited by the VAR to check a pitch-side monitor to reconsider the decision.

How do you define 'clear and obvious'? And what about 'subjective'?

Subjective decisions are part of refereeing. Football is a contact sport and it's the significance of contact that counts rather than the fact it happened. It's impossible to write a Law that defines this because it's often about the context of a potential offence; referees, let alone fans, won't necessarily agree no matter how many times a replay is shown. As for defining 'clear and obvious', it's not always as clear and obvious as it sounds. One supporter's hard but fair tackle is another's reckless hatchet job. So, it's left to on-field referees to make instant assessments. After viewing a replay, they can still decide that they were right and the VAR wrong, because reviews aren't meant to be about 're-refereeing' play. (Refs will almost always take VAR advice for factual rulings though, such as offside.) It's important to note that referees can't independently use the monitor to check their own decisions.

What happens if …

directly before a goal, a potential offence occurs in the 'attacking phase', or the ball is suspected to have gone out of play? If either is confirmed on review, then the goal is disallowed and the game restarts in line with the Laws. The 'attacking phase' is defined as the moment an attacking side takes possession and moves forward. If an opponent nips in and hoofs the ball back to them it doesn't end the attacking phase; rather defenders would need to control the ball or pass to a teammate. It is even possible for a goal to be scored but then disallowed because a penalty offence has been spotted at the other end. This can lead to a 'two-goal swing', as Bournemouth discovered to their cost with the VAR system only six months old. Playing at Turf Moor, the Cherries were a goal down after 53 minutes but equalised on the hour, through a flowing counterattack emanating from their own penalty area. Burnley claimed Bournemouth's Adam Smith had handled a cross in the area as he started the move. VAR agreed, Bournemouth's goal was annulled, Burnley were awarded a penalty, Jay Rodriguez converted and the score swung from 1-1 to 2-0 to the hosts.

THE GOOD, THE BAD AND THE VAR-CICAL

Autumn 2023 produced a veritable windfall of VAR rows and we've gathered up the most triggering into the basket of controversy below. A VAR row doesn't necessarily mean the system failed – although in at least a couple of these matches it did, big time – but it inevitably leaves fans, players, managers, pundits and referees themselves questioning its application. Watching and playing football is, or should be, all about the action. When video interventions start to take over the flow of a game and its talking points, there are going to be questions for Professional Game Match Officials Limited, the not-for-profit company responsible for refereeing all Premier League, English Football League and FA matches. Non-interventions can, of course, produce just as much breast-beating – witness the worst VAR of the 2023–24 autumn crop at the Tottenham Hotspur Stadium. But we're going to start at Old Trafford on the opening weekend of that season for the first of Wolves' Woes.

Wolves' Woes I:
Manchester United 1-0 Wolverhampton Wanderers

This wasn't a great start for the VAR (bad error), Wolves (victims of bad error) or Manchester United (outplayed). United, with much of their midfield still mentally on the beach, had gone ahead against the run of play in the 76th minute when Raphaël Varane headed in Aaron Wan-Bissaka's cross. But Wolves continued to make the running, and in the fifth minute of injury time that pressure told as United's on-rushing keeper André Onana flapped at a cross, missed emphatically and poleaxed Saša Kalajdžić. The ball stayed in play but the clattered Kalajdžić was in no position to play it, on account of lying prone in the six-yard box. Referee Simon Hooper saw no penalty, Stockley Park saw no clear and obvious error. Wolves' disbelieving manager Gary O'Neil saw a yellow card and United gratefully saw out three points. That, of course, was not the end of it. In one post-match interview O'Neil told reporters:

> I thought live that it was a penalty. I thought it looked like the goalkeeper almost took our centre-forward's head off ... and when I watch it back it looks the same. Really, really surprised. I think it's a foul. When you go for the ball and clatter into an attacking player that hard I think it *has* to be a foul ... as he [the referee] jogged over towards us I thought he might be going to the screen but as it turned out he booked me and not Onana.

United manager Erik ten Hag was more cautious. 'It was the judgement of the officials and lucky for us no penalty,' he said. 'I think you can debate it but I think no penalty.'

There was no debate as far as former Premier League ref Jon Moss, PGMOL's Select Group 1 manager, was concerned. O'Neil said,

> I was told live that they didn't think it was a clear and obvious error but having just spoken to Jonathan Moss – and fair play to him for coming straight out – he apologised and said it was a blatant penalty and should have been given ... he can't believe the on-field referee didn't give it and he can't believe VAR didn't intervene.

PGMOL gave Hooper, the VAR Michael Salisbury and Assistant VAR Richard West the next gameweek off. But they couldn't give Wolves back their penalty. Or, probably, a well-deserved point.

Tottenham Hotspur 2-1 Liverpool

The game that has provided nailed-on evidence for the prosecution in the case against VAR. Liverpool, already down to ten men after a questionable 26th minute straight red for Curtis Jones, appeared to have taken the lead eight minutes later through a brilliant finish by Luis Díaz. However, the on-field assistant referee raised his flag for offside and referee Simon Hooper (him again) ruled the goal out, fully aware that his VAR Darren England and Assistant VAR Daniel Cook would check the lino's decision. And check it they did. Unfortunately, they hadn't seen the flag go up. They thought Hooper had *awarded* the goal, their check showed Díaz was onside, and therefore in their eyes no action was necessary. 'Check complete, check complete. That's fine, perfect,' says VAR. Hooper replies 'Well done boys, good process,' and blows the whistle to restart. Seconds later it becomes clear that neither decision nor process is fine, perfect, or even good. A transcript of the officials' conversation, which PGMOL deserves credit for releasing, captures the mounting feeling of dread. The video replay operator – the tech guy with no role in decision-making – chirps up: 'Wait, wait, wait, wait. The on-field decision was offside. Are you happy with this? The image that we gave them is onside?' There's an audible sigh followed by an expletive. Then the tech guy says 'Oli's calling to delay the game' – that's VAR hub operations executive Oli Kohout – 'the decision is onside ... Oli's saying to delay ... to delay the game, stop the game.' The VAR replies: 'They've restarted the game. Can't do anything. Can't do anything.' Things got worse for Liverpool. Two minutes later Son Heung-min put Spurs in front and although Cody Gakpo equalised just before half-time, Diogo Jota's quickfire double booking left the visitors scrambling to survive. A Joël Matip own goal in the sixth minute of stoppage time summed up their day.

Later that Saturday evening PGMOL apologised to Liverpool and fessed up. 'The goal by Luis Díaz was disallowed for offside by the on-field team of match officials,' it announced. 'This was a clear and obvious factual error and should have resulted in the goal being awarded through VAR intervention, however, the VAR failed to intervene.' This was a complete vindication for Simon Hooper. His lino thought Díaz was offside and his VAR apparently agreed. What else could he do? Three days later PGMOL issued a fuller statement confirming that 'significant human error had occurred' and that the VAR system had fallen 'short of expectations'. England and Cook would be stood down from the next round of matches and a new VAR communication protocol would be developed to 'enhance the clarity of communication between the referee and the VAR team in relation to on-field decisions.' England and Cook were, however, correct in deciding they couldn't ask Hooper to stop the game once it had restarted. The tenth principle of the International Football Association Board's VAR protocol is,

> If play has stopped and been restarted, the referee may not undertake a 'review' except for a case of mistaken identity or for a potential sending-off offence relating to violent conduct, spitting, biting or extremely offensive, insulting and/or abusive action(s).

So what of the fallout? Jürgen Klopp was clear but measured in his response, refusing to target any of the officials. 'It's really important that as big as football is, and important as football is, we deal with it in a proper way,' he said.

All the people involved, the on-field referee, linesman, fourth official and especially in this case VAR, didn't do that on purpose. It was an obvious mistake and I think there would have been solutions for it afterwards. Some people probably don't want me to say, but not as the manager of Liverpool so much, more as a football person, the only outcome should be a replay. That's how it is. It probably will not happen. The argument against [a replay] would probably be if we open that gate, everybody will ask for it. The situation is so unprecedented that I'm 56 years old and I'm absolutely used to wrong decisions, difficult decisions but something like that as far as I can remember never happened, and so that is why I think a replay would be the right thing.

Wolves' Woes II:
Wolverhampton Wanderers 2-2 Newcastle United

Whereas the Old Trafford game denied Wolves a penalty, this fixture saw one awarded against them in dubious circumstances. With the game at 1-1, and seconds away from half-time, the hosts' Hwang Hee-chan was adjudged by referee Anthony Taylor to have tripped Newcastle's Fabian Schär. Contact was minimal but after a protracted review the VAR decided there was not enough clear and obvious evidence to overturn the on-field decision. Callum Wilson duly dispatched the spot-kick, and although Wolves fought back to a 2-2 draw the feeling of injustice niggled away at Molineux. When Taylor was downgraded to Championship duty the following week, manager O'Neil seized on it as vindication. 'I saw the numbers in the [independent post-match] review they do ...

which was 5-0 in favour of a penalty not being given on-field and 4-1 in favour of it not being overturned,' he said.

> I think Anthony Taylor's doing a Championship game this weekend – that's three referees who've been relegated on the back of refereeing us so you need to be careful when you referee Wolves.

The review figures he quoted suggest that while Taylor may have made a mistake – in that good, old-fashioned way before pitch-side technology – the VAR was right to keep schtum. O'Neil's comment was presented in the media as a light-hearted joke although perhaps it was a not-so-subtle message to refs to give Wolves a break.

Wolves' Woes III:
Sheffield United 2-1 Wolverhampton Wanderers

If that was the message, there was no sign of it getting through to Bramall Lane the following week. As November's VAR circus got underway, Wolves lost as the direct result of a questionable penalty after Fábio Silva was ruled to have fouled George Baldock in the area. Blades' skipper Oliver Norwood converted with the last kick of the game and little wonder that the Old Gold felt aggrieved. Having a point controversially snatched away when you're denied even a sniff of a comeback is particularly harsh. Silva did leave a foot in but, really? As Gary Lineker posted on Twitter/X: 'Another stinking decision goes against @Wolves. Exactly the same as last week v Newcastle. Another error from VAR'. *Match of the Day* pundits Martin Keown and Danny Murphy agreed: 'This is almost deja-vu, it's in the same part of the penalty box,' said Keown, 'it's incredible to be honest, and of course, this cost them any kind of result today.' Murphy felt that in both cases attacking players went down too easily. 'They're both really poor decisions,' he said. 'The problem is, it's encouraging people to keep trying to manipulate.'

Gary O'Neil was predictably incandescent, though more critical of referee Rob Jones and VAR's 'rules of engagement' than the VAR officials themselves. His post-match diatribe typified the feelings of many at the sharp end of questionable, match-defining moments: 'terrible decision ... hardly any contact ... never, ever a penalty ... if you give a foul for that contact there would be one million fouls in the 90 minutes ...' and so on. You have to forgive him the hyperbole because he'd just watched the incident back with Rob Jones, who was insisting his decision was correct. But O'Neil also made some astute points about the rules governing VAR and their effect on the careers of managers and players. He continued: 'Because of the wording we use, VAR can't intervene because it is not deemed clear and obvious,' he said.

> Craziness. I don't expect anything, we didn't get an apology last week and apologies don't help me. We are six points down maybe from refereeing decisions. I have said a million times we need to be better so decisions don't affect us as much, but the facts are they have had a big impact on our points total. A big impact on where we are in the league, the feel of the place, an impact on how well I am deemed to have done as a new manager arriving at Wolves, and 12 points is a big difference to 18. To sit and have a conversation with the referee and him still think that is a penalty is absolutely crazy.

Yet former Premier League referee Mike Dean supported Jones, pointing out that while the penalty may have been 'soft', Silva's boot had landed on top of Baldock's toes. 'There's contact,' he said.

> The referee has given the penalty so it's not a wrong decision and VAR would not have overturned it ... last week there was no contact. That's more of a penalty than last week in my opinion.

Newcastle United 1-0 Arsenal

Meanwhile, with social media still in meltdown over that Wolves defeat, things were getting tasty at St James' Park in the 4 November late kick-off. And now it wasn't the on-field officials taking the flak but the entire VAR system: rules, cameras, officials – the whole caboodle. No apologies for dwelling on this particular November VAR because the circumstances encapsulate the whole debate.

It was always going to be a rufty-tufty midfield scrap, with both teams in the top six and Arsenal keen to replace Spurs as league leaders. VAR incidents became a source of animosity between the sides, starting in the 37th minute when Kai Havertz scythed down Sean Longstaff on the touchline. Longstaff had the ball under control as Havertz leapt off the ground, leading foot high enough to crunch his ankle. Fortunately, it missed and instead Havertz's trailing leg made contact. This might still have been seen as a reckless and dangerous red card tackle but referee Stuart Attwell settled for yellow, and VAR decided that was credible. Newcastle's fuming players thought differently, and the resulting melee resulted in Havertz getting pushed into advertising hoardings while both

Anthony Gordon and Fabian Schär got booked for dissent. It was never going to end there and, as the first half entered added time, the Magpies' Bruno Guimarães jabbed a forearm into Jorginho's head. This looked remarkably like it was (a) intentional and (b) violent but, just as remarkably, went unpunished – a scenario which would have cleared the way for VAR to review on the grounds that Attwell had either missed it or made a clear and obvious error. Stockley Park decided neither was the case and it was Arsenal's turn to seethe. But not as much as they were about to.

In the 62nd minute the formidable Joelinton stormed into the Arsenal box and set up Jacob Murphy. His shot was sprayed harmlessly across the face of goal but was then retrieved from the far corner by Joe Willock. Arsenal, believing the ball had gone out of play, made the standard Under-12s error of failing to play to the whistle. There was no whistle. Willock bent in a teasing cross, goalkeeper David Raya executed a mid-air flap, Joelinton and Gunners centre-back Gabriel battled for the scraps and the ball ricocheted to Gordon who stabbed in from close range. And so the VAR-fest began. Was the ball out when Willock crossed? Did Joelinton foul Gabriel by pushing him in the back as they both went up? Did the ball touch Joelinton's hand before it reached Gordon? And was Gordon onside? There then followed a triple VAR check, which probably should have been a quadruple given the potential handball. As sports artist Paul Trevillion's celebrated *You are the Ref* comic strip challenge in *Shoot!* magazine used to ask, 'WHAT NOW?' What indeed.

The goal stood. Audio of the conversation at Stockley Park revealed that VAR Andy Madley could find 'no conclusive evidence' that the whole of the ball had crossed the line before

Willock retrieved it. He goes on: 'I don't see a specific foul on Gabriel. I see two hands on his back but I don't see anything of a push that warrants him flying forward like that.' What about offside? Assistant (AVAR) Stuart Bell says:

> I don't know where the ball is because the ball is being hidden [by] Joelinton here. So you don't know where the ball is. And you've got no conclusive evidence of Gordon being ahead of the ball. So with the reverse angle that you've got, you have not got any opportunity there of where the ball is. With that, in my opinion, I think you have to award the goal on the evidence.

At this point you might ask yourself why the Premier League doesn't adopt the same VAR protocol as rugby union. There's no obvious answer to that ... If a rugby ref is unsure whether a try is valid you'll hear him ask his VAR team: 'Is there any reason why I cannot award a try?' Had Stuart Attwell been able to ask the same question for Newcastle's goal, the answer would have been no, no and no.

Initial TV stills appeared to show the ball *had* gone out of play before Willock curled in his cross. But these were hardly definitive. While there are generally more cameras at a Premier League ground than a Taylor Swift 'Meet the Press' do, the cameras can't be everywhere and not one of them was any help. So, no clear and obvious error.

Secondly, did Joelinton foul Gabriel? Well, maybe, maybe not. Joelinton certainly had two hands on the defender's back, but Gabriel had also arched his body into Joelinton. The on-field decision was no foul and in a 50:50 call, VAR deemed that to be fair enough.

Next, the 'handball'. A still image of this emerged only after full-time and so it never formed part of VAR's deliberations. While it may have added to the post-match outrage at the Emirates, it was not a factor in any decision-making.

Finally, the offside. And here there was no available camera angle to conclusively show the point of contact between Joelinton and the ball and, *ipso facto*, whether Gordon was or wasn't offside. You can see it from Arsenal's point of view. There were four possible reasons to rule out the goal, and yet it stood. But then from Newcastle's point of view: Why *should* it be ruled out when none of those reasons were valid? The Laws of football don't work like that. You can't have a free kick just because there are four 'almost fouls' in the preceding few seconds. Not that any defence of VAR would have quelled the inferno raging in Gunners' manager Mikel Arteta's belly (readers will need to strap themselves in for that later). A more considered view came from *MOTD's* guest pundit, the redoubtable Martin Keown, who felt his old team had been royally turned over by VAR. Here's a summary of his comments and exchanges with Gary Lineker.

Did Joe Willock keep the ball in play? Keown: 'This isn't really conclusive. We haven't got the technology yet around the perimeter of the pitch.'

Did Joelinton foul Gabriel by putting both hands on his back as they fought for the ball? Keown: 'I was screaming "that's a foul". That's two hands. Anywhere else on the pitch, Gary, you put two hands on the back of a player's shirt and it's a foul. And it's a foul there. Why they've not seen that ... '

Lineker: 'Well, they may have seen it but they may have decided it's not a clear and obvious absolute howler.'

Keown: 'Well, I disagree with that. Look at that – two hands on his back, he [Joelinton] is off the ground, that's why Gabriel is stooping. He can't get off the ground.'

Was Anthony Gordon onside when the ball fell to him? Keown: 'We haven't got the camera angles available, we're told, to draw the lines for what's potentially an offside. So that one is inconclusive and that's maybe where the manager is feeling the technology simply isn't good enough.'

Did Joelinton handle the ball as he jumped? Keown: 'It might even have hit his hand in that particular buildup. There may have been an offside, I mean virtually everything is wrong with that particular goal that you can think of.'

Mikel Arteta agreed. As you can probably tell from his post-match interview:

> How the hell did this goal stand up? It's incredible. I feel embarrassed. It's an absolute disgrace that this was allowed. For many reasons it's not a goal. It's so difficult to compete at this level. This is nowhere near the [refereeing] level to describe this as the best league in the world. I feel sick to be part of this.

He went on: 'The question is it's not a goal, it's simple. For a goal there are certainly things that are not allowed in football.' The following day, his employers also waded in:

> Arsenal Football Club wholeheartedly supports Mikel Arteta's post-match comments after yet more unacceptable refereeing and VAR errors on Saturday evening ... the Premier League is the best league in the world with the best players, coaches and

supporters, all of whom deserve better. PGMOL urgently needs to address the standard of officiating and focus on action which moves us all on from retrospective analysis, attempted explanations and apologies. We support the ongoing efforts of Chief Refereeing Officer, Howard Webb and would welcome working together to achieve the world-class officiating standards our league demands.

Two days later Arteta was back in the fray, saying the only way to improve refereeing was to call out mistakes, which seemed at odds with his response after the Tottenham-Liverpool fiasco which was that 'officials are trying to make the best decisions' and 'mistakes happen'. He explained the apparent contradiction using a phrase destined to become a classic – the 'stinking drawer' – saying,

I stand for the same words, that mistakes are part of football. [I will] give my voice and opinions in the managers' meetings in the most constructive way to get a better game. If you have a problem and you put it in your drawer, the problem is in the drawer and it's going to stink at some point. Let's talk about it, try to improve it.

Journalists asked whether his outspoken words were an attempt to deflect criticism of Arsenal's play – they had managed just one shot on target – but Arteta's reply was robust. 'One thing is saying it externally,' he said. 'Internally to my players it is how we can play better, be more dominant and play the way we want so we give no chance to the opponent.' He still wouldn't define how Newcastle's goal buildup was wrong, but declared:

My duty is to defend my players and club in the best possible way and this is what I'm going to do time after time, and I do it with the evidence and being as clear as possible. Everyone wants the same thing but we have to understand that [managers] have to be there.

The final official word on – let's call it VAR-gate – came on 9 November when the Premier League's Independent Key Match Incidents Panel handed down judgement on the rights and wrongs of that Newcastle goal. IKMIP comprises three former players or coaches and a representative apiece from the Premier League and PGMOL. The aim is for the panel to divorce itself from the passion and controversy surrounding VAR and make clinical judgements based on the known facts. In summary, it decided VAR was right to award Gordon's goal, because there was no conclusive evidence to the contrary, but both on- and off-field officials missed clear red card offences committed by Havertz and Guimarães. The panel also unanimously agreed that the Sheffield United and Newcastle penalty awards against Wolves were mistakes. None of which would have soothed Mikel Arteta and Gary O'Neil's hurt feelings.

Tottenham Hotspur 1-4 Chelsea

The 'maddest game ever', screamed one headline, and in terms of top-flight English football this London derby must at least be a candidate. It managed to be both a captivating game of a football and a VAR-fest which in its 111 minutes saw five goals scored, five disallowed, two Spurs players sent off and an attack-versus-defence climax in which Chelsea – still eleven-strong – were showered with scoring chances.

Through all this, VAR John Brooks had to work harder than a Duckett's Green potboy on match day to keep up. It had all started so well for the hosts when in the sixth minute Dejan Kulusevski cut in from the right to score a deflected goal. Son thought he'd added a second, only to be ruled offside by VAR, whereupon it was Chelsea's turn to get the Stockley Park treatment, as first Raheem Sterling's equaliser was ruled out for handball, followed four minutes later by Moisés Caicedo's effort, disallowed after a series of video replays which showed, eventually, that Nicolas Jackson was offside. From this point on, things went mostly downhill for the hosts. Cristian Romero was sent off for a dangerous challenge, allowing Cole Palmer to level from the penalty spot, then Romero was joined in the dressing room by two more key players in James Maddison and Micky van de Ven, both injured. There was a brief respite for increasingly bewildered home fans when VAR cancelled out a Jackson goal (another offside), but the second half was just ten minutes old when Spurs' Destiny Udogie departed courtesy of a second yellow. For the next 20 minutes the nine men held out impressively, playing a brave if naive defensive line, until Jackson put Chelsea ahead. Even then the drama wasn't over. Eric Dier blasted in the volley of his life, only for another lengthy VAR check to conclude that he was offside, and it was left to Jackson to score twice deep in added time to secure his hat-trick and the three points. The surreal quality of the night was captured at the final whistle when, despite shipping four at home to their fans' second-most despised rivals, Spurs players got a standing ovation.

In truth, this was a VAR controversy only because everyone had to hang about for mind-numbingly long reviews. At one stage you suspected both sets of fans had knocked goal celebrations on the head because what was the point? Who wants to hear exaggerated laughter from the other lot if VAR says no goal? Many commentators feel that 'celebration chilling' and interminable delays are two of the biggest problems with the system: fans are left wondering what the issue is, what officials are saying to each other, how an incident looks slowed down. Why not let supporters waiting patiently for a decision to at least see key video frames on stadium screens and, for those who want it, even hear VAR discussions via a 'ref link' earpiece? Who knows, it just might defuse controversy. But we digress, VAR controversies are what this November chapter is all about and we haven't finished yet. At least there aren't any more Wolves' Woes. Oh, wait.

Wolves' Woes IV:
Fulham 3-2 Wolverhampton Wanderers

Three penalties, a headbutt too 'soft' for a red card and yet more VAR agony for Wolves manager Gary O'Neil. He was aggrieved at both the penalties awarded against his side, and felt the one they got should have resulted in a second yellow for Fulham defender Tim Ream. But, like it or not, penalties are subjective. The degree of contact matters. O'Neil's biggest gripe centred on the moment in the 87th minute when Fulham's Carlos Vinícius raised his head into Max Kilman's face. It looked like a headbutt, and had Kilman gone down to exaggerate the impact it might have been treated as one by referee Michael Salisbury. But Kilman stayed honest, Vinícius was merely booked and VAR saw no reason to get involved. A Fulham side reduced to ten at that stage of the game would, you might think, have been disinclined to push for the win. But with a full 11 they pushed, and in the 94th minute Harry

Wilson went down in the penalty area under a challenge from João Gomes. Salisbury waved play on, but the VAR advised a pitch-side monitor check, Salisbury reversed his decision and Willian put away Fulham's winner. Once again O'Neil was left to pour out his anger publicly after seeking a private post-match explanation from the referee. 'We discussed the headbutt, which it was,' said O'Neil,

> but he debated that a little bit with me and said that it was a soft headbutt. That's crazy. We can headbutt people as long as it's deemed soft, or not hard enough? So my son at home watching that – millions of children watching that – we're telling them that you can headbutt people on a football pitch, as long as it's not too hard?

The following day the International Football Association Board announced it was considering a 'sin bin' trial in which referees would be handed a third card to flourish – somewhere between red and yellow – to send players off temporarily. VAR would also be able to advise on its use. This didn't go down well with former England international Chris Waddle, who told BBC Radio 5 Live Drive:

> I cannot stand VAR, I think it's the worst thing that's happened to football. If they bring in a sin bin now, and three [types of] cards, will you get to use a joker as well? It's absolutely killing the game of football. You cannot celebrate, you cannot enjoy it, you wait six minutes to see whether there's a line and offside ... if they're going to do anything, get rid.

Wolves tried to do precisely that. At the end of the season, they submitted a proposal to all 20 Premier League clubs calling for VAR to be scrapped. To succeed, this would have required 14 clubs to vote in favour but in the end only one – Wolves – did so. The club said it was 'disappointed with the outcome of the vote' but encouraged by the Premier League's 'commitment to improve VAR'. The League said refinements would include semi-automated offside technology (SAOT), in which both players and ball are digitally tracked. There would also be instant in-stadium announcements by referees to explain VAR decisions to fans.

Lineker says: I don't like VAR

After November's blizzard of VAR controversies you could sense the frustration on *MOTD*. Presenters and pundits were having to discuss match-defining moments based on checks and reviews rather than the show's *raison d'être* – action. When VAR disallowed a scrambled, dying-seconds equaliser for Arsenal in their 9 December top-of-the table clash away at Aston Villa, Gary and Ian Wright waded in, highlighting the bizarre VAR-inspired handball rule, which is applied differently according to whether the offender is an attacker or defender. They had just watched a slow-motion replay of Gunners forward Kai Havertz and Villa defender Matty Cash battling to control a ball at close quarters as it pinged around the Villa goalmouth. It struck Cash's arm first, then Havertz's, before the German stabbed it into the net. You might have thought that was potentially a penalty to Arsenal because the first offence was Cash's. Or that, because neither handball was deliberate, the goal could stand. Not a bit of it. After a review of several minutes the VAR confirmed Jarred Gillett's decision. But why?

It comes back to our old friend Subjectivity. There are plenty of subjective Laws, but handball is the only one which adds the word 'deliberate' as a factor. Law 12 of the International Football Association Board's 'Rules of the Game' specifies three scenarios which govern the ref's interpretation: the player (a) deliberately handled the ball; (b) made his or her body 'unnaturally bigger' in the positioning of hands and arms; or (c) was in the act of scoring a goal. Cash and Havertz were inches away from both a fast-moving ball and each other, so a deliberate act seems unlikely. Neither was attempting to make their body bigger – Cash was falling and Havertz was swivelling – which leaves only option (c), that the ball touched Havertz's hand in the act of scoring a goal. Therefore, a free kick and, effectively, three points to Aston Villa was correct.

'So, defenders can actually handle the ball, but forwards can't,' said Gary, 'Why are we trying to stop goals? The people who make the Laws of the game. Why are they doing that?' Ian Wright had no idea. But he was excoriating in his view of IFAB: 'It's the most ridiculous law,' he said. 'In all law. Not just in football. All law in the whole world of law – the multiverse and everything.' Gary admitted: 'I have to say, I really don't like VAR very much anymore. I was one of the people who advocated it and I actually feel quite guilty. I was definitely wrong and it's spoiling the game.' Most fans would agree with that. But PGMOL can rightly argue that the system does prevent result-changing mistakes, and it's improving. Statistics released by IKMIP in April 2023 showed that since the end of the Qatar World Cup in December, VAR made 33.3% fewer mistakes, with incorrect interventions dropping from once every 24.3 games to once every 37.5. So there is hope. As Greek mythology students well know, Hope is the one blessing which never escaped Pandora's box.

DECEMBER: SANTA BRINGS THE SACK

Why is it that UK football fans regard the Christmas football programme as sacrosanct? Sure, Boxing Day is a bank holiday, but there are parlour games to play, leftovers to eat, *Dr. No* showing somewhere, maybe a visit to the in-laws for more unwanted presents …

Oh, alright, you can see why. But while fans may love a Christmas fixture, managers hate them. That's partly because they're training or strategising on the big day, partly because a relentless number of games adds to the injury list, but mostly, in the case of those under pressure, the fear that Santa will bring the sack. More on that later in this homage to festive football. But let's start with how we got here.

Christmas football has been around for almost a millennium, initially taking the form of mass participation events in which mobs of players would try to kick a pig's bladder or leather ball into their opponents' goal. It was often played along a town or village street, goals could be almost anything – a town gate, harbour, river or even a church balcony – and with no VAR available there must have been some dodgy tackling. Among the best-known surviving examples is the ba' Game, played in the town of Kirkwall, on the Orkney Islands, on various days between Christmas and the New Year. The competing teams are known as the Uppies and the Doonies (short for Up-the-Gates and Doon-the-Gates) and once the winning side has emerged, its players decide, through the democratic process of shouting loudly, which of their number should 'claim the ba'' as their own – an innovative departure from the Premier League's current process for determining man of the match. This 2022 Boxing Day Ba' game report from the *Orcadian* suggests the five-hour encounter – no added-on time here; it finishes when it finishes – was a cracker: 'It was an intensely fought game on both sides, with a number of injuries, a wall falling foul of the pack, and an hour-long holdout by the Uppies down a lane by Kiln Corner,' writes the *Orcadian's* ba' correspondent.

> It was just after 5.30pm when the ba' finally hit the water of Kirkwall Bay, marking the Doonies second win of the day. A tense discussion ensued for over 25 minutes, with a number of players shouting to claim the ba' as their own. The loudest cries by far, however, were for Mr [David] Johnstone, who was finally held aloft above the pack in the basin at 5.58pm.

Brilliant though this must have been as a spectacle, it comes a distinct second to the legendary first ever ba' game, recounted in a colourful snippet of folklore published by *Orkneyjar*.

The story goes that a Scottish tyrant called Tusker (named for his protruding teeth) was killed by a young Orcadian lad who crossed the Pentland Firth to confront him. The lad decapitated Tusker, strapped the head to his saddle, returned to Orkney and galloped back to Kirkwall to celebrate his victory. The head must have been bouncing around because on the journey home one of Tusker's teeth scratched our hero's leg; the wound became infected and he arrived in town close to death. In his final moments he hurled the head into the midst of the assembled townsfolk who booted it through the streets, simultaneously assuaging their anger at Tusker and inventing the ba' game.

Throughout the medieval period there were numerous attempts to ban football, particularly over Christmas and other religious holidays. In 1314 Edward II issued a decree warning that

> For as much as there is great noise in the city, caused by hustling over large balls from which many evils might arise which God forbid, we command and forbid, on behalf of the King, a pain of imprisonment, such game to be used in the city in the future.

Things didn't end well for Edward if you believe the stories surrounding his demise – let's just say it involved a hot poker – but his unpopularity seems to stem from propaganda about his private life, and the fact that he was no good at war, rather than his dislike of football. His son Edward III did a whole lot better on the battlefield, but in 1363 also banned the game as an 'idle' pastime. In common with the other kings who reigned over the Hundred Years' War with France, he felt football distracted subjects from archery practice at a time when England needed good archers.

Other opponents included the burghers of Manchester, who complained about sliced passes smashing windows, but Christmas football's biggest knock came when Puritan Oliver Cromwell banned both football *and* Christmas following the Roundhead victory in the English Civil War. Research by historian Professor Bernard Capp for the University of Warwick has revealed that when the Mayor of Canterbury proclaimed Cromwell's ban on Christmas Day 1647, an angry crowd reacted by producing footballs and having a kick around. As Professor Capp explains:

> Across the country, enemies of the Puritans saw football as a symbol of rebellion ... football became a flashpoint for social and political tensions between Puritan authorities and their enemies. Football originated as a seasonal sport, often played between rival villages on Shrove Tuesday or Easter, so during traditional times of seasonal festivities, which were then prohibited, such as during Christmas or before Lent, differences flared.

The national obsession with football even inspired Shakespeare, who in Act II, Scene 1 of *The Comedy of Errors* has the servant Dromio complaining that he is spurned – literally meaning 'kicked with the foot' – by his betters:

> *Am I so round with you as you with me,*
> *That like a football you do spurn me thus?*
> *You spurn me hence, and he will spurn me hither.*
> *If I last in this service, you must case me in leather.*

By the Victorian era festive football was played regularly, in keeping with a tradition that the working classes participated in public events on official holidays. Christmas Day had long been established as one of these, and when the 1871 Bank Holidays Act designated Boxing Day a bank holiday, clubs saw a chance to cash in. Christmas was one of the few times of the year when big attendances could be guaranteed, and they were keen to cram in as many matches as possible. This led to the kind of fixture congestion unheard of in the modern game. On Christmas Day 1913 Liverpool beat Manchester City 4-2 at home, lost the return 1-0 on Boxing Day then drew 3-3 with Blackburn Rovers on 27 December. Not hard to imagine what today's Premier League managers and players – particularly those from abroad – would make of that. The British love affair with festive football is not shared by the rest of Europe: Ligue 1, Bundesliga, Serie A and La Liga all usually pause fixtures before Christmas Eve and don't restart until after the New Year (La Liga has played the odd game on New Year's Eve).

In the Covid-delayed 2019–20 season both Jürgen Klopp and Pep Guardiola hit out at the Premier League's Christmas fixture list, with Klopp arguing that, while Liverpool weren't the worst affected, it was a 'crime' for clubs to face two games in two days. 'Obviously we can say what we want but no one is listening,' he told a press conference. 'The body needs a specific amount of time to go again. That is science. But we ignore that completely. We just say "Oh, they look strange running around again today."'

One club that did face a Christmas two-in-two was Manchester City, scheduled to play Wolves at Molineux on the evening of the 27th before hosting Sheffield United less than 48 hours later. Speaking sarcastically, Guardiola told reporters his players would have to 'go to the fridge' to reduce muscle pain and soreness. 'I wrote a letter to the Premier League to say thank you and we are going to the fridge after Wolves to get ready for Sheffield United,' he said. 'We are training on the 23rd and 24th. The night of 24th is off, the morning of 25th off. Then 26th training, and 27th Nuno [Espírito Santo]'s team.' City went on to lose 3-2 at Wolves – as much due to goalkeeper Ederson being sent off in the 12th minute as to fixture congestion – before beating the Blades 2-0. Meanwhile Liverpool secured a 4-0 win at Leicester on Boxing Day and saw off Wolves 1-0 at Anfield on 29 December. Klopp and Guardiola at least had the luxury of managing large squads with high quality cover; Liverpool ended up runaway winners of the 2019–20 title on 82 points, 25 ahead of runners-up Manchester City and 29 ahead of third-placed Leicester. But even well-resourced managers know that clubs show precious little Christmas spirit if things aren't going well. As our list of Premier League festive season sackings demonstrates.

'TIS THE SEASON TO BE JOBLESS …

Managing a Premier League team is a cut-throat business, never more so than when you're in a relegation battle. Defining the moment that battle commences is sometimes straightforward – many a club promoted from the English Football League would say it starts in August – but for those perpetually occupying lower league positions the spectre of the drop often doesn't appear until the first quarter of the season is done. Chairmen of the so-called 'big clubs' tend to use the same marker to decide whether expectations are being fulfilled. Either way, we're talking December, Christmas and the Sacking Season.

A change of manager is perceived as the chance to try something different, better channel a squad's talents, bring in tactical changes and re-energise players who have upset the existing gaffer. The table on **page 130** lists the 30 Premier League managers for whom Santa brought the sack during the 30 years between 1993 and 2023. We've defined the festive season as the whole of December, but haven't included the full twelve days of Christmas, some of which fall in January. We've also discounted caretaker managers and managers who genuinely resigned, as opposed to leaving with loaded expressions such as 'mutual consent' or 'best for both sides' ringing in their ears. We could find no December sackings in 1995, 2021, 2022, or between 1997 and 2003. The analysis shows that Christmas period sackings have, however, risen sharply overall since the Premier League got underway in 1992. In the ten Decembers between 1992 and 2001, just two managers got P45 forms; between 2002 and 2011 there were ten out the door, while between 2012 and 2021 the toll was 16. This almost certainly reflects a general speeding up of the managerial merry-go-round – powered by clubs desperate to trouser the millions bestowed by Premier League status, and the associated TV money. Patience is not considered a virtue in many boardrooms these days.

But was it ever really? In *Match of the Day*'s first season (1964–65) Stan Cullis, by far Wolves' most successful manager, got the chop as early as 15 September. Sackings also tend to come in clusters. When one chairman hires a new boss to improve his struggling team's chances others tend to get trigger-happy, fearing they too need a freshen-up. Our dataset shows December 'sacking clusters' on the 1st, 14th, 16th and 27th in 2013 and the 1st, 5th and 28th in 2019 but, if you include the weeks immediately either side of any December, you can find more and larger clusters. Add late November to December 2019 and the tally becomes five in as many weeks, while January 1994 saw four clubs replace their managers in 24 days, a scale of carnage reminiscent of the Red Wedding in *Game of Thrones*. Spare a thought too for managers who've felt Santa's boot more than once: step forward José Mourinho, Alan Pardew and Mark Hughes, who have all experienced two Christmastime dismissals.

CHRISTMAS CARNAGE: 30 PREMIER LEAGUE DECEMBER SACKINGS

John Lyall: Ipswich Town, 5 December 1994

Lyall took over the Ipswich hot seat in May 1990 after an unceremonious dismissal by West Ham, the club he'd served as player and manager for 34 years. Although he secured only a 14th finish during his debut season in what was then the Second Division, he brought the club's iconic striker John Wark back for a third stint at Portman Road and the following year guided the Tractor Boys to the Championship and promotion to the new Premier League. In January 1993 they stood fourth but then careered downwards to finish 16th: a particularly painful slump as arch-rivals Norwich had ended in third place. The following season saw a similar trend – good start followed by dire results – and they survived relegation only through an injury time winner for Chelsea which sent Sheffield United down instead. By December 1994 Ipswich were bottom of the league, angry fans were staging post-match pitch demos and the board were pushing Lyall to quit. He resigned two days after a 2-1 home defeat to Manchester City and never returned to football management. Ipswich were relegated.

Frank Clark: Nottingham Forest, 19 December 1996

Replacing God – Forest fans' nickname for their rightly-revered manager Brian Clough – was a monumental task. But the club had been relegated in Clough's final 1992–93 season, and if anyone had the CV to revive them it was Frank Clark. The defender had signed for Forest on a free from Newcastle and been a stalwart in the Clough team which won promotion from the Second Division in 1976–77 before claiming the First Division title the following year. Clark had retired at the end of the 1978–79 season and after a managerial apprenticeship in the lower leagues had returned to the City Ground in 1993. He'd inherited a team still packed with talent – the likes of Stuart Pearce and Steve Stone – added shrewd signings such as Stan Collymore and restored Forest to the Premier League at the first time of asking. They finished third in 1994–95, but with Liverpool snapping up Collymore in the close season Clark found himself without the kind of striker who turns draws into wins. Collymore's replacement Andrea Silenzi, the first Italian to play in the Premier League, failed to fire and by mid-December Forest were back in the relegation zone having won only one of their 16 games. Clark was shown the door and took a job at crisis-stricken Division One side Manchester City, where he would last 14 months.

Steve Wigley: Southampton, 8 December 2004

This always looked a vulnerable berth for Steve Wigley, promoted in 2004 in the wake of Gordon Strachan's departure. He started as caretaker manager, was demoted a few weeks later when Paul Sturrock was recruited from Plymouth Argyle, reportedly tried to act as peacemaker when Sturrock's style didn't wash with senior players then, when Sturrock departed just two games into the 2004–05 season, was re-promoted to full-time manager. The Saints notched up just one win in 14 under his tenure, albeit a massive one against deadly south coast rivals Portsmouth, and he returned to academy duties. Chairman Rupert Lowe then brought in Harry Redknapp from Portsmouth to save the Saints from relegation (which he didn't), causing mass discombobulation among Pompey fans, who printed up a load of T-shirts bearing unkind sentiments about their former manager. Redknapp lasted a year at Southampton before heading back to coach Portsmouth, now themselves threatened with relegation from the Premier League. He kept Pompey up and the following season secured them a ninth-place finish – their best for half a century. By then, the T-shirts were in the recycling.

Alan Pardew: West Ham United, 11 December 2006

Pardew joined West Ham from Reading in September 2003 with a brief to win promotion from the Championship. He didn't quite manage it, losing the play-off final to his former club Crystal Palace. But the Hammers won the following season's play-off against Preston and in 2005-06 Pardew steered them to a ninth-place Premier League finish and an FA Cup final against Liverpool, which they narrowly lost on penalties after the match ended deadlocked on 3-3. The start of the 2006 campaign began with great Tevez-and-Mascherano-inspired anticipation but quickly disintegrated into an eight-game losing streak – last experienced at Upton Park in the 1930s. The Hammers were knocked out of the UEFA Cup in the first round by Palermo, suffered an embarrassing League Cup defeat to Chesterfield and with the takeover by Eggert Magnússon's consortium in November time was running out for Pardew. His denouement followed a 4-0 rout at Bolton on 9 December, after which the manager admitted his club was 'in a tight spot'. Two days later he was gone.

Les Reed: Charlton Athletic, 24 December 2006

Christmas Eve has to be the worst day of the year to be sacked, but this didn't affect the Scrooge-like focus with which the Charlton Athletic board handed Les Reed his cards (for avoidance of doubt, they weren't Christmas ones). It gave Reed the unfortunate distinction of having the shortest tenure of any full-time Premier League manager, and his 41 days in charge produced just one win and a humiliating League Cup defeat to League Two side Wycombe Wanderers. Reed had come through the ranks of the Addicks coaching staff and was handed the top job after Ian Dowie – who popularised the infamous phrase 'bouncebackability' during a previous stint at Crystal Palace – failed to bounce back from his own disastrous start: Charlton won only two out of 15 during Dowie's brief spell at the helm. It seems Reed, author of a manager's manual titled *The Official FA Guide to Basic Team Coaching*, was partly a victim of his own Christmas spirit. His decision to give the squad Christmas Day off ahead of their 27 December home game against Fulham was reportedly the last straw for chairman Richard Murray. Alan Pardew became his third manager of the season. Charlton were later relegated.

Lawrie Sanchez: Fulham, 21 December 2007

Northern Ireland manager Sanchez was initially hired as caretaker manager by Fulham under a job-share agreement with the Irish Football Association. At Craven Cottage he replaced Chris Coleman, sacked in April 2007, and was tasked simply with avoiding relegation. He had 32 days to pull it off and succeeded, just, thanks to a home win against of all teams a Liverpool side three weeks out from a Champions League final. Sanchez was rewarded with a permanent contract but never managed to find momentum in the following season. With key players like Jimmy Bullard and Brian McBride nursing long-term injuries his side managed only two wins in 17, and a 1-0 home defeat by Newcastle on 15 December meant he was toast. Interviewed a few weeks later, he felt that having kept Fulham up he had faced 'the biggest rebuilding of a Premier League club that's ever been attempted' and had deserved more time to see it through. But there was no ill will towards his successor, Roy Hodgson, the man who had once coached him as a 12-year-old.

Roy Keane: Sunderland, 4 December 2008

Be honest, would *you* fancy being the chairman responsible for telling Roy Keane he's fired? Nor did Sunderland's Niall Quinn. This was one of those managerial departures officially presented as a resignation, although statements from both men suggest there was no way Keane could have carried on. Quinn said he'd tried for two years to relieve pressure on his manager but added:

> Obviously the Premier League is the Premier League and I guess it came to the point where Roy thought he

had reached the end of that journey. Reluctantly,
I accepted that. It was not the easiest thing to do, but I
think it was the best thing to do in the circumstances.

Keane later cited a rift with Sunderland's principal shareholder, the Irish-American businessman Ellis Short, as the underlying factor. 'It didn't upset me, what happened at Sunderland,' he said. 'It was a business decision. Even for me I suppose it was a business decision. I couldn't give my heart and soul with this fella on my shoulder. That, I'm sure, is how he works.' At the time Sunderland sat 18th in the Premier League having lost five of their previous six games. Keane and his team were booed off after the latest of those – a 4-1 home defeat to Bolton – and when news of his departure emerged some Black Cats players reportedly celebrated. But it would be unfair to characterise Keane's time in charge as a failure. In 2006–07 he took a side rock bottom of the Championship into the Premier League as Champions and secured their survival the following year. Quinn praised him for bringing new thinking, discipline and a 'winning mentality' to the club and plenty of supporters backed his insistence on professionalism. When in March 2007, as Sunderland were fighting for automatic promotion, three players turned up late for an away trip to Barnsley, they found the coach had left without them. Sunderland won the game 2-0.

Paul Ince: Blackburn Rovers, 16 December 2008

Another act-in-haste, repent-at-leisure decision by a Premier League club. For all his tremendous qualities as a player, Paul Ince was more than unproven as a top-flight manager because he hadn't even acquired all his coaching badges.

The Premier League gave him special dispensation to move from League One side Milton Keynes Dons, and only on condition he undertook extra homework to catch up. In June 2008 Blackburn, who were replacing Manchester City-bound Mark Hughes, handed Ince a three-year contract. It was torn up in six months. The record showed a mere 13 points from 17 games and with Rovers already five points adrift from relegation rivals, chairman John Williams opted to cut the club's losses. 'Three wins in 17 games has seen a squad, which finished seventh last season, fall to 19th position,' he noted.

> We are currently in real danger of becoming detached from the pack. The survival of the club in the Premier League is paramount and our focus now is on finding a replacement who will be able to maintain our top division status.

Sam Allardyce took over. Blackburn finished 15th.

Mark Hughes: Manchester City, 19 December 2009

Seeing the manager touted as your successor watching from the stands is football's equivalent of the bit in *Treasure Island* where Blind Pew hands Billy Bones the dreaded Black Spot. For those unfamiliar with Robert Louis Stevenson's classic, the Black Spot is a burnt piece of paper used to deliver a verdict of judgement or guilt. City chairman Khaldoon Al Mubarak and owner Sheikh Mansour didn't need to get the matches out though: Roberto Mancini gazing down from the stands at Eastlands was quite sufficient to pronounce both judgement *and* guilt. Within two hours of beating Sunderland 4-3, Hughes was gone, his heavy spending on the likes of Emmanuel Adebayor, Joleon Lescott and Carlos Tevez having failed to provide the required payback. 'A return of two wins in 11 Premier League games is clearly not in line with the targets that were agreed and set,' read a City statement.

> Sheikh Mansour and the board felt that there was no evidence that the situation would fundamentally change. This is a particularly difficult announcement given the personal investment over the past 15 months on all sides.

It still seemed harsh given that City lay sixth, had lost only twice all season and were in the semi-finals of the Carling Cup. But in the Premier League, ambition trumps patience every time. As Gary Megson soon discovered at the other end of the table.

Gary Megson: Bolton Wanderers, 30 December 2009

Some axed managers walk away quietly. Others, in the words of Dylan Thomas, 'do not go gentle into that good night.' Gary Megson certainly did not go gentle, describing the manner of his sacking – a phone call from chairman Phil Gartside – as 'galling'. The club was, he said, in a lot better state than when he joined in October 2007, adding that 'they seem to think it was tantamount to taking over at Real Madrid and then it not going too well. That place was in a huge mess and most people didn't realise it.' In an interview with BBC Radio 5 Live he also pointed out that, while Wanderers lay 18th at the time of his dismissal, they were only four points off 11th-placed Everton and had two games in hand over most of the table's bottom half.

> If we had won one of those two games we would have been 12th, the highest position the club would have

reached for two or three years. We have scored the most goals from set pieces in the Premier League and had one of the best away records. The problem was that the club is one of the lowest spending.

Bolton's statement read: 'The decision has been taken in the light of the position the club finds itself in ... at the halfway point of the season.' Steve Wigley, who must have been used to all of this by now, took temporary charge until Owen Coyle took over on 8 January.

Chris Hughton: Newcastle United, 6 December 2010

'The players are sure to be asking themselves, "What the hell is going on?"' said Magpies defender Sol Campbell after Hughton's departure was announced. What indeed. Hughton had been one of Newcastle's most loyal and effective servants since arriving in February 2008 as assistant coach to Kevin Keegan during Keegan's brief second spell as manager. When Keegan quit in September 2008, Hughton acted as caretaker until the appointment of Joe Kinnear, then stepped in again when Kinnear was taken ill to help Alan Shearer and Iain Dowie in their ultimately doomed attempt to save the club from relegation. He was placed in temporary charge for the start of Newcastle's 2009–10 Championship season but started so well that his role was made permanent in October 2009. He won the Championship title and on return to the Premier League saw the Magpies to a respectable 11th place when owner Mike Ashley called time. Newcastle said they wanted 'an individual with more managerial experience ... to take the club forward.' Alan Pardew got the job.

Sam Allardyce: Blackburn Rovers, 13 December 2010

Another Christmas, another sacking at Blackburn. This time it was Big Sam in the firing line as new owners Venky's decided 13th wasn't good enough for Rovers, despite them being only one win off a European place. Venky's said they had taken the decision 'as part of our wider plans and ambitions for the club'. Sam said he was 'very shocked and disappointed', while League Managers Association chief executive Richard Bevan said,

> It is extremely difficult to understand the thinking behind the dismissal. It is ironic that one minute Sam can be proposed as the next England manager and the next, finds himself out of work.

Six years later Allardyce did, very briefly, go on to manage England (that's another story) while Blackburn entered a decade of decline. They were relegated from the Premier League in 2012, dropped to League One in 2017, bounced back to the Championship in 2018 and were still there in 2023–24.

Martin Jol: Fulham, 1 December 2013

Jol was another victim of New Owner Syndrome, sacked five months after Shahid Khan took control at Fulham. It was not entirely unexpected. The Cottagers had been in a death-spiral since April that saw them lose 16 out of 24 matches in all competitions and had been bobbing around the bottom three on ten points since September. A desperate performance at Upton Park on 30 November was their fifth defeat on the bounce and the Dutchman, who had arrived from Ajax in June 2011, seemed resigned to his fate in his post-match interview.

Khan first appointed René Meulensteen to run the first team then, from February 2014, German manager Felix Magath. It was all too late and an ageing, underperforming team was deservedly relegated.

Steve Clarke: West Bromwich Albion, 14 December 2013

Steve Clarke's first season in charge of the Baggies started well, and by mid-September 2012 they sat a lofty third in the League. They tailed off during the following spring but still finished 8th, Albion's best Premier League performance. Yet this effort disguised a creeping malaise. In the calendar year 2013 Clarke's record was 31 points from 34 games – a lukewarm 20% win rate – and a fourth straight loss convinced hard-headed chairman Jeremy Peace that he had to go. In a statement, West Brom highlighted a 'generally disappointing points return' and a wage bill which was 'the highest in the club's history'. However, *Match of the Day*'s Alan Shearer felt Clarke had been unlucky. 'They overachieved last year and that put pressure on him,' said Shearer.

> When you have a slow start to the season questions will always be asked. The chairman might look at it and think other clubs have improved [after changing manager]. But even so, you have to say it's extremely harsh.

André Villas-Boas: Tottenham Hotspur, 16 December 2013

Sometimes it's not so much the points that matter but the results against your key title rivals. So it proved for Villas-Boas whose team had emerged smoothly from their Europa League group and sat seventh in the Premier League, only five points behind fourth-placed Manchester City, when

Spurs chairman Daniel Levy wielded the axe. The former Porto manager's problem was the humiliating manner of certain defeats: a dismal 3-0 home loss to West Ham in early October had angered Levy, while a 6-0 thrashing at the Etihad Stadium on 24 November was clearly unacceptable – particularly given the £109 million spent on new players during the summer. When, three weeks later, Liverpool trounced Spurs 5-0 at the Lane there was no way back, although in media interviews immediately afterwards the Portuguese insisted he would not resign. Within hours he found that he had ... by 'mutual consent.'

Malky Mackay: Cardiff City, 27 December 2013

Mackay led the Bluebirds through two cracking seasons following his recruitment from Watford in 2011, reaching a League Cup final, which Cardiff lost on penalties to Liverpool, and narrowly missing out on promotion from the Championship. In 2012–13 he pushed on, securing Cardiff the Championship title and a berth in the Premier League for the first time in their history. But it all went pear-shaped at pace. Owner Vincent Tan fell out with Mackay over his playing style, results, signings and budget management (just about everything then), and emailed him demanding he quit. Mackay stood his ground but after a 3-0 home defeat to Southampton on Boxing Day 2013 he was out. Five months later he reached a compensation settlement and issued a statement expressing gratitude to Tan, who he said had 'invested heavily in the club and supported our decisions in our push for promotion to the Premier League.' By then, though, Cardiff were effectively back in the Championship. They finished rock bottom under Mackay's successor, Ole Gunnar Solskjær.

Neil Warnock: Crystal Palace, 27 December 2014

At this point, in a career spanning 34 years and 14 managerial appointments, you can see why Neil Warnock had a philosophical attitude to dismissal. After becoming the first Premier League boss to get the chop in 2014–15 he was quick to take the positives, telling one interviewer: 'I've watched seven episodes of *Downton Abbey* in the last few days – you miss out on things like that ... things are not all doom and gloom.' His second stint at Selhurst Park was fairly gloomy, however; brought in on the eve of the new season after Tony Pulis quit, he posted only three wins in 17 games and a 3-1 Boxing Day home defeat to Southampton forced the hand of co-chairman Steve Parish. In the rarefied world of Premier League management it's rare for chairman and manager to part amicably, but this was a notable exception. Parish spoke of Warnock as a 'great guy' who 'wanted to do it at Palace.' Alan Pardew took over and Warnock went on to manage another five clubs over the next decade.

Alan Irvine: West Bromwich Albion, 29 December 2014

Another Christmas sacking at the Hawthorns and one so well trailed it barely raised an eyebrow among Albion fans. Having lost Steve Clarke the previous December, watched Clarke's successor Pepe Mel produce underwhelming performances in the spring and then winced at Irvine's record of four wins in 19 games, they just wanted someone, *anyone*, to steady the ship. The former Everton academy manager was dismissed following a 2-0 away defeat to Stoke City – Albion's seventh defeat in nine matches – a move described as a matter of 'regret but necessity' by technical director Terry Burton. 'Securing a sixth season in the Premier League is the over-riding target,' he said. 'Sometimes unpleasant decisions have to be taken to serve that imperative.' Tony Pulis took the helm and the Albion ship of state ended the season in calmer waters.

Garry Monk: Swansea City, 9 December 2015

The departure of Garry Monk is a case study in the fickle nature of Premier League football. Having joined Swansea as a player in 2004, he was part of a League Two squad that achieved three promotions and won the Capital One Cup. His 270 appearances ensured plenty of terraces' goodwill when he took over as manager from Michael Laudrup in February 2014 and he soon led the Swans from drop-zone flirtation to an eighth-place finish. The 2015–16 campaign also started well with wins against Manchester United and Newcastle, and there was even talk of Monk as a future England manager. Then an autumn run of one win in 11 did for him. In announcing the decision chairman Huw Jenkins cited a drop in performance levels but admitted, 'Nobody foresaw the position we would be in at this moment.'

José Mourinho: Chelsea, 17 December 2015

Then-Chelsea owner Roman Abramovich was well used to dumping managers by this time – seven since his 2003 takeover – but the eighth must have been unusually difficult. Mourinho had brought him three league titles, the FA Cup and three League Cup wins during two spells at Stamford Bridge, making the Special One easily the most successful manager in the club's history. The last of those

title trophies had been lifted only seven months previously,
but in the Premier League stats trump sentimentality.
With just four wins in 14, a 2-1 surrender to a rampant
Leicester City was the final act. Afterwards José said he
had been 'betrayed' by players who failed to follow orders.
Abramovich heard that as, 'I've lost the dressing room.'
Guus Hiddink took over and Chelsea went on a 15-match
unbeaten run to finish tenth.

Alan Pardew: Crystal Palace, 22 December 2016

From a manager's perspective, if there's one thing worse
than a pre-Christmas bad run of form it's the knowledge
that new owners are watching with increasing alarm. Pardew
found himself in exactly this predicament as the Palace squad
assembled for their Christmas party at Quaglino's restaurant
on 20 December. Defeats in eight of their previous ten games
– including a 5-4 debacle at Swansea – had left them just a
point off the drop but Pardew was still expecting to oversee
the Eagles' visit to Watford on Boxing Day. He never got
the chance. American major shareholders David Blitzer and
Josh Harris, who had each taken an 18% stake in the club 12
months earlier, knew Sam Allardyce was available and wanted
to pounce before anyone else got him. Allardyce lived up to
his, at the time, 'relegation-proof' reputation and secured
Palace a 14th-place finish.

Bob Bradley: Swansea City, 27 December 2016

Bob Bradley made his name in Major League Soccer and did
a decent job coaching the US men's national team for five
years. But he was the first American to manage in the Premier

League and his appointment by the Swans in October 2016 was greeted with trepidation by supporters and pundits – rightly, as it turned out. His three-month tenure at the Liberty Stadium comprised 11 league matches, seven defeats and a jaw-dropping 29 goals against. His last game in charge was a 4-1 Boxing Day home capitulation to West Ham, by which time fans were chanting for 'Bobley''s dismissal. American co-owners Steve Kaplan and Jason Levien duly obliged. Was this fair? The *New York Post* didn't think so, accusing the Swans of being 'too impatient for a winning formula to boost a historically mediocre team'.

Paul Clement: Swansea City, 20 December 2017

The message is clear. If you're in charge of a struggling Swansea City team, come December do feel free to go ahead and book your January break in the sun. Paul Clement was plonked into the ejector seat vacated by Bradley on 3 January and although he kept the club up – earning a Manager of the Season nomination for a return of 29 points from 19 games – he didn't see out the year. Swansea ended the summer transfer window with the League's lowest net spend and the sale of Fernando Llorente and Gylfi Sigurdsson meant the Swans, like their namesakes, were toothless. With ten defeats from 13 during the Christmas run-in, and four points from safety, chairman Huw Jenkins said Clement's dismissal offered the best chance of a turnaround. 'To change the manager, especially at only the halfway point of the season, is the last thing we wanted to do as a club,' he said. Three Decembers in a row suggests Huw was getting used to it.

Mark Hughes: Southampton, 3 December 2018

When the axe is swinging madly, your club has one win in 14 and the season's goal tally is a parlous 15, it's important to keep taking the positive pills. Which is exactly what Mark Hughes did on learning that Les Reed, the vice-chairman who had handed him a new contract six months earlier, had been dismissed by Chinese owner Gao Jisheng. Hughes told a press conference that

> All the board and the ownership itself made that decision to offer me that contract so ... there's still a lot of people here that felt I was the right man for the job. I don't think my position has been diminished too much in that regard.

Brave words. And wrong. A month later Hughes had joined the procession out of St Mary's – part of a 'restructuring' plan which conveniently overlooked the way his stewardship had saved Saints the previous season.

José Mourinho: Manchester United, 18 December 2018

Mourinho won a League Cup and a Europa League title during his two-and-a-half years in charge at Old Trafford but this fell well short of expectations. Losing 3-1 at Liverpool on 16 December left United 19 points behind the league leaders and, in terms of points, closer to the relegation zone than top spot. The board was less than impressed after investing nearly £400 million on Mourinho signings for, well, what exactly? Media reports spoke of a failure to develop young players or embrace the club's philosophy of attacking football. Ole Gunnar Solskjær took over but failed to magic up the new dawn.

Quique Sánchez Flores: Watford, 1 December 2019

Watford's Honorary Life President Sir Elton John scored a smash hit with his 1973 festive classic 'Step into Christmas', an invitation not extended to Flores by the Hornets' hierarchy as they lay anchored at the foot of the Premier League on 30 November. The Spaniard had been hired for a second spell at Watford after a full season in 2015–16. This time he lasted 90 days, with a record of one win in ten and a paltry eight points. Vicarage Road was clearly no place for the nervous. Since Gianfranco Zola's exit in 2013 Watford had seen off nine managers (if you count both Flores stints). Former Leicester boss Nigel Pearson became the tenth, although he didn't make it to the end of the season either.

Marco Silva: Everton, 5 December 2019

Marco Silva was one of those departed Watford managers – appointed by Everton in 2017 after the Toffees paid around £4 million to buy out his contract. He was midway through a three-year deal at Goodison when a run of eight defeats in 11 matches persuaded majority shareholder Farhad Moshiri to make him the club's fourth managerial casualty in as many years. Carlo Ancelotti was in charge by Christmas.

Manuel Pellegrini: West Ham United, 28 December 2019

As a Premier League title winner with Manchester City, Pellegrini looked a good catch when he took control at the London Stadium in May 2018. Co-chairmen David Sullivan and David Gold backed him through two summer transfer windows and acquisitions such as Felipe Anderson, from Lazio, and Sébastien Haller, from Eintracht Frankfurt –

a combined cost of £80 million – heralded much promise. But neither player fired consistently and Pellegrini's total spend of £155 million was never justified by results. He was sacked with the Hammers in 17th place and only five league wins on the board. New boss David Moyes kept them up on goal difference.

Slaven Bilić: West Bromwich Albion, 16 December 2020

If any manager deserved a club prepared to cut him some slack it was Slaven Bilić. Admittedly things did not look good: the Baggies had won just one game all season and that was against Sheffield United, the only team below them. Nonetheless, Bilić had restored Albion to the Premier League in 2019–20, been given a miserly (by Premier League standards) summer transfer budget of £20 million and then told his key centre-back Ahmed Hegazi was being sold against his wishes. The depth of Albion's malaise was such that not even new manager Sam Allardyce – who had managed seven top-flight clubs without once being relegated – could save them. The Baggies equalled Norwich City's record of five Premier League relegations.

Paul Heckingbottom: Sheffield United, 5 December 2023

When travelling supporters sing that their team isn't good enough – we're paraphrasing you understand – not many managers would consider joining in. But Paul Heckingbottom got close after the Blades' 5-0 thrashing at Turf Moor on 2 December. It was United's 11th defeat in 14 games, unsurprising given the 39 goals they'd conceded, and Heckingbottom could see what was coming. He'd been frustrated at financial restraints preventing him from tying in key players but also understood the club's need to sell. 'If the fans start, it changes the dynamic,' he said after the game. 'The fans are right to shout, say we're not good enough. You can't kid them. I was as angry as well and almost singing along with them.'

MANAGERS SACKED IN DECEMBER DURING THE 30 YEARS OF THE PREMIER LEAGUE

Among relegation-threatened clubs, a **bold** entry indicates that the sacking made no difference to the club's end-of-season fate: they still went down.

Manager	Club	Date left	Pos.	Finished
John Lyall	**IPS**	**5, 1994**	**22nd**	**22nd**
Frank Clark	**NTG**	**19, 1996**	**20th**	**20th**
Steve Wigley	**SOU**	**8, 2004**	**18th**	**20th**
Alan Pardew	WHU	11, 2006	18th	15th
Les Reed	**CHA**	**24, 2006**	**19th**	**19th**
Lawrie Sanchez	FUL	21, 2007	18th	17th
Roy Keane	SUN	4, 2008	18th	16th
Paul Ince	BBR	16, 2008	17th	15th
Mark Hughes	MCI	19, 2009	6th	5th
Gary Megson	BOL	30, 2009	18th	14th
Chris Hughton	NEW	6, 2010	12th	12th
Sam Allardyce	BBR	13, 2010	13th	15th
Martin Jol	**FUL**	**1, 2013**	**18th**	**19th**
Steve Clarke	WBA	14, 2013	16th	17th

Manager	Club	Date left	Pos.	Finished
André Villas-Boas	TOT	16, 2013	7th	6th
Malky Mackay	**CDF**	**27, 2013**	**16th**	**20th**
Neil Warnock	CRY	27, 2014	18th	10th
Alan Irvine	WBA	29, 2014	16th	13th
Garry Monk	SWA	9, 2015	15th	12th
José Mourinho	CHE	17, 2015	16th	10th
Alan Pardew	CRY	22, 2016	17th	14th
Bob Bradley	SWA	27, 2016	19th	15th
Paul Clement	**SWA**	**20, 2017**	**20th**	**18th**
Mark Hughes	SOU	3, 2018	18th	16th
José Mourinho	MUN	18, 2018	6th	3rd
Quique Sánchez Flores	**WAT**	**1, 2019**	**20th**	**19th**
Marco Silva	EVE	5, 2019	18th	12th
Manuel Pellegrini	WHU	28, 2019	17th	16th
Slaven Bilić	**WBA**	**16, 2020**	**19th**	**19th**
Paul Heckingbottom	**SHU**	**5, 2023**	**20th**	**20th**

BOTTOM THREE AT CHRISTMAS: BEAT THE DROP (1992-2024)

Three teams have always been relegated from the Premier League. The only exception to this rule since the league was founded in 1992 was the 1994–95 season, when four teams were relegated from the division. This is because the league was restructuring from including 22 clubs to 20. The bottom quartet of clubs were relegated with only two promoted from the second tier.

Between 1992 and 2024, there were 94 occasions when teams were in the drop zone on Christmas Day and 38 of those teams went on to escape relegation – a survival rate of almost 36%. Only four sides have stayed up after being rock bottom on Christmas Day: West Brom in 2004–05, Sunderland in 2013–14, Leicester in 2014–15 and Wolves in 2022–23. They each had ten points – the lowest a team has had at Christmas and survived. In the table below, **bold** type indicates that no bottom-three side at Christmas beat the drop that season.

Year	Club	Xmas Pos.	Final Pos.
1992–93	AWM/MKD	21st	12th
1993–94	SOU	21st	18th
1994–95	EVE	19th	15th
	AVA	20th	18th
1995–96	AWM/MKD	18th	14th
	CVC	19th	16th
1996–97	BBR	19th	13th
1997–98	TOT	18th	14th
	EVE	19th	17th
1998–99	SOU	19th	17th
1999–2000	DRB	18th	16th
2000–01	MID	19th	14th
2001–02	**DRB**	18th	19th
	LEI	19th	20th
	IPS	20th	18th
2002–03	BOL	19th	17th
2003–04	PTM	18th	13th
2004–05	WBA	20th	17th
2005–06	PTM	18th	17th

Year	Club	Xmas Pos.	Final Pos.
2006–07	WHU	18th	15th
2007–08	SUN	18th	15th
	WIG	19th	14th
2008–09	MCI	18th	10th
	BBR	19th	15th
2009–10	BOL	18th	14th
	WHU	19th	17th
2010–11	WIG	18th	16th
	WLV	19th	17th
2011–12	WIG	18th	15th
2012–13	**WIG**	18th	18th
	QPR	19th	20th
	RDG	20th	19th
2013–14	CRY	18th	11th
	SUN	20th	14th
2014–15	LEI	20th	14th
2015–16	SWA	18th	12th
	SUN	19th	17th
2016–17	SWA	19th	15th
2017–18	BOU	18th	12th
2018–19	BUR	18th	15th
2019–20	AVA	18th	17th
2020–21	**FUL**	18th	18th
	WBA	19th	19th
	SHU	20th	20th
2021–22	NEW	19th	11th
2022–23	NTG	18th	16th
	WLV	20th	13th
2023–24	**LUT**	18th	18th
	BUR	19th	19th
	SHU	20th	20th

TOP ON CHRISTMAS DAY – WIN THE TITLE?

It's an arbitrary thing of course, a date plucked midway through the season and seized on by the media as a bellwether for who will ultimately win the league. You could pick any date and run the stats and come up with slightly different results. But Christmas Day is a good a date as any to play the game. The chart below shows that over the first 60 years of *Match of the Day*, 28 of the teams that were top at Christmas went on to claim that year's title, a success rate of 48.27%. If you analyse just the 31 Premier League years, the success rate rises to 51.6%. In the case of the latter, it's worth pointing out that, typically, teams top at Christmas still face the bulk of their fixture programme – perhaps 23 or 24 games. So for roughly half of them to bring home the bacon is a decent return. Chelsea have the best record when it comes to converting Christmas top spots into titles: they've managed it on all five occasions that they led on 25 December. Manchester City also have a 100% record with three from three, while Liverpool have a 50% conversion rate, winning eight titles after leading on 16 Christmas Days. Manchester United have managed 7 out of 13, a 53.8% return, although they've also nursed a couple of painful post-Christmas hangovers. In 1970–71 they steadily slipped from Division One leaders on Christmas Day to finish eighth. And in 1997 they were a whopping 13 points clear of Arsenal, with bookmakers paying out punters who had backed Alex Ferguson's side. Then the Gunners found new ammo, put together a 15-match winning run (including a 1-0 win at Old Trafford), reined in the Red Devils and secured a third top-flight Double. Arsenal fans should, statistically speaking, pray that they're *not* top as

Santa starts his rounds. During the *MOTD* years, on the six occasions they've occupied pole position on 25 December – 1986–87, 1989–90, 2002–03, 2007–08, 2022–23, and 2023–24 – they never got to wear the crown. But being second-best at Christmas seems to work. Of the six titles they've won since 1965, five came off the back of a 25 December second place. The only exception was that incredible 1997–98 run when they climbed from sixth to overtake United.

Season	Top at Xmas	Finished
2023–24	ARS	2
2022–23	ARS	2
2021–22	MCI	1
2020–21	LIV	3
2019–20	LIV	1
2018–19	LIV	2
2017–18	MCI	1
2016–17	CHE	1
2015–16	LEI	1
2014–15	CHE	1
2013–14	LIV	2
2012–13	MUN	1
2011–12	MCI	1
2010–11	MUN	1
2009–10	CHE	1
2008–09	LIV	2
2007–08	ARS	3
2006–07	MUN	1

Season	Top at Xmas	Finished
2005–06	CHE	1
2004–05	CHE	1
2003–04	MUN	3
2002–03	ARS	2
2001–02	NEW	4
2000–01	MUN	1
1999–00	LEE	3
1998–99	AVA	6
1997–98	MUN	2
1996–97	LIV	4
1995–96	NEW	2
1994–95	BBR	1
1993–94	MUN	1
1992–93	NOR	3
1991–92	MUN	2
1990–91	LIV	2
1989–90	ARS	4
1988–89	NOR	4
1987–88	LIV	1
1986–87	ARS	4
1985–86	MUN	4
1984–85	TOT	3
1983–84	LIV	1
1982–83	LIV	1
1981–82	SWA	6
1980–81	LIV	5

Season	Top at Xmas	Finished
1979–80	LIV	1
1978–79	LIV	1
1977–78	NTG	1
1976–77	IPS	3
1975–76	MUN	3
1974–75	IPS	3
1973–74	LEE	1
1972–73	LIV	1
1971–72	MUN	8
1970–71	LEE	2
1969–70	EVE	1
1968–69	LIV	2
1967–68	MUN	2
1966–67	MUN	1
1965–66	LIV	1
1964–65	MUN	1

JANUARY: THE IMPROBABLES – FA CUP GIANT-KILLERS

It's not often that fans of lower league teams get to feast at the same table as football's aristocracy. The reality of life in the cheap – well, cheaper – seats is usually long motorway journeys, mediocre service station sandwiches and two hours in a freezing stadium dating from the Relief of Mafeking. All in the certainty that another season of dashed hopes lies ahead. The one sustaining factor is that your team gets to enter the FA Cup. Put together a run and suddenly the terraces are a bit busier, the atmosphere a touch rowdier and the players slightly more interested. And perhaps, just occasionally, you might experience the visceral joy of the upstart peasant bringing down a lordly opponent. Maybe your team will never be title-winners. But they *can* be giant-killers. Sixty years of *Match of the Day* proves it. Never mind the Invincibles – meet the Improbables.

On 10 January 2022, the final day of Emirates FA Cup third round fixtures, an intriguing piece of Cup research was released by the FA. Working with the Institute for Mathematical Innovation at the University of Bath, Opta data from 8,152 FA Cup results was fed into a bespoke mathematical model which used probability theory to calculate the least likely FA Cup final scores over the previous fifty years. Those games are listed below. After that we've added our 'best of the rest' giant-killing acts, using no mathematical calculations whatsoever, because we can. The University of Bath study, by Dr Adwaye Rambojun and Professor Andreas Kyprianou, factored in the overall probability of a lower tier team reaching the third round, the gulf in league status, current league positions, goals scored and the sequence and timing of goals in any one tie. This produced a top ten of the unlikeliest winners – the FA Cup's band of Improbables. Helpfully, the boffins added real-life examples to illustrate quite how improbable these Cup shocks were. For readers who are not maths nerds, probability and odds are essentially different ways of stating the chances of something happening. The probability that an event will occur is the number of times you'd expect to see that event happen relative to a given number of trials. For example, the 4-2 defeat of West Bromwich Albion in their FA Cup third round home tie against Woking in January 1991 should statistically have occurred once every 15,959,312 games, assuming all the games had identical teams and conditions. Woking nailed it on the first attempt.

1 West Bromwich Albion 2-4 Woking, 5 January 1991

Probability: 1 in 15,959,312.
Chance of conceiving identical quadruplets: 1 in 15,000,000.

This looked a massive mismatch with Second Division West Brom taking on Isthmian League side Woking at the Hawthorns. That said, the Baggies league form was abject, they stood three points off the drop zone and manager Brian Talbot was under mounting pressure. The home side went 1-0 up at the break but the second half saw an extraordinary transformation in which Woking's Tim Buzaglo completed an 11-minute hat-trick and Terry Worsfold added a fourth on 88 minutes. A consolation goal for Albion somehow added to the embarrassment – the locals were disinclined to celebrate anything – and came way too late to spoil the Surrey side's party. When the Bath mathematicians put their findings to former Woking manager Geoff Chapple he said,

> I always told the team we had hope, even if it was a one in 16 million chance. I remember sitting there after the match thinking: "Am I dreaming? This can't be happening. We're from Surrey, nobodies, what's going on here?" Our players were part-time. We had couriers, painters, decorators and builders. But I always used to instil in them that anything was possible, especially in the FA Cup, and this result proved it.

Chapple remarked that his football management career 'will forever be defined by this match'. It certainly defined Talbot's season. He was sacked the following week and West Brom were relegated in May, having drawn each of their last five matches 1-1. In his analysis Dr Rambojun observed that

Woking's achievements in winning the match were remarkable enough but the fact that they went behind in the match and then scored four second-half goals before West Brom's late consolation is what makes this result and scoreline so improbable.

2 Hereford United 2-1 Newcastle United, 5 February 1972

Probability: 1 in 32,449.
Chance of growing to over seven feet tall: 1 in 26,315.

We touched on this third-round replay earlier. It famously supercharged a 26-year-old John Motson's *MOTD* career and perhaps it is the combination of his commentary and Ronnie Radford's thunderbolt of a goal which made this result the definition of Cup giant-killing for generations to come. Today's fans might roll their eyes and mutter that the Premier League is awash with fantastic goals. Yet how probable is it that today's pros could wallop in a thirty-yarder on a pitch the consistency of Herefordshire pig farm slurry? The University of Bath maths supremos could no doubt tell us precisely. As a rough guess though, wildly improbable.

3 Stevenage Town 3-1 Newcastle United, 8 January 2011

Probability: 1 in 7,712.
Chance of rolling five sixes consecutively with a dice: 1 in 7,776.

Newcastle manager Alan Pardew had been in post barely a month when the Cup banana skin otherwise known as Stevenage FC was cast in his path by the draw. Perhaps mindful that he had work to do in building a relationship with Toon fans – one poll of 40,000 had only 5.5% favouring him as replacement for the popular Chris Hughton – Pardew played pretty much his strongest team. It didn't work. The Premier League side's attacking tactics consisted of just one: hoofing long balls to Leon Best. While Best had slotted a hat-trick in his previous game against West Ham he offered nothing like the aerial threat of the injured Andy Carroll. Not that he got much service anyway. Stevenage's midfield comprehensively bossed the likes of Alan Smith and Kevin Nolan and in the 49th minute their work was rewarded, albeit fortuitously, when Stacy Long's powerful strike was deflected in off Michael Williamson. Six minutes later they were two up courtesy of a 25-yard daisy cutter from Michael Bostwick and although Joey Barton pulled one back in injury time, Peter Winn had time to nudge in a third for the League Two outfit. Afterwards Pardew apologised for an insipid performance, not helped by Cheick Tioté's second-half red card, and blamed a packed Christmas fixture list. 'I thought we were running on empty,' he said, 'it's been such a tough sequence of games.' Stevenage boss Graham Westley observed that his team had also been busy over Christmas but had benefitted from seven-hour daily training sessions. 'Our focus before the game was how we would win 5-0,' he said. 'We established that if we did just 20% of what it would take to win 5-0, we'd win.' Maybe not a robust mathematical formula. But effective.

4 Birmingham City 1-2 Altrincham, 14 January 1986

Probability: 1 in 4,376.
Chance of being dealt four-of-a-kind in poker: 1 in 4,165.

During the seventies and eighties few league clubs would have fancied drawing Altrincham in the FA Cup. The Gola League outfit saw off 12 league opponents during those two decades, posted draws against both Everton and Tottenham and were the only non-league side to have qualified for the third round over four consecutive seasons. Besides which, Alty had a point to prove against loftier opponents. Despite winning the Alliance Premier League Championship in both 1980 and 1981 they failed to get elected to the Football League – these were the days before automatic promotion – and dark rumours of voting skulduggery still swirled around Moss Lane. For fans, the prospect of turning over a First Division Birmingham side which had taken just two points from a possible 48 was not to be missed and Kevin Ellis' 63rd minute goal sent them on their way. Robert Hopkins equalised but then, from a narrow angle, somehow slotted a gentle pass beyond on-rushing goalkeeper David Seaman into his own net. 'What has happened here tonight has been coming for the last two years,' seethed Birmingham manager Ron Saunders after the game. 'I hope this result shakes things up and I can get some money from the board.' Altrincham's boss John King was unmoved: 'I haven't any sympathy for him,' he said. 'In fact, I'd swap places. Hasn't he got a contract worth £150,000?' He had, but not for much longer. Saunders resigned two days later.

5 Oxford United 3-2 Swansea City, 10 January 2016

Probability: 1 in 3,487.
Chance of scoring a hat-trick in the FA Cup final to win the Cup: 1 in 2,993.

Going into this game Oxford were 54 places below their top-flight opponents in the league pyramid – although you wouldn't have known it. Several of the U's team that day were cast-offs from bigger clubs who now seemed intent on showing their former coaches what they'd missed. The pick of the crop was 23-year-old Kemar Roofe who had not made a single first team appearance in his four years with West Bromwich Albion, the Baggies preferring to put him perpetually out on loan in a kind of Grand Tour of the lower leagues and, in one case, Iceland's Besta deildin league. Here, he oozed Premier League quality. After Jefferson Montero scored a clever opener for the visitors, and Liam Sercombe equalised from the penalty spot, Roofe fed on Oxford's momentum. His brace of goals – a curling 20-yard shot which squeezed inside the far post followed by a breakaway sprint and finish – proved enough to seal victory, despite Bafétimbi Gomis' reply. Swans manager Alan Curtis admitted his players couldn't cope with the hosts' energy and passing game, adding: 'We didn't even look anything like a team until after we went 3-1 down.' Roofe said,

> I just never got the chance at West Brom. I believe
> I should have had that chance. I did all I could.
> [Leicester City's] Jamie Vardy started lower and he got
> the scoring record in the Premier League. It can be
> done given the time and [the] chance.

6 Sutton United 2-1 Coventry City, 7 January 1989

Probability: 1 in 3,260.
Chance of dropping the FA Cup from space and it landing in the UK: 1 in 2,103.

In his programme notes Sutton's manager, former history teacher Barrie Williams, quoted this Rudyard Kipling verse to summarise the secret of battlefield success:

> *It ain't the individual*
> *Nor the army as a whole,*
> *But the everlastin' teamwork*
> *of every bloomin' soul.*

His Sutton United team may have been viewed as cannon fodder by some Sky Blues fans – after all, the visitors to Gander Green Lane had won the trophy outright 18 months previously and sat securely mid-table in the First Division – but if so it was a big mistake. Sutton had a strong team ethos and the best part of 8,000 maniacal fans behind them, they played good football and they had been well prepped by the cerebral Williams. Cannon fodder they were not. Just before half-time the GM Vauxhall Conference side took the lead through a Tony Rains header and although David Phillips equalised for Coventry, master bricklayer Matthew Hanlan gleefully volleyed home the winner 15 minutes from time. Afterwards Williams' press conference sounded a little like a history lecture. 'The enormity of this result,' he said, 'will reverberate throughout the whole of soccer.' Coventry manager John Sillett offered sporting congratulations and admitted 'It's been a very hard day for my players. Sunday is going to be worse when they read the papers and realise that they have made history the wrong way round.'

7 Burnley 0-1 Wimbledon, 4 January 1975

Probability: 1 in 2,515.
Chance of becoming a NASA astronaut: 1 in 1,525.

At the time, this Cup result rivalled Hereford's derring-do against Newcastle. Burnley lay seventh in Division One, two points off the top, and had a formidable attacking lineup including Welsh international midfielder Leighton James and centre-forward Paul Fletcher. Wimbledon were nobodies from the Southern League – still 13 years away from their incredible Wembley triumph. Yet by the end of this encounter the Dons had become the first non-league side in 55 years to defeat a top-flight opponent away from home, and the footballing world started paying attention. Manager Allen Batsford's strategy had been to frustrate the Clarets and hope for chances to hit them on the break or, even better, get a lucky break. The winning goal certainly had an element of luck when, in the 49th minute, striker Roger Connell's miscued shot fell perfectly for 30-year-old PE teacher Mick Mahon to sweep home. But the game still had to be closed out and over the next 40 minutes it took an inspired goalkeeping display by Dickie Guy, backed by some typically feisty defending, to see Wimbledon home. Years later Guy revealed that Batsford had convinced his team they could beat anybody. 'Allen had built up lots and lots of confidence in the squad and we went up there in high spirits,' he said.

We were used to playing in front of 3–4,000 at Wimbledon, so when we ran out in front of 20,000 or so it felt like we were playing at Wembley. But to be honest, as soon as the game kicked off, we realised it was still only 11 men against 11.

8 Harlow Town 1-0 Leicester City, 8 January 1980

Probability: 1 in 1,800.
Chance of being born on a leap day: 1 in 1,461.

When you're Gary Lineker, one of the few downsides of presenting *MOTD* is that mischievous pundits can pore over a vast library of historic football action in which you featured. Lineker started his career at Leicester City, his boyhood club, and so when the show headed for Newport in 2019 for live coverage of the Foxes' 2019 third round match (spoiler alert, that one's on the Improbables list too), Alan Shearer recalled the last time Leicester lost an FA Cup tie to a team outside the top three divisions. Inevitably, this included footage of Harlow's 1980 winning goal, in which the teenage Lineker, back to 'help' his defence, didn't seem to try terribly hard to challenge for an incoming free kick. 'It's all about attitude,' lectured Alan. 'Did you have the right attitude … ?' Gary took it well. 'It was a replay,' he said,

> and I wasn't [usually] in the side back then, I was only 19. We travelled to the ground, I was in the squad but I knew I wasn't going to play – I was really ill, I had terrible tonsillitis, and I was so scared of [Jock Wallace] the manager that when he read out the team and I was in it I went 'oh no'. But I didn't have the courage to tell him. That's my story – good excuse, isn't it?

He did manage to get his own back on the grinning Shearer. 'Eleven years later I went on to win the FA Cup – how about you Alan?' For all his league prowess, it was a trophy Shearer never won. As for the Hawks' victory, it was a great performance from a semi-pro Isthmian Premier League side up against a Leicester team destined for promotion back to the First Division. John MacKenzie's scrambled toe-poke saw the visitors off and Harlow only narrowly missed out on further progress in the competition, losing 4-3 in the fourth round to Watford.

9 Derby County 1-3 Bristol Rovers, 6 January 2002

Probability: 1 in 397.
Chance of tossing eight heads in a row: 1 in 256.

Rovers sat 87th out of 92 league clubs as this fixture got under way and even Derby, in the midst of a desperate season at the foot of the Premier League, must have fancied their chances. In fact County were comprehensively outplayed by the Pirates who showed guile, creativity, tactical awareness, team spirit and, thanks to Nathan Ellington, clinical finishing. The striker put Rovers in front on 14 minutes, doubled the advantage just before half-time and completed his hat-trick midway through the second half with a superb volley on the turn. Pride Park was by now not a pleasant place for Derby players, with striker Fabrizio Ravanelli the main recipient of advice from the terraces following three wasted free kicks. He did pull one back to add undeserved respectability to the scoreline, although the tie could easily have ended 4-1 when Mark Walters' crisp shot hit the post. This was the game that did for Rams manager Colin Todd, a former England international and one of the club's finest defenders. He was sacked 12 days later after only three months in charge with chief executive Keith Loring confirming that the board 'was not happy with the way things have been going'. Sadly for Rovers, they never managed to replicate their Pride Park performance in remaining Division Three games and finished second-bottom.

10 Newport County 2-1 Leicester City, 6 January 2019

Probability: 1 in 337.
Chance of conceiving identical twins: 1 in 250.

Leicester were still casting around for a long-term replacement in the wake of 'Saint' Claudio Ranieri's departure two years earlier. Craig Shakespeare's eight-month tenure hadn't worked, and the board's recruitment of French manager Claude Puel had worked only for a bit. By early 2019 Leicester, with a squad still containing most of their title-winning heroes, had won only nine out of 21 games, and patience was running thin. Puel fielded an under-strength team for this tie, a decision which infuriated Foxes fans who had seen another second-string outfit lose to Manchester City on penalties in the Carabao Cup a few weeks previously. Whatever, Puel was right to point out afterwards that he had eight title-winners in his team, which should have been sufficient to beat a side sitting 13th in League Two. In reality Newport, fuelled by a packed Rodney Parade in which fans celebrated every tackle and header, were simply too good for their opponents. Jamille Matt's header to finish Robbie Willmott's outstanding wing play could have graced any Premier League ground, and although Rachid

Ghezzal's belting 20-yard strike brought Leicester level, the visitors never looked comfortable. When Pádraig Almond sealed victory with a late penalty it triggered a frenzied, and thoroughly deserved, knees-up for the Exiles faithful. Manager Michael Flynn neatly summed up the improbability of FA Cup giant-killing. 'We couldn't beat [League Two] Stevenage, who had 10 men, on New Year's Day,' he said. 'It's crazy how the players can raise their levels and keep concentrating for 95 minutes against a team that is seventh in the Premier League.' Puel was sacked the following month.

BEST OF THE REST:
SHOCKS WHICH ROCKED THE FA CUP

Newcastle United 1-2 Bedford Town, 4 January 1964

Cometh the hour, cometh the Tim. When Bedford Town were handed the financial windfall of a third-round FA Cup tie at Newcastle they knew they would be heading into the game without a manager. The incumbent, Reg Smith, had resigned four months earlier and although he'd agreed to stay on until a replacement was found, that replacement was Yeovil Town boss Basil Hayward. But Yeovil were also in the third round and Hayward felt he had to stay put until their Cup run ended. So, the call went out to Town's former coach Tim Kelly, who had been out of football for 18 months. The strange thing about this scenario is that while Kelly must have felt pressure, there wasn't really any. Newcastle were ten times Cup finalists, and although a mid-table Second Division club, remained a 'sleeping giant'. Bedford Town were a Southern League Premier Division outfit who had gone unbeaten in the league all season, thanks largely to goalkeeper Jock Wallace (the very same Jock Wallace who would terrify Gary Lineker 16 years later). There was no expectation of success for the Eagles (note to Palace fans: there are only so many decent nicknames) and Kelly's job was simply to make sure they gave their all and did right by an estimated 3,000 travelling supporters. For the first 20 minutes it was all Newcastle, and only a succession of fine saves from Wallace kept them in the tie. But then John Fahy put the visitors in front and, just before half-time, Toon full-back Billy McKinney deflected a cross into his own net. Stan Anderson, the only player to have captained all three major north-east clubs, pulled one back in injury time, but it was far too late and Bedford saw out a famous victory.

Newport County 3-2 Sheffield Wednesday, 4 January 1964

Meanwhile, down at Rodney Parade, Newport County were busy writing a few of their own back page headlines. Standing a modest 15th in Division Four, they faced a Sheffield Wednesday side which included England winger Eddie Holliday and long-serving star Alan Finney. Wednesday were genuine Division One title contenders and would eventually finish sixth, but on a chilly January night in South Wales the febrile atmosphere generated by home fans seemingly got to them. Journeyman striker Joe Bonson emerged as County's two-goal hero with Ralph Hunt contributing a third, and while Holliday and Finney both got on the scoresheet for Wednesday the Exiles held out. Over half a century later, a teenage ball boy at the game, Les Thompson, told the *South Wales Argus* that a 'fantastic save' by Len Weare had proved crucial in the final minutes. 'I was on the touchline opposite the dugouts,' he said. 'Our winger kept asking me, "How long to go?" I kept saying, "Just a couple more minutes." At full time everyone was on the pitch and all the players were up on people's shoulders.'

Wrexham 1-1 Blyth Spartans, 18 February 1978

Full disclosure. This is not on the list for being a giant-killing feat *per se*. It's there because it so *should* have been. Northern League Blyth were seconds away from a place in the quarter-finals when they were denied by a refereeing howler and a nerdy corner flag technicality which, though specified in the Laws, was no less heartbreaking for Spartans fans. This was not so much a football match as a dark 90-minute drama, in which the plucky underdogs were first toyed with and then crushed by the cruel fist of fate. Blyth had travelled to the Racecourse for the 11th game of one of the great non-league FA Cup runs. They hadn't managed this through luck. Here was a side with arguably the best non-league goalkeeper in the country in Dave Clarke, a full-back, Ron Guthrie, who had won the trophy outright with Sunderland in the 1973 final, and front man Terry Johnson, a prolific scorer with both Brentford and Southend. Blyth had spent a decade building strength in depth, as Stoke City discovered in the process of losing 3-2 to them in the previous round. But Wrexham were no mugs either. They were on their way to the Third Division title, had comprehensively dismantled Newcastle 4-1 in the fourth round and started this game strong favourites. Yet the semi-frozen pitch proved a leveller. When full-back Alan Hill played the ball back to keeper Dai Davies he weighted the pass in the belief the ball would run, only to discover he hadn't put quite enough on it. Johnson pounced like a stray cat on a kipper and the visitors were one up. They maintained that lead until the final moments when skipper John Waterson tackled

Wrexham forward Bobby Shinton close to Blyth's goal line.
The ball clearly came off Shinton but referee Alf Grey whistled
for a corner. The drama was about to enter its tragi-comic
final act. Midfielder Les Cartwright shaped to take the kick
but, feeling he needed more room, moved the corner flag to
poke up at an angle. His cross was collected comfortably by
Clarke but Grey spotted the pole had fallen over and ordered
a retake. Cartwright plunged it back into the icy ground,
delivered a second cross, the Blyth defence cleared with the
final whistle now seconds away. Yet, once more, the corner
flag had toppled. At the third attempt the ball was legitimately
delivered, Dixie McNeil bumbled it over the line, the ref blew
up, the tie went to a replay and Wrexham won 2-0. Brutal.

Bournemouth 2-0 Manchester United, 8 January 1984

'Beware the savage jaw of 1984', sang David Bowie. He was
obviously predicting the result of this game – Robbie Savage
was in Bournemouth's lineup(not to be confused with the
younger Leicester City and Welsh international midfielder,
Robbie Savage). Even though the Cherries were becalmed
at the foot of the Third Division they had no need for either
savagery or Savagery to dispense with the current Cup holders
who sat second in Division One. Everald La Ronde was
calm personified against the attacking creativity of Norman
Whiteside and Frank Stapleton, allowing 25-year-old Ian
Thompson, who had only just turned pro, and Milton Graham
to contribute the goals. But the mastermind behind this
extraordinary win was Bournemouth's young manager Harry
Redknapp who took his players to a local hotel on the eve of
the game, treated them to a slap-up Italian supper and then
fired them up with a concocted story about United's players

watching horse racing prior to the game. He also flagged up a pre-match TV interview given by Ron Atkinson. 'Atkinson did an interview and it came across like this game was an exercise,' Graham later told the BBC.

> That was Harry's first team talk to us that day. He said, "Did everyone see that interview last night? ... They are all in there, laying their bets, believing this is going to be a run-out and they think they will beat us comfortably."

York City 1-0 Arsenal, 26 January 1985

This is how giant-killing legends are made. Division Three York City, assembled for around £19,000, versus an Arsenal side stuffed with stars such as Charlie Nicholas, Tony Woodcock, Kenny Sansom and Viv Anderson and collectively worth £4.5 million. Throw in a snowbound Bootham Crescent, local radio appeals for volunteers to grab spades and clear the pitch (200 answered the call), a Gunners side who clearly didn't want to play and a finale so fraught as to be painful, and you have the magic of the Cup encapsulated. That old cliché about the pitch being a great leveller was a factor in Arsenal's defeat but it doesn't explain why, in the final minute, midfielder Stevie Williams took it upon himself to wrap both arms around Minstermen striker Keith Houchen before engaging in a ten-yard exhibition wrestling match in front of the ref. The ball was nowhere near them but as the pair entered the Arsenal penalty area Houchen finally went down. John Motson's *MOTD* commentary said it all:

> The referee has given a penalty. In the last minute. You couldn't ask for a more dramatic finale. Houchen,

the man who was fouled, has put the ball on the spot.
And he could put York City in dreamland.

Houchen obliged and York played out time by winning their
first corner of the game. The *MOTD* footage of that moment
is priceless. As left-back Alan Hay prepares to take the kick you
can see two white-jacketed blokes pushing a tea trolley around
the touchline – impressive dedication given the snow – who
have to move out of his way.

Wrexham 2-1 Arsenal, 4 January 1992

Apologies to Arsenal fans for another reminder of not-so-
glorious Cup runs but it would be criminal to overlook this
gem. The Gunners were reigning league champions – their
second title in three seasons under manager George Graham
– while the Welsh side were bottom of the Fourth Division
and would only escape relegation to the Conference through
Football league reorganisation. For the entire first half the
90 places between the teams looked an accurate measure
of their respective abilities. The Red Dragons were battered
but somehow managed to hold out until a minute before
half-time, when Alan Smith poked in Paul Merson's assist.
Wrexham's Mickey Thomas, who had played for Manchester
United against the Gunners in the 1979 FA Cup final, later
admitted he was dreading the second half. However, manager
Brian Flynn was relaxed and upbeat, telling his players 'Stay
in the game – something's always going to happen.' Eight
minutes from time, Wrexham got a free kick on the edge of
the Arsenal box, Thomas stepped up, two of his teammates
vamoosed from in front of the defensive wall and the 37-year-
old Welshman drilled the ball though the gap into the top

corner. 'Oh, could you imagine a free kick struck sweeter than that?' drooled commentator Tony Gubba. 'Or at a more important time? [Arsenal goalkeeper David] Seaman had no chance.' Two minutes later Tony Adams, racing back to defend, overstepped the ball, slipped and allowed Wrexham youngster Steve Watkin to slide in the winner. 'Arsenal's world is falling around their ears,' observed Gubba.

Shrewsbury Town 2-1 Everton, 4 January 2003

In fairness, Everton had defensive problems. Injuries to Kevin Campbell and Joseph Yobo had forced manager David Moyes to play a quartet of centre-backs. Even so, how a team fifth in the Premier League could be quite so comprehensively demolished by one 80 places below them, with a league goals-conceded record of 47, the worst in the Third Division, is puzzling. The explanation, of course, is that Shrewsbury were (a) outstanding and (b) having a right go at their illustrious visitors. But for the brilliance of Toffees' goalkeeper Richard Wright it would have been all over in half an hour. As it was, veteran captain Nigel Jemson put the Shrews ahead on the 37th minute and, despite Niclas Alexandersson's equaliser, went on to seal victory with a last-minute header. Afterwards Town manager Kevin Ratcliffe, a former Goodison hero, revealed his tactics: 'The last thing I said was, "Don't show them any respect. Get out there and get at them."' Simple. And effective.

Manchester United 0-1 Leeds United, 3 January 2010

It's not hard to imagine how cross Sir Alex Ferguson was when the ref blew full-time on this one. Losing at home to League

One Leeds, United's despised cross-Pennine rivals, was bad enough, but to fold when you're second in the Premier League, with a team sheet that listed Giggs, Owen, Berbatov and Rooney, smacked of both carelessness and complacency. And yet. Leeds were top of their division and in Jermaine Beckford had a striker on fire. He later recalled how he was spurred on by 9,000 Leeds fans making all the noise inside Old Trafford, and when his chance came on 19 minutes he didn't want to fail them. 'I've hit it, I've looked, it's going in, then it's going wide, then it's going back in. I'm thinking, "Please go in. Please, please go in."' It did, and the Whites defended their lead like men possessed. 'After the game, a couple of the boys had family who were Manchester United fans,' Beckford later told the *Daily Mail*. 'They tried to get a couple of shirts from their players and Alex Ferguson said, "Absolutely not, under no circumstances are you giving any of them your shirts."' Alex was cross alright.

Crawley Town 3-0 Leeds United, 10 January 2021

In truth, that heady FA Cup day at Old Trafford was a rare and precious thing for Leeds United. In the two decades before this trip to West Sussex they'd managed to make it past the third round on only five occasions and in a couple of cases (look away now Leeds fans) they didn't even *get* to the third round, losing to the likes of Hereford and a Cambridgeshire village team called Histon FC. Here Crawley were all over the visitors from the off, although the rout didn't properly get going until the second half when Nick Tsaroulla, Ashley Nadesan and Jordan Tunnicliffe banged in the goals. The last time Leeds manager Marcelo Bielsa suffered a 3-0 defeat this devastating was at the 1999 Copa América, when his

Argentina side was beaten 3-0 by Columbia and striker Martín Palermo missed three penalties.

Ipswich Town 1-2 Maidstone United, 27 January 2024

A tie which saw National League South Maidstone United become the first team outside the top five tiers to make it to the fourth round since Blyth Spartans in 1978. It was nip and tuck against an Ipswich side challenging for promotion to the Premier League, and United survived three first-half shots onto the woodwork before Lamar Reynolds put them ahead with a sumptuous dink over onrushing Town goalkeeper Christian Walton. Ipswich levelled in the second half through Jeremy Sarmiento before Sam Corne hit a breakaway winner. Stones ended the match with two goals from two attempts while Ipswich had one from 28 – an indication that the visitors would have been skewered without goalkeeper Lucas Covolan's 12 excellent saves. Afterwards manager George Elokobi offered an FA Cup maxim for all would-be Improbables: 'Always believe there is hope ... and fate.'

FIERY FEBRUARY: RED CARDS AND TROUBLE

Grudge matches are the beating heart of domestic football. Win one, and an entire season of bewildering tactics, abject performances and painful thrashings can be airbrushed from memory. Like politicians flinging red meat to their mercurial supporters, managers know that arming fans with bragging rights after a grudge-match victory means pretty much everything else is forgiven, at least for a few weeks. Some grudges are built into a club's DNA – no one knows quite how or why they started but you have to keep them going anyway – others simmer away for years with minimal animosity until suddenly, out of nowhere, a seemingly minor bit of banter between players reverberates into the following season. Or, in the case of Manchester United and Arsenal, the next eight seasons. Between February 1997 and February 2005, encounters between these two great clubs saw no fewer than seven red cards as players and managers and, it has to be said, journalists, ramped up notions of injustice. There were so many 'Battles of Old Trafford' that the media gave up trying to think of new monikers for them, and it became hard to work out which particular BoOT was being referenced. But before we get to all that, let's take a trip back to pre-Premier League days and a chill autumnal afternoon at the Theatre of Dreams.

Manchester United 0-1 Arsenal, 20 October 1990: The 21-Player Brawl

The genesis of this altercation, known as the '21-Player Brawl', can be traced back to the previous season, when Gunners full-back Nigel Winterburn gave United striker Brian McClair the verbals for missing a penalty. Nothing too heinous then – a batter gets similar or worse every five minutes in professional cricket – but it niggled away at McClair and in this game he made sure he didn't fluff a kick, landing several emphatically on Winterburn as the latter executed an agricultural tackle on Denis Irwin. Irwin himself retaliated, giving Winterburn a boot for good measure, whereupon goal scorer Anders Limpar pitched in, landing a right on McClair's head. In fairness, most players were trying to calm things down: United goalkeeper Les Sealey had both arms around David Rocastle, while Tony Adams teamed up with Alex Ferguson to try to separate the protagonists. It all fizzled out with just two bookings – Winterburn and Paul Davis – but off the pitch the ramifications were considerable. The FA fined both clubs £50,000 for bringing the game into disrepute, United were docked a point, Arsenal two (they had form, with an altercation with Norwich players the previous season) and the Highbury board took a particularly dim view of the whole business. Rocastle, Limpar, Winterburn, Davis and Michael

Thomas were all fined two weeks' wages while manager George Graham had his bank balance relieved of £9,000. Eighteen years later Winterburn told the *Independent* it was 'all because of something I'd said to Brian McClair' after that missed penalty at Highbury. 'I shouldn't have done it, and it was one of those things you end up wishing you hadn't done,' he said. 'It probably caused a lot of the bad blood between the sides that has lasted for years but I was just competitive and desperate to win.' He and McClair niggled away at each other for several more encounters until they agreed to disagree and shook hands. In his autobiography *Odd Man Out: A Player's Diary*, McClair wrote:

> I tangled with Nigel Winterburn, and all hell broke loose. Within a few minutes the red mist had disappeared, and I was looking round in disbelief. I couldn't believe what I'd just done. The worst thing of all was watching myself on television behaving very badly. My perceptions had been so badly distorted by rage I hadn't actually remembered what happened accurately. I was convinced that I'd only kicked Nigel once but that wasn't the case at all.

The docked points mattered little to Arsenal – they ended the season top with seven to spare – and it made no difference to the Red Devils who finished sixth, still waiting for that elusive first title under Ferguson.

Arsenal 1-2 Manchester United, 19 February 1997: Wright v Schmeichel

Hostility between the two sides didn't exactly vanish after the 21-Player Brawl although it did ratchet down. For the next six years they confined themselves to settling matters through football rather than fisticuffs. But in October 1996 Arsenal appointed Arsène Wenger to replace the embattled Bruce Rioch and, while it would be wrong to suggest his arrival from Japanese side Nagoya Grampus Eight reignited the enmity, it certainly put fire into his team. As United full-back Gary Neville would later observe, Ferguson 'knew [Wenger] was going to be his biggest challenge as Manchester United manager.' Plainly, the men didn't get on, and for both sets of players this placed a premium on winning head-to-head fixtures. That said, the Wright v Schmeichel affair appears to have started as a purely personal dispute which got out of hand. Ian Wright's two-footed challenge on Peter Schmeichel in this midweek game – surprisingly considered fair by referee Martin Bodenham – caused uproar in the visitors' camp. *Match of the Day* cameras showed a livid-looking Ferguson stomping up the touchline as Schmeichel lay injured, while John Motson's commentary hinted at some personal baggage:

> There's been a bit of history between Wright and Schmeichel, and Alex Ferguson is concerned, to say the least, about the condition of the goalkeeper and maybe about the challenge ... Schmeichel and Wright have been at each other's throats once or twice before – figuratively anyway.

At the final whistle police moved in to keep the players apart, and in the aftermath, Wright complained he had been verbally abused by the United goalkeeper at the previous league encounter three months earlier. Schmeichel emphatically denied this, and the allegation was later dismissed by both the Football Association and the police for lack of evidence.

The two players were persuaded to call a fragile truce which unfortunately didn't encompass their managers. With United pushing for the title in the face of a punishing run-in of four games in eight days, Ferguson called on the League to extend the fixtures schedule. Wenger, whose team had only two to play, objected. This mattered because although United sat top on 2 May, only four points and a goal difference of one separated the teams. Wenger was never going to retreat, and Ferguson didn't hold back. 'I think it is only fair that the season be extended, but I see Arsène Wenger has had a swipe at Manchester United again,' he said.

> He's certainly got plenty to say. He's at a big club, well Arsenal used to be a big club, and maybe next year he could be in the same situation. I wonder what his story will be then? Arsène Wenger has been in Japan. He doesn't know anything about English football and the demands of our game. Unless you have been in the situation and had the experience, then he should keep his mouth shut – firmly shut.

United went on to win the title after Arsenal's hopes evaporated in a 1-0 home defeat to Newcastle. But the Ferguson-Wenger grudge was up and running. After the Gunners won the League and Cup Double the following season, pipping United to the title by a point, there was no going back. Over the next six seasons Ferguson's team claimed four titles and Wenger's two. They produced some of the best teams ever seen in English football and, with feisty characters like Roy Keane, Patrick Vieira, Rio Ferdinand and Martin Keown around, they also produced the best tantrums.

Manchester United 0-0 Arsenal, 21 September 2003: The First Battle of Old Trafford

There aren't many landmark 0-0s, but this one is on the list. It is remembered not just for *MOTD* pundit Martin Keown's unrestrained jig of joy around Ruud van Nistelrooy following the striker's penalty miss but also because, had that kick gone in, there would have been no Arsenal Invincibles. More on the Invincibles in our **May** section on title-defining games but, for now, it's enough to note that this was the season a magnificent Gunners side completed their entire English league programme without a single defeat, a feat previously achieved only by Preston North End in 1888–89. This First Battle of Old Trafford hinged on a single incident in the 81st minute when Van Nistelrooy jumped into Vieira. He was correctly penalised, but when the Arsenal midfielder jabbed out a foot from his prone position on the ground the Dutchman theatrically jumped away. Although no contact was made there was obvious intent and referee Steve Bennett was within his rights to brandish a card. However, Vieira's teammates believed Van Nistelrooy had deliberately exaggerated his reaction, and swarmed around him to pass on their views. Minutes later, Bennett awarded a soft injury-time penalty to United, the result of a Keown challenge on Diego Forlán, and Van Nistelrooy stepped up only to hit the bar with his kick. Cue further bedlam, Keown's in-your-face celebration and further pushing and shoving at the final whistle as, amid a swarm of players, the Arsenal defender's forearm made contact with Van Nistelrooy's back. Keown was later banned for three games and fined £20,000 for violent conduct. Ashley Cole, Ryan Giggs and Cristiano Ronaldo were also fined while Ray Parlour, Lauren, and Vieira received bans. Almost two decades later Keown told the *Daily Mail* he couldn't contain his emotions. 'It was a raw reaction in the middle of a match that had so much riding on it between two great Premier League rivals,' he said.

> I felt like justice had been served and so did my teammates. Looking back, perhaps we could have toned down our reaction. But it happened in the heat of the moment and I don't regret anything I did.

Manchester United 2-0 Arsenal, 24 October 2004: The Second Battle of Old Trafford, aka The Battle of the Buffet, or Pizzagate

This was the season *MOTD* regained rights to the Premier League's highlights package, although sadly there were no cameras in the tunnel to record the best of the post-match action. The result showed the Invincibles were vincible after all, because it ended Arsenal's record 49-match unbeaten run in the Premier League. That fact might have been mentioned by United players at the final whistle and would have niggled an Arsenal side already grumpy after Wayne Rooney won a controversial penalty which Van Nistelrooy – who else – converted. Rooney also got a late goal so by the time the teams were back in the tunnel tempers were running hot. A fight broke out between players and staff, in the midst of which Arsenal's 17-year-old substitute Cesc Fàbregas lobbed a slice of pizza from the buffet laid on in the visitors' dressing room out of the door and onto Sir Alex. In an interview with ITV Sport years later he denied targeting the United supremo and claimed he resorted to a pizza offensive because he didn't fancy a proper fight. 'We were 49 games unbeaten,' he said.

They were so competitive but they were very smart people. I was getting a lot of stick as well. So, I was very frustrated. You're warming up and didn't play. You're annoyed you lost. I just went in quickly to the dressing room and there was some food there, I was starving ... I took a slice of pizza and we started hearing noises. You started seeing players and Arsène Wenger everywhere. The first thing that occurred to me was to throw the pizza because I didn't have the power or the courage maybe to go into that fight. They were monsters in there. They were super, super big guys.

Sir Alex, who also sustained collateral damage from flying soup, reportedly tried to get into the dressing room but was restrained by a security guard. In an interview with the *Independent* the following year he claimed the Arsenal manager was 'publicly criticising my players, calling them cheats.' He went on:

I went out into the tunnel and said to him: "You get in there and behave yourself, leave my players alone". He came sprinting towards me with his hands raised saying: "What do you want to do about it?" He was standing right there. To not apologise for the behaviour of the players to another manager is unthinkable. It is a disgrace. But I don't expect Wenger to ever apologise.

In fact, Wenger did later apologise, describing his player's actions as 'unacceptable'. He added:

Pizzagate was a little bit of unrest in the tunnel area. Mike Riley was the referee and he didn't have the best day, Rio [Ferdinand] shouldn't have been on the pitch after 20 minutes. Yes, it was aggressive, to lose after such a long undefeated run and the way we did was not acceptable.

It's impossible to say whether the Second BoOT caused these two sides to lose focus. But whereas Arsenal were top of the League when it happened, they were five points behind Chelsea two months later. Neither the Gunners nor United were able to catch José Mourinho's outstanding Chelsea champions.

Arsenal 2-4 Manchester United, 1 February 2005: Vieira v Keane

Another fractious encounter that started, rather than ended, in the tunnel. Viewers saw referee Graham Poll trying to calm warring captains Roy Keane and Patrick Vieira as he prepared to lead out the teams, telling them, 'Leave it in here, leave it in the tunnel' (optimistic, given that a wild-eyed Keane had just shouted at Vieira – not in a friendly way – 'I'll see you out there'). According to Wayne Rooney, one of the players waiting in the Highbury tunnel that day, Arsenal players verbally targeted Gary Neville during the warm-up and Vieira chased him into the visitors' dressing room. Writing in the *Sunday Times*, Rooney went on:

[Neville] told us what happened and when the teams lined up to go out, Roy went straight to Vieira. "If you're going to pick on someone, try me," he said. You can see on the footage that I'm laughing because it was quite funny – though, inside, I was thinking: "Roy, don't do anything silly here, don't get sent off." As it happened, Roy had a magnificent game – as did Vieira.

Neither got so much as a yellow card, unlike Ryan Giggs, Gabriel Heinze, Cristiano Ronaldo and Rooney himself, while Mikaël Silvestre was sent off near the end. But perhaps the day was most memorable for the Gunners' young mascot. Footage shows the lad obviously enjoying the tunnel ructions, although he looked decidedly nervous when shaking Keane's hand before kick-off.

The most public of managerial meltdowns in the annals of Wenger-Ferguson rivalry occurred at the start of the 2009–10 season. Rivalry between the clubs was less intense, not least because the bill for Arsenal's new stadium had left them relatively strapped for cash in the transfer market. Nonetheless, when the Gunners' Robin van Persie looked to have scored a last-minute equaliser at Old Trafford on 29 August, Wenger was quick to celebrate. Then RVP's effort was disallowed on account of William Gallas being offside in the buildup, and the manager took out his frustration on a plastic water bottle, booting it down the touchline. Fourth official Lee Probert alerted referee Mike Dean to this heinous crime, whereupon Dean sent Wenger off. But it wasn't clear where he was supposed to go. This resulted in Wenger standing among supporters, arms spread, incredulous at the absurdity of it all. *MOTD*'s guest pundit and former United midfielder Gordon Strachan had great fun with these farcical scenes in his running commentary:

> he boots the plastic bottle somewhere, that's not causing any harm, and then the fourth official decides, "I'm going to make a name for myself." [He tells Wenger]: "You can't kick a plastic bottle away like that. I'm going to tell the referee you've kicked a plastic bottle away … right we'll send you off for that."

Wenger later got an apology from the Professional Game Match Officials board, and told journalists, 'I didn't kick the bottle because I thought Gallas had been onside. I kicked it because I was disappointed. I did not know that was not allowed. Although, it was a good kick.'

There's a comforting footnote to this protracted Arsenal-United antipathy. However nasty things may get in the heat of battle, it seems the passage of time can soothe even the most stubborn of grudges. During *MOTD's* 2002 World Cup coverage, Schmeichel and Wright made up live on air after years of avoiding each other. Former *MOTD* editor Paul Armstrong recalls how they'd both been booked as panellists, initially to work separately. But after they bumped into each other at the BBC's hotel, they had 'a long grown-up chat' and decided they wanted to work together, which they did, very amicably. According to Paul, 'Wrighty even managed to refrain from gloating too much when England eliminated Denmark 3-0.' As for Sir Alex and Arsène, all is now sweetness and light. When in 2023 they jointly became the first managers to be installed in the Premier League's Hall of Fame, there were lovey-dovey exchanges which would have been inconceivable two decades earlier. 'I feel Arsène is a very worthy inductee as he transformed Arsenal Football Club fantastically,' gushed Sir Alex.

> They became a tough team to compete with and we both wanted to win, which motivated us further. Through the years since retirement, we'd go for dinner together in a little restaurant he knows well in Switzerland. He is a really interesting man and I enjoy his company, but it is still my job to pick the wine.

Wenger was equally magnanimous: 'To share this with Sir Alex is a great honour for me,' he said.

> It's like two boxers, you fight like mad and go the distance together. At the end of the day, you have respect, and it will be a great opportunity to meet with him, share a good bottle of wine and memories of our old battles.

You do wonder though, during their cosy chats, whether Sir Alex ever touches on his Premier League record – played 810; won 528; drew 168; lost 114; win rate 65.2% – and compares it to that of his new bestie – played 828; won 476; drew 199; lost 153; win rate 57.5%. Surely he wouldn't. Would he?

WHO'D BE A REF?

At least if you're the referee placed in charge of an Arsenal-Manchester United game you know what's coming. And getting that one on your CV means your boss at Professional Game Match Officials Limited must rate you as a 'big hitter', valued for your calm demeanour and meticulous preparation. That said, there's only so much prep you can do. Top-flight football is a fickle mistress, exulting in bizarre twists, red mists and things teachers at referee school never thought to mention. Here we dip into the *Match of the Day* selection box of refereeing conundrums.

Leeds United 1-2 West Bromwich Albion, 17 April 1971: Leeds Don't Play to the Whistle

A game that saw arguably the most controversial offside decision of England's professional pre-VAR era. Eighteenth-

placed Albion hadn't won an away match in 16 months
while top-of-the-league Leeds, with a home record of only
seven defeats in five years, were on course to pip Arsenal
to the title. By the 65th minute of this encounter they were
a goal down and pressing hard for an equaliser when a dire
Norman Hunter pass was intercepted by Tony Brown and
booted into the Leeds half. Colin Suggett was standing in an
offside position but, under Law 11, that is not an offence. The
question is rather: is the offside player 'active' or somehow
'interfering with play'? In this case, Brown chased his own kick
forward and Suggett immediately ran ahead, but crucially *away*
from the ball. Had his action drawn a Leeds defender into
following, he might indeed have been interfering with play.
But the entire Leeds defence had gone AWOL. Almost every
player was camped in Albion's half, and when the linesman
raised his flag they stopped running. Referee Ray Tinkler
rightly waved play on and Brown passed to Jeff Astle for a tap-
in or, as Leeds fans still prefer to call it, a 'title-denier'. Cue a
pitch invasion involving middle-aged Yorkshiremen sporting
unfeasibly large sideburns, police chasing them round the
centre circle Benny Hill-style, Whites manager Don Revie
pleading with the linesman, and *MOTD*'s Barry Davies siding
with Leeds, kind of, as he tried to make sense of the mayhem:

> Leeds will go mad. And they've every right to go mad,
> because everyone stopped with the linesman's flag.
> Leeds have every justification for going mad although,
> one must add, that they played to the linesman and
> not to the whistle.

United did pull a goal back, and had they drawn this game
they would have finished the season tied at the top with

Arsenal on 65 points but with a 3.4% better goal average. Tinkler had no time for the whingers. 'What people forget is that Leeds were already losing before that goal was scored, and they were playing badly,' he told the *Guardian*.

> Now it's true that one of the West Bromwich players, Colin Suggett, had been standing in an offside position when Tony Brown intercepted a pass and raced clear of the Leeds defence. My linesman raised his flag straightaway but I waved him down – the ball never went anywhere near Suggett. He saw my signal, but the problem was he didn't move. He should have lowered his flag and tried to keep up with play. Because he didn't move, several Leeds players wrongly assumed that play had stopped.
>
> I was known for always playing advantage, that was the way I refereed. This was no different. Of course now it wouldn't be an issue – everyone would know that Suggett wasn't interfering with play.

Maybe Ray, maybe.

Crystal Palace 1-1 Manchester United, 25 January 1995: Eric Cantona's Kung Fu Kick

In terms of consequences, this is the granddaddy of them. Things were going well for Cantona – three days earlier his goal against Blackburn had put United within two points of Kenny Dalglish's pace-setters – but opposing teams now realised that to blunt the Red Devils' attack you first had to stifle, and preferably wind up, Eric. At Selhurst Park Crystal Palace players warmed to the task, and when centre-back

Richard Shaw made yet another vigorous challenge the Frenchman petulantly kicked out. With intent clear, ref Alan Wilkie had no choice but to brandish a red card. As Cantona walked disconsolately along the touchline to the dressing room he was triggered by a choice piece of crowd abuse, freed himself from the steely grip of his escort, United kit man Norman Davies, delivered a mid-air kung fu kick to the body of Palace fan Matthew Simmons and followed up with a punch. Football genius he may have been, but this was plain thuggery. He later gave a ludicrous statement to the press: 'When the seagulls follow the trawler it is because they think sardines will be thrown into the sea. Thank you.' How very Confucian, Eric. Magistrates thought Cantona should be thrown into prison, but his two-week sentence was commuted on appeal to 120 hours community service. He was banned by the FA for nine months, fined £20,000 by his club and £10,000 by the FA. Could you say his stupidity probably cost United the title? Yes, you could.

Coventry City 3-1 Crystal Palace, 6 September 1980: Clive Allen's Goal That Never Was

Billed 'the most expensive teenager in sport', Clive Allen's arrival at Palace in the summer of 1980 suggested he was worth every penny. After scoring in the 47th minute of this match, defensive mistakes allowed the Sky Blues' Gerry Daly to put the hosts back in front, only for Allen to apparently equalise in the 55th minute with a humdinger of a 20-yarder into the top corner of Jim Blyth's goal. It hit the supporting stanchion and rebounded so hard that both referee Derek Webb and, initially, commentator John Motson were deceived. 'Clive Allen hammered that and it came back off the woodwork,' said Motson. 'Palace say it was over the line and the referee says no goal. Well, there's a talking point.' Back in the *MOTD* studio a slow-motion replay revealed the ball had indeed hit the back of the net. Eagles manager Terry Venables was seething:

> It was a disgusting decision. I've never seen anything like it. Clive is choked and he is entitled to be. That goal would have brought us back to 2-2 with a fighting chance of taking a point. It was a goal. End of story. We lost the game after that. It knocked us for six.

Daily Express correspondent John Davies neatly summed things up, writing that 'Clive Allen was robbed of what might have been BBC's Goal of the Month by what was certainly the Boob of the Season.' For poor Derek Webb there was no hiding place. 'No doubt I'll hear more about it,' he said. 'It was a split-second decision I had to make, and I must stand by it.'

Sheffield Wednesday 1-0 Arsenal, 26 September 1998: Paolo's Push

Stereotypes are rarely true but in this case hot-blooded Italian Paolo Di Canio proved that sometimes they're bang on. He claimed later he was trying to act as peacemaker when Arsenal's Patrick Vieira and Wednesday's Wim Jonk tumbled over in a midfield tussle before engaging in a playground shoving match. Paolo pushed them, Martin Keown pushed him (simultaneously poking an elbow in his face) and Paolo reacted unwisely. 'I tried to grab [Keown's] neck, his eyes, and kick his leg,' he later told Sky Sports. 'That was a stupid but instinctive reaction.' When referee Paul Alcock reached for the inevitable red, things rapidly got worse.

> When I saw Paul Alcock, in a rash moment, put in my face the red card, I lost my temper. I lost everything. I thought, "I had received this elbow in the face, I feel pain and also you punish me in this way?" ... I pushed him away, but without any violent conduct, because it wasn't a push, which is absolutely wrong.

Caught by surprise, Alcock took several tottering steps backwards before collapsing in a heap. Some of the tabloids ludicrously accused him of 'taking a dive', and the referee conceded that it 'looked silly'. But he insisted: 'At the time I was off balance. There was no way you would feign something like that on national TV.' Hit with an 11-match ban and £10,000 fine, and cold-shouldered by Wednesday, Di Canio was snapped up by West Ham in the January transfer window and scored his first goal for them against Blackburn on 27 February 1999. He became a Hammers favourite, and his battered reputation was restored the following year at Goodison. With Everton keeper Paul Gerrard lying injured on the ground, and the goalmouth gaping, Di Canio decided to catch an incoming cross rather than try to score. He later received the FIFA Fair Play Award for 'a special act of good sportsmanship'.

Liverpool 2-2 Chelsea, 21 April 2013:
Suárez Does *Jaws*

> Luis Suárez went from hero, villain to hero in one half of football. You just cannot keep him out of any game for a second. Rafael Benítez is left frustrated on his first return to Anfield as a manager. But it is another game that, for all sorts of reasons, is about Luis Suárez.

MOTD commentator Guy Mowbray was understandably cautious in his summary – it's easy to jump to conclusions in the heat of action – but in the aftermath his 'all sorts of reasons' phrase became a whole lot clearer. In the 52nd minute Suárez had provided a sublime assist for Daniel Sturridge's equaliser before conceding a penalty with a blatant handball. Minutes later, as Liverpool pressed for a second equaliser, he bit Blues Serb defender Branislav Ivanović on the upper arm as the two of them challenged for the ball. Suárez had previous – as Ajax captain in 2010 he had been banned for seven games after sinking his gnashers into PSV Eindhoven midfielder Otman Bakkal's shoulder – however at Anfield, referee Kevin Friend hadn't spotted his antics. Although an aggrieved Ivanović revealed the toothmarks, the moment had passed. If VAR been around there's little doubt the Uruguayan would have been sent off, but his continued involvement, allowing him to score a 97th minute equaliser, added to the controversy. Fortunately, justice was served. TV cameras had picked up the bite and an FA-appointed independent review panel imposed a 10-match ban, ending Suárez's season.

Sunderland 1-0 Liverpool, 17 October 2009: The Beach Ball Goal

If you're not a 'Laws-of-the-Game' nerd you can skip the next bit. As this encounter got under way, stewards at the Stadium of Light noticed that a Liverpool-branded beach ball had been thrown onto the pitch by an away fan. They retrieved it, but somehow it found its way back on, ending up stationary on Reds keeper Pepe Reina's six-yard line, in front of his goal. The relevant bit of Law 5 defines this as 'outside interference' and – deep breath here – states that if

an extra ball, other object or animal enters the field
of play during the match, the referee must: stop play
(and restart with a dropped ball) only if it interferes
with play unless the ball is going into the goal and
the interference does not prevent a defending player
playing the ball, the goal is awarded if the ball enters
the goal (even if contact was made with the ball)
unless the interference was by the attacking team.

We'll try and unpick that in a moment, but what actually
happened is a whole lot simpler to grasp. With five minutes
on the clock the Black Cats broke down the right. Andy Reid
crossed the match ball which deflected to Darren Bent. He
struck an innocuous shot straight at Reina but en route the
match ball hit the beach ball, knocking it behind the goal line,
before spinning past Reina's left hand into the net. It was like
snooker-soccer. Referee Mike Jones awarded the goal and got
duly lambasted by most of the ex-referees plying their trade as
media pundits.

But was that fair according to the Law? Bear with us here.
Jones could have stopped play and ordered the beach ball
to be removed *only* if was interfering with play. But if that
interference resulted in the match ball entering the goal, didn't
stop a defender from playing it and wasn't instigated by the
attacking team, then Jones was not at liberty to blow up. In
which case, the goal had to count. The counterargument is
that the beach ball prevented defender Glen Johnson, who
was standing alongside it, from playing the match ball. Slow-
motion replays show that he had a boot in place to block Bent's
shot but, because it struck the beach ball a fraction earlier, his
block was ineffective. As Johnson later told talkSport:

I stuck my foot out to routinely block the shot. I was in line with it, so I knew I wouldn't miss it, but all of a sudden I didn't touch the ball. I'm looking around and the first thing I saw was a beach ball in the air, but I didn't realise it had hit that at the time. It was one of those crazy moments. It was madness.

All this is easy to analyse from the armchair; less so in the milliseconds granted to Jones. He was demoted to the Championship the following week but went on to referee a total of 202 league and cup matches. It should also be noted that this wasn't the first 'outside interference' controversy of the modern game. The previous year, Luton Shelton's strike for Sheffield United in a 2-1 FA Cup fourth-round win over Manchester City deflected to him off a light-blue balloon, wrong footing City defender Michael Ball. That one counted too.

Arsenal 1-0 Manchester City, 22 October 2005: The Comedy Penalty

A candidate for the worst penalty ever taken, anywhere, at any level of the game. This was a jaw-dropping mistake by Arsenal Invincible Robert Pires in consort with fellow Invincible Thierry Henry. The pair decided to show off by agreeing that, instead of shooting direct at goal, Pires would pass the ball from the penalty spot to Henry running in from the edge of the box. They were trying to emulate a penalty taken by Johan Cruyff for Ajax in the 1982–83 season, when the Dutch maestro swapped passes with teammate Jesper Olsen before scoring. This is all fine under the Laws provided that (a) the ball moves forward from the spot, and (b) the penalty taker doesn't kick the ball a second time until another player has touched it. Pires, who had earlier managed to put away a penalty more conventionally, never got as far as (b). He scuffed his pass so badly that the ball moved, almost imperceptibly, square, Henry arrived, Sylvain Distin cleared, Pires and Henry spread their arms appealing for a retake and referee Mike Riley correctly awarded an indirect free kick to City. What Arsène Wenger made of it, given that his side were only a goal up, isn't hard to imagine.

BEWARE THE IDES OF MARCH

Readers who know their Roman history will be familiar with the Ides. They served as a fixed point in every month from which you counted back to work out the rough date. A bewildering system for diary entries you might think, but compared to determining 'clear and obvious' via VAR it was surely a cinch. The significance of the Ides of March – or 15 March as we now call it – is that this was the date in 44 BC that Julius Caesar, ignoring warnings from a soothsayer, was ambushed by his enemies and stabbed to death (23 times if you want the actual stats). 'Beware the Ides of March', a phrase from Shakespeare's *Julius Caesar*, subsequently passed into popular culture as synonymous with risk and danger. Which is a convenient, if admittedly tenuous, link to top-flight football's very own version of the Ides. Here we recall two of the greatest financial scandals to hit the game during the *Match of the Day* years, both of which emerged from investigations prompted by March events. They would have far-reaching ramifications for an England international star and a revered Double-winning manager.

1964: The Match-Fixing Scandal

As we've seen, *MOTD*'s debut year was a time of great upheaval in the game, with changes to transfer rules, player wage demands and acrimonious debate over the merits of televised football. But there was also a darker side to professional football, with more serious implications. By mid-March 1964, reporters at the *Sunday People* were finalising a 12-month investigation into match fixing, and were set to publish their scoop. Enquiries had focused on a betting syndicate run by Jimmy Gauld, a former Everton striker whose journeyman career encompassed ten clubs. Gauld's playing days had ended and he needed extra income. He knew several former teammates at Mansfield Town had been bribed by Tranmere Rovers players to throw a game, and in 1962 he launched a similar scam himself. He asked Sheffield Wednesday striker David 'Bronco' Layne, whom he'd once played alongside at Swindon, to help throw a game. Layne identified the 1 December fixture at Ipswich Town, reasoning that Alf Ramsey's side was Wednesday's bogey team, even though the Owls were then eighth in Division One, 13 places above their relegation-threatened hosts. During training, Layne recruited teammates Peter Swan and Tony Kay, telling them that Gauld needed to ensure Wednesday's defeat to bring in a treble on the back of match-fixed Fourth Division games between Lincoln Town and Brentford, and York City and Oldham. The players each staked £50 at 2-1 and each collected £100. Swan told *The Times* in a 2006 interview that Wednesday lost their game 'fair and square', adding: 'I still don't know what I'd have done if we'd been winning. It would have been easy for me to give away a penalty or even score an own goal. Who knows?' Ipswich players detected no sign of sharp practice. Their striker Ray Crawford, who scored twice in the 2-0 win, told the *East Anglian Daily Times*:

> If you watched that match you'd never think those players were on a back-hander. They all had fairly good games. Peter Swan always used to kick me when we came up against each other and it was certainly no different that day I can tell you. And Tony Kay was the stand-out man-of-the-match, he was that good.

Gauld's syndicate was emboldened. The result was never questioned, at least publicly, and if bookmakers spotted a suspicious betting pattern they didn't let on.

Yet by the spring of 1963 rumours of match fixing were rife. Following a tip-off, the *Sunday People* accused two Bristol Rovers players – goalkeeper Esmond Million and forward Keith Williams – of trousering bribes to throw a match against Bradford Park Avenue. Both were fined and banned from football for life along with Mansfield Town's Brian Phillips, who had brokered the deal. Then, in August 1963, Hartlepool United player Ken Thomson admitted to the newspaper that he'd bet through Gauld's syndicate on his side losing a game against Exeter City. The following weekend the *People* named Gauld as the match-fixing 'mastermind' and for the next eight months focused attentions on him, eventually persuading him to turn principal tipster for a fee of £7,000 (equivalent to around £145,000 in 2024). As part of the deal Gauld secretly taped conversations between himself and Layne, and by the end of March 1964 the newspaper's investigations and legal checks were complete. The story finally broke on 12 April, and this time it was a full-blown scandal. By naming the three Sheffield Wednesday players Gauld had shown that, far from being the preserve of the lower leagues, match fixing had penetrated English football's top flight, and no result could be considered safe. Besides which, left-sided midfielder Kay, who was transferred to Everton shortly after the fateful Ipswich Town game, and Wednesday defender Swan, were England internationals. These players were household names who fully expected to be selected for Alf Ramsey's 1966 World Cup squad. Swan had played 19 successive games for England and been flagged in the Italian media as the best centre-back in the world. He had even been assured by Ramsey that he was 'top of the list' for a position that eventually went to Jack Charlton. Kay had only one international cap but had been pivotal in Everton's title-winning 1962–63 season and was Toffees' team captain. As for David Layne, he was Wednesday's top scorer for both the 1962–63 and 1963–64 seasons with 52 goals in 74 league appearances. Now these players' careers lay in ruins.

'David and I have asked ourselves many times why we did it,' Swan said decades later.

> What fools we were. I was banned from going to all football matches. When the wind blew you could hear the roar from Hillsborough at our house and that was hard. I played for a pub side and they got fined for having me. I wasn't even allowed to go and watch my son, Carl, play. It was like they'd cut my legs off. You think about what you could have done and you feel like busting a vein. I was happy for the England team

in 1966 and Big Jack did a great job, but you can't help thinking about what might have been.

In January 1965 ten current and former players, including Gauld himself, went on trial at Nottingham Assizes in a case that made English legal history as the first to admit taped evidence. All were jailed, with Gauld, whose tapes served as the prosecution's ace card, handed the heaviest sentence of four years. Layne, Kay and Swan all got four months and were among seven defendants banned for life from football, although Swan and Kay successfully appealed seven years later and returned to play for Sheffield Wednesday. In all, the British Betting Scandal, as it became known, saw 33 players prosecuted.

1994: The Bung Scandal

In March 1994 tax inspectors at the Inland Revenue were investigating unusual payments into the personal bank accounts of senior Arsenal FC members of staff. One was Steve Burtenshaw, a former caretaker manager and now the club's chief scout. The other was an iconic figure, George Graham, former Gunners player and the revered manager who had brought six major trophies, including two league titles, to Highbury. A month later, on 22 April 1994, Arsenal's accountants received a letter from the Revenue raising concerns that 'coaching staff have received payments or moneys … which have emanated from transfer fees paid by your client.' It was a neutral phrase, but everyone knew what it meant. The payments looked like 'bungs'. Four days later, Graham and Burtenshaw were summoned to a meeting with Arsenal's long-serving managing director, Ken Friar, who was understandably keen to know more. Burtenshaw admitted that he'd received money from Rune Hauge, a Norwegian football agent. Life was about to get very uncomfortable for those doing business in the dark and grubby corners of football's transfer market. Within ten months the FA would launch a Commission of Inquiry. A Premier League inquiry into illegal payments was already underway.

The story begins, though, in the summer of 1988, when Rune Hauge arrived in London on a business trip, part of which involved meeting Arsenal's vice-chairman David Dein. Hauge was informally introduced to Graham as a potential future contact but not regarded, yet, as a key mover and shaker. While agents had been around for decades, their role in international transfers was relatively minor because European leagues restricted the number of foreign players on a club's books. Most deals were agreed through one-to-one meetings between managers or directors, with players involved only in the final stages. But as the international market matured, agents assumed greater importance. Hauge had good contacts across Europe, particularly in his native Scandinavia, and became closer to Graham after overseeing Anders Limpar's move from to Arsenal in 1990. Graham later summed up their relationship in his book *The Glory and the Grief*:

> I saw him as a good contact to have in Europe because he was so well connected, and he saw me as a man who could help him do business in England. We worked together on the understanding that I would tell him which clubs might be interested in his players, only after I had been given first choice for Arsenal.

Evidence submitted to the FA inquiry would later show how two more of Hauge's clients were transferred to Highbury –

Norwegian full-back Pål Lydersen and Danish midfielder John Jensen. Lydersen was signed from IK Start for £500,000, with the deal completing on 9 December 1991, while Jensen moved from Brøndby for £1.57 million, the fee landing in Brøndby's Copenhagen bank account in late July 1992. The timings are significant. On 23 December 1991, 13 days after Lydersen became a Gunners player, Hauge met Graham in the bar of London's Park Lane Hotel, where he handed over a briefcase containing £140,500 in £50-note bundles. The following August, a month after Jensen's transfer, Graham opened his morning post to discover a banker's draft in the sum of £285,000, made out in his name, together with a compliments slip from Hauge. Graham would later insist that these payments were unsolicited gifts in recognition of the help he'd given Hauge in making contacts among England's leading clubs. He hadn't mentioned them to Arsenal and didn't for a further two years. To see how things played out we need to return to 1994 and the aftermath of that Inland Revenue letter.

On 19 September 1994 Graham was invited to another meeting with the Arsenal hierarchy. But this time it wasn't just Ken Friar asking awkward questions. Also present was the club's chairman, Peter Hill-Wood, the third generation of his family to serve in that role and a man not inclined to see his beloved Arsenal dragged through the dirt. Hill-Wood was old school. He would defend club colleagues to the hilt in public but any deviation from the straight and narrow would result in a 'quiet word' in private. His *Times* obituary recalled an FA disciplinary hearing in the 1989–90 season when Arsenal players were hauled up to explain themselves following an altercation with Norwich at Highbury. Hill-Wood told the panel that after viewing the footage three times all he saw was teammates defending each other. But as he waited outside for the verdict, he beckoned over team captain Tony Adams. 'Look, you tell your buddies, I don't much enjoy spending my afternoons at places like this,' he scolded Adams. 'I don't want it to happen again.' The same season he watched four Arsenal players remonstrating animatedly with a linesman as they tried to get an Aston Villa winner ruled out for offside. Hill-Wood promptly fined all four of them on the grounds that officials were 'decent and honest men' who 'do not deserve to be abused.'

The September 1994 meeting was the first time Graham admitted to his bosses that he'd received £425,500 from Rune Hauge. He hadn't mentioned it, he said, because the money wasn't in any way connected to the transfers of Lydersen and Jensen. This explanation cut little ice with Hill-Wood, a respected City banker, who suspected it very much was. Graham paid back £465,500, comprising the sum he'd received plus two years' interest, and transferred this to Arsenal's bank account on 1 December. For the manager, it was the end of the matter. He felt a line had been drawn, a view seemingly confirmed when he was given additional transfer funds to revive a jaded squad. But by now Arsenal had passed details of the Hauge affair to the FA and Premier League, and those investigations were ticking along. On 21 February 1995, Graham returned from a morning jog to find a voicemail message summoning him to the club. On his arrival, discussion lasted less than three minutes before Hill-Wood ushered him into the boardroom to present a letter confirming his immediate dismissal. Minutes later, the club released a statement:

> Arsenal Football Club have now been informed
> by the FA Premier League Inquiry of the results of
> their investigations into the alleged irregularities
> concerning certain transfers and the board have
> concluded that Mr Graham did not act in the best
> interests of the club. The board have therefore
> terminated Mr Graham's contract as manager.
> The chairman said it was sad that Mr Graham's
> distinguished career with Arsenal FC should have to
> end this way and paid tribute to Mr Graham for the
> success he had brought the club.

Not acting in Arsenal's best interests was an internal matter
between employer and employee. Damaging the reputation of
the game was altogether more serious. The FA established a
Commission of Inquiry to consider disciplinary proceedings
against Graham and, uniquely at the time, decided the
hearing would be conducted on courtroom principles, with
prosecution and defence barristers. This was in part to send
a message to other managers, several of whom were also
suspected of accepting bungs, that there would be severe
consequences if they were caught. But it also ensured that any
complex financial evidence could be properly tested by skilled
lawyers. In Brian Leveson QC the FA had engaged one of the
Bar's most experienced and respected prosecutors. George
Graham may have been adept at fielding tricky questions
from journalists but in Leveson he faced an altogether more
formidable, and forensic, inquisitor. On 9 November 1995
the FA Commission published its verdict. Graham was
guilty under Rule 26(a)(x) covering 'misconduct ... or any
improper behaviour likely to bring the game into disrepute'
and consequently would be suspended from all football

activity until 30 June 1996. In its Statement of Reasons, the Commission said it was not convinced that Graham and Hauge conspired to make a personal profit from the Lydersen and Jensen deals. However, it found that Graham knew the payments were made in connection with those transfers.

> Mr Graham gave evidence about the payments being unsolicited, however, even if this is right, as a respected manager of a Premier League team, and a senior figure in the League Managers' Association, we find that he must have known just how serious a matter it was for him to be receiving this amount of money from an agent. When it happened for a second time after the Jensen deal, this must have struck him even more forcefully ... Mr Graham's evidence that he made only brief enquiries as to the reason for the payment ... is, we find, wholly unconvincing. When he received the bundles of cash in the Park Lane Hotel he must have reflected on the fact that he had only recently succeeded in negotiating a cut for Mr Hauge in relation to the Lydersen deal. Similar thoughts must have occurred to him when he received another payment so soon after the Jensen deal.

After serving his suspension, Graham returned to management: first with Leeds United and then – to the horror of Highbury – as manager of Tottenham, for whom he secured victory in the 1999 League Cup final. With the passing of time, he is now remembered as one of the great Arsenal managers, a man who took a rudderless team and instilled in them a burning desire to succeed. It should also be said that, despite a Premier League bung inquiry that lasted years, and implicated other leading figures, no other manager was ever charged – let alone punished.

BALANCING THE BOOKS

Today, the shiny new scandal hovering over England's leading clubs is Financial Fair Play, or rather a lack of it. The Premier League stopped using the term almost as soon as it was coined, and now prefers 'Profit and Sustainability Rules' (PSR). Some commentators have drily pointed out that this amounts to a tacit recognition that there is nothing 'fair' about the rules, which effectively prevent clubs running up large debts by shelling out millions more on transfers and facilities than they generate in income. Unsurprisingly, if you happen to own a rich, successful and well-supported club with a massive stadium you can trouser more profit and, therefore, afford better players to keep you rich and successful. Critics say PSR allows 'big' clubs to pull up the ladder and stop smaller rivals climbing up to challenge them. PSR supporters retort that there must be *some* restraint on owners with bottomless bank balances to prevent them further distorting transfer markets and 'buying trophies'. It's an important debate but it's also nerd-level dull. So, we'll stick to a brief-ish rundown of the Premier League rules and the implications as they stand in *Match of the Day*'s 60th anniversary year. In simple terms, clubs must not record a loss greater than £105 million over any consecutive three seasons' worth of accounts. There are caveats and exemptions aplenty – owners can, for instance, pump up to £90 million into clubs by buying more shares (as opposed to lending money) and headline debt figures can be reduced through investment in youth development, infrastructure, or community football projects. But, after all that, if a club still exceeds the £105 million limit it risks being dragged before an independent tribunal to face a points deduction.

And here's where things start to get tricky. Take the case of Everton. In February 2024 the Toffees were handed a six-point deduction, effective for the 2023–24 season, as punishment for exceeding the £105 million loss limit over the three financial years ending 2021–22. It can be argued that this excess allowed them, for instance, to sign better players and so avoid the drop (Everton finished four points clear of relegated Burnley in 2021–22). Then, in March 2024, Everton received a second penalty deduction of two points for a similar transgression in the 2022–23 season, when they finished just two points above relegated Leicester City. At the same time Leicester were *themselves* charged by the Premier League with breaching PSR and were facing potential action from the English Football League over an alleged breach linked to their 2023–24 Championship season. Other clubs in the firing line included Nottingham Forest (also charged by the Premier League) and Chelsea, who were said to be 'sailing close to the wind'. And we haven't even touched on the big one, Manchester City, who at the time of writing are strongly contesting 115 charges relating to alleged PSR breaches, deception to circumvent the rules, failure to provide accurate information and lack of co-operation. If found guilty – and at the time of writing it remains a big 'if' – the implications for City are huge. Will teams be relegated or denied titles on the basis of financial accounting? Time will tell.

PARTIES, PASTA AND PETULANCE

There's nothing better than an off-the-field drama – especially if it upsets the tightly-controlled, smoke-and-mirrors world of professional football. The Bung and Betting Scandals were massive news stories not just because there were serious implications for the game's reputation but because, for fans, they offered glimpses behind closed doors. As the case studies below show, clubs can deploy all the spin doctors they like to keep a multibillion-pound global industry 'on brand'. But football's rumour factory rarely sleeps.

Chelsea's Partygate

Tommy Docherty arrived at Chelsea as player-coach in September 1961 and replaced Ted Drake as manager a few weeks later. He inherited a club in decline – the Blues finished bottom that season with only nine wins – but he successfully brought on a young squad known as Docherty's Diamonds (so called because in the world of sports journalism any reference to a manager's young squad must *de facto* be alliterative, as in the Busby Babes). The Diamonds bounced straight back to Division One in 1962–63, and the following season won the League Cup before securing a fifth-place finish. But it was in *Match of the Day*'s 1964–65 debut season that Docherty's side found themselves in with a sniff of becoming champions. On 17 April 1965 they sat top of the table on goal average with three to play. Both Leeds United and Manchester United had a game in hand but Chelsea's run-in – away games at Liverpool and Burnley, both mid-table, and away at struggling Blackpool – was do-able for an in-form team with 15 wins from its last 22 matches.

Docherty had promised his players a night out after the Liverpool game but when they lost 2-0 he changed his mind, perhaps conscious that word would get out about them 'celebrating' a defeat. He put his team under curfew at their hotel, but eight players – Terry Venables, George Graham, Eddie McCreadie, John Hollins, Barry Bridges, Marvin Hinton, Bert Murray and Joe Fascione – briefly sneaked out for a couple of beers. When they got back a furious Docherty suspended them for the rest of the season, effectively ending any faint chance of silverware. Sure enough, Chelsea suffered an embarrassing 6-2 defeat at Turf Moor and although the errant eight were picked for the trip to Blackpool, by then it was all over. The Blues' 3-2 defeat mattered little as Manchester United pipped Leeds to take the title. Docherty's decision outraged Venables, whose relationship with the Scot was already bumpy. He later described it as 'crass, stupid and self-defeating', and at the end of the following season signed for Spurs.

Bobby's Night Out in Blackpool

For years, top footballers tended to get away with the occasional eve-of-match night out, sometimes even sharing a few beers with journalists. No sports reporter was going to dob in a handy contact to a club's gaffer or risk becoming the pariah of the press room. But as football crept onto the news pages this age of innocence vanished. Some commentators have even put a precise date on the culture change – the freezing cold New Year's Day of 1970 when West Ham players arrived at their Blackpool hotel for an FA Cup third-round tie the following afternoon. Bizarrely, and indirectly, members of *MOTD*'s outside broadcast team played a key role in the events which unfolded. Two cameramen bumped into Hammers icon Bobby Moore in the hotel as he and fellow star Jimmy Greaves headed for an early night. One of the *MOTD* men mentioned that the Bloomfield Road pitch was ice-bound and there was virtually no chance of the game going ahead. Seizing on this, Moore and Greaves, both fond of a drink, decided to abandon their early night and instead make for the nearby 007 nightclub owned by one of Moore's pals, the former boxer Brian London. They were accompanied by two other players – senior pro Brian Dear and 19-year-old teetotaller Clyde Best – but, as Best insisted to the BBC years later, they were all tucked up in bed by midnight.

Unfortunately for the quartet that was literally and figuratively too late. To everyone's surprise the match went ahead, Blackpool smashed West Ham 4-0, thanks to a stellar performance by Scottish midfielder Tony Green, and the Hammers got duly monstered in match reports. It was the perfect cue for a local news reporter who hurriedly tipped off Fleet Street that he'd seen the four boozing in Brian London's club. When the story broke, manager Ron Greenwood called his players in, fined them all a week's wages and suspended Moore, Greaves and Dear. Recalling the incident in 1985, Moore said:

> It was a completely innocent couple of hours. We only drank two or three glasses of beer. Best drank orange juice. After that, things were never the same between myself and West Ham. I had claret-and-blue blood, but I could never forgive the club for the way they treated me.

He moved to Fulham three years later.

Boiling in the Bath

He'd not had the greatest start to the 1974–75 campaign. Although he'd scored for Leicester City in their 2-1 defeat at Anfield on 24 August, Keith Weller had been furious to see two penalty decisions go against his side. He'd unwisely sought out the referee to pass on 'insulting comments', a decision which earned him a £100 fine plus £60 costs for bringing the game into disrepute. As the season wore on, and the Foxes looked increasingly worn out, Weller slapped in a transfer request, only to have it immediately rejected by the board. By the time Ipswich Town arrived at Filbert Street on 20 December, City were lying third from bottom, having lost five of their previous six league games. With home fans getting on his back, Weller started rowing with teammates. At the break he flounced down the tunnel, ran a bath, jumped in and refused to get out for the second half. Leicester lost the match 1-0, Weller was fined and soon got his wish to be transfer-listed. But eventually everyone kissed and made up, and he stayed with the Foxes for another four years. He remains a strong candidate for Leicester's all-time greatest XI.

Fergie Boots Beckham

Dressing room bust-ups always make great copy so when, on 16 February 2003, David Beckham was seen leaving Old Trafford with a cut above his left eye – an injury he certainly *didn't* get during Manchester United's humiliating 2-0 FA Cup defeat to Arsenal – the tabloids were soon on the case. Reports emerged that Sir Alex Ferguson had been so dischuffed with Beckham's shift that he'd kicked a stray boot on the dressing room floor straight into his player's head.

Becks made no attempt to hide the injury during training the following week and the papers were plastered with plaster pictures highlighting his wounded brow.

The incident was seen as further evidence of a rift between the two men, fuelled by rumours of Beckham's interest in a move to Real Madrid. Ferguson believed Beckham had both betrayed the sanctity of the dressing room and hyped up his injury. 'Whatever happens in a dressing room is sacrosanct,' he told a press conference the following week.

> Taking anything out of the dressing room for whoever's benefit – it never works that way. Loyalty is 100% ... having said that, the publicity it has caused, the only reaction I have to that [is that it was] an incident which was freakish. If I tried it a hundred times, a million times, it could not happen again. If I was [able to do it] I would carry on playing. Contrary to a lot of reports, David did not have two stitches put in his head. He had no stitches. It was a graze.

Twenty years later Beckham laughed off the incident in his eponymous Netflix documentary: 'We walked in the changing room and the boss is fuming, I can see by his face,' he said.

> And when you see the boss' face like this, you don't want to be anywhere near him . . . It is a face that no one can do, trust me. [Ferguson starts swearing and criticising Beckham's performance] and I went back at the boss and said "no" ... and then I swore. I said the F-word. And then I saw him change, and I was like, "S**t, I really shouldn't have said that" ... I think I said the F-word too many times.

Beckham signed for Real in the summer although he claimed he wanted to stay at United. 'It was my home,' he said. 'My relationship with the boss was always special. We had our moments, but I still loved him.'

Lasagne-gate

'Pasta 1 ... Spurs Ill', chortled one back page headline, as news emerged that half of Tottenham Hotspur's team had fallen sick after eating lasagne and spaghetti bolognese on the eve of a season-defining game at West Ham. Spurs needed only to match Arsenal's result at Highbury against Wigan Athletic to luxuriate in the knowledge that they would qualify for a final Champions League place at the expense of their North London nemesis. But as Sunday, 7 May 2006 dawned, Martin Jol's side suddenly went from narrow favourites to also-rans with the runs. Word reached the media that at least seven, and perhaps ten, players had become violently ill after a meal at the Canary Wharf hotel where they were staying pre-match. The view within the camp was that anyone who had tucked in to the lasagne or spag bol was at risk, and soon a conspiracy theory was gathering traction among Spurs supporters. They were convinced one of the hotel chefs must have been an Arsenal fan. He'd grasped an opportunity to give the Gunners a head start by sneaking something nasty into the pasta sauce.

Soon the incident had a jovial moniker – Lasagne-gate – but for those affected there was no funny side. Key starters such as Robbie Keane, Aaron Lennon, Michael Dawson, Edgar Davids and Teemu Tainio were all struck down, but poor Michael Carrick suffered worst. In his 2018 autobiography *Between the Lines* he recalled, 'I'd never endured agony like this. It felt like a fire was lit in my guts with petrol poured on it again and again. The pain kept flaring up and I curled up on bed, praying for it to pass.' Writing for *Yahoo Sport* a decade later, Spurs midfielder and *MOTD* guest pundit Jermaine Jenas explained that it was not normal practice to assemble the squad in a hotel the night before a match. But the West Ham game was considered so important that Jol felt encouraging team togetherness was worth it. 'Lasagne and spaghetti Bolognese were on the menu, we ate, and then in the middle of the night we started dropping like flies,' he wrote.

> It was mayhem. The club tried to get the match called off, but in vain, so we just had to play through it feeling like death. A lot of the lads were running on empty – literally. Even while the gaffer Martin Jol was giving his team talk before the game, players were being sick in the toilets. Once the game started players were literally running off the pitch. It was carnage.

It was also the end of Spurs' Champions League dream. They lost 2-1 to West Ham while Arsenal, determined to sign off their final match at Highbury with a win, beat Wigan 4-2 to claim the qualifying place. As for Lasagne-gate, like most conspiracy theories it was entirely wrong. The Health Protection Agency found no evidence of any food poisoning emanating from the hotel, and attributed the outbreak to a highly contagious virus.

The Tevez Sub Sulk

At the end of September 2011 Manchester City went into their Champions League away game at Bayern Munich in confident mood. Level on points with Manchester United at the top of the Premier League, and unbeaten in six games, they looked good for a draw at least. But, stunned by two first-half goals from the hosts, City appeared toothless and late in the second half manager Roberto Mancini decided to bring on Carlos Tevez to liven things up. Problem was, Carlos refused. He was still smarting at having his close-season transfer request rejected and was unhappy at being left on the bench for City's previous Premier League game. After Munich closed out the win, City manager Roberto Mancini said: 'He refused to come on. One player refused to go on – I can't accept this.' The following day Tevez apologised to fans but claimed he had been 'warmed up and ready to play'. It mattered not. He was fined two weeks' wages and sent on gardening leave until February 2012. But football clubs are, above all, pragmatists. Tevez was far too good a player to ignore, and after City lost 1-0 away to Arsenal on 8 April, he was thrust back into the starting XI to try and revive a flagging title push. The rest is history. Tevez scored in a 4-0 demolition of West Bromwich Albion, bagged a hat-trick in the 6-1 defeat of Norwich and inspired his side to six straight wins, including that incredible final day 3-2 win over QPR, to emerge as champions.

APRIL:
GREAT ESCAPES

Defining a Great Escape isn't easy. It's not enough to merely face the mathematical possibility of relegation and then scrabble clear. That's a scenario endured and accepted by supporters of around half a dozen clubs most seasons. Nor can you count a couple of must-wins in April which turn out, surprisingly, to be actual wins. No, for an escape to be classed as *truly* great, the escaping club must surely first dump fans into a pit of total despair before hauling them up through a sustained and unexpected rearguard action enlivened by the occasional jammy, drop-dodging goal. Readers will have their own definitions, but for the purposes of our **April** chapter we're going to divide escapee clubs into three broad categories: Usual Suspects (hopeless, but marginally less hopeless than the clubs around them); Sleepwalkers (big-name clubs which stumble into relegation territory and suddenly realise they're not too big to go down); and Miracle Workers (play like lemons, or should that be lemmings, for much of the season but somehow produce the form of champions during the run-in). Whatever the category, escapes are often subject to the unpredictable – the nervy performance of a rival struggler, a missed penalty, a goalkeeping howler, a dodgy refereeing decision, technology failure or, in one notorious case (pay attention Coventry City, Bristol City and Sunderland fans), traffic mayhem on the A444. One thing's for sure though. By April a struggling club needs to at least be in the mix. No one wants to join Huddersfield Town or Derby County as Premier League teams relegated before the end of March. Neither do you want to be in the drop zone after your penultimate game. In the Premier League era, the bottom three has changed on only seven occasions following the final round of matches – perhaps because those above can go into Matchday 38 with the psychological advantage of being (at least theoretically) in control of their fate.

Here we look at the greatest escapes of the *Match of the Day* years and show how their April results impacted on their eventual survival. Our Hall of Fame table below sets out, left to right: escapee; season; points per game (PPG) up to 31 March; position on 31 March; PPG from 1 April; and final league position. Some of the stats tell you all you need to know. In Leicester City's extraordinary 2014–15 escape the Foxes managed just 0.65 PPG up until the end of March – the worst position of any escapee in our Hall of Fame. But from 1 April they pocketed 22 points from nine games for a PPG of 2.44, making them the best run-in performers on the list. Wigan Athletic were similar spring wonders, pushing their PPG up from 0.9 prior to April to 2.14 by season's end. Contrast these efforts with Coventry City, who somehow managed to produce a worse PPG in April and May (0.78) than they had managed over the previous seven months (0.85), yet still beat the drop. While the stats are illuminating, it's the stories that matter. Before we get on to those, a reminder that it was two points for a win until season 1981–82, when it became three, and that top-flight football comprised 42 games per season until the end of 1994–95, after which it dropped to 38 games.

THE HALL OF FAME

Club, Season	PPG to 31/03; Position	PPG from 01/04; Final position
FUL, 1965–66	23 from 33 = 0.69; 21st	12 from 9 = 1.33; 20th
AVA, 1965–66	29 from 34 = 0.85; 14th	7 from 8 = 0.87; 16th
TOT, 1974–75	28 from 37 = 0.75; 20th	6 from 5 = 1.20; 19th
CVC, 1976–77	24 from 28 = 0.85; 17th	11 from 14 = 0.78; 19th
BSC, 1976–77	22 from 29 = 0.75; 19th	13 from 13 = 1.00; 18th
CVC, 1984–85	34 from 31 = 0.91; 19th	16 from 11 = 1.45; 18th
OAT, 1992–93	35 from 34 = 1.02; 18th	14 from 8 = 1.75; 19th
EVE, 1993–94	36 from 33 = 1.09; 15th	8 from 9 = 0.88; 17th
CVC, 1996–97	30 from 32 = 0.93; 19th	11 from 8 = 1.37; 17th
WBA, 2004–05	24 from 30 = 0.80; 19th	10 from 8 = 1.25; 17th
BDC, 1999–00	26 from 30 = 0.86; 18th	10 from 8 = 1.25; 17th
PTM, 2005–06	24 from 30 = 0.80; 19th	14 from 8 = 1.75; 17th
WHU, 2006–07	26 from 31 = 0.83; 19th	15 from 7 = 2.14; 15th
WIG, 2010–11	30 from 30 = 1.00; 20th	12 from 8 = 1.50; 16th
WIG, 2011–12	28 from 31 = 0.90; 19th	15 from 7 = 2.14; 15th
LEI, 2014–15	19 from 29 = 0.65; 20th	22 from 9 = 2.44; 14th
AVA, 2019–20	25 from 28 = 0.89; 19th	10 from 10 = 1.00; 17th

Escapee: Fulham.
Category: Miracle Workers
Season: 1965–66

Nothing encapsulated Fulham's late-season turnaround
in form like their 2-0 victory over Liverpool on 26 February
1966. *Match of the Day* was at Craven Cottage – handily, the
outside broadcast team had only to make a quick dash from
their earlier camera position covering the Boat Race – and
in his introduction commentator Kenneth Wolstenholme
suggested the result was a *fait accompli*. After a jovial
comment about the weather ('I don't know what force of
wind a typhoon is but whatever it is we've got it here'), he
observed that 'if anything is certain in Association Football,
this is a clash of certainty because it looks like Fulham
will go down and Liverpool will become champions.' He
noted that Fulham had just one victory in their last 15
league games, while Liverpool had been undefeated since
Boxing Day. It was looking 'bright for Liverpool and black
for Fulham'. Finally, to leave *MOTD* viewers in no doubt
that the Cottagers faced a right tonking, he noted that
Fulham manager Vic Buckingham was 'away today looking
at new players', admittedly hardly a vote of confidence from
the gaffer. Nonetheless, the hosts defied Wolstenholme's
downbeat assessment of their chances with goals from
midfielder Steve Earle securing a deserved 2-0 victory.
Fulham went on a run of seven wins in eight to reach
safety by a two-point margin, sending Wolves down
with Birmingham.

Escapee: Aston Villa
Category: Sleepwalkers
Season: 1965–66

Whereas Fulham pulled themselves up by their bootstraps in 1965–66, Aston Villa spent the final matches of the season inflicting collective psychological torture on their supporters. The Villains sleepwalked into peril perhaps because a few good performances reassured them that all would be well. Unfortunately, the good didn't offset the abject. For example, on 19 March centre-forward Tony Hateley bagged four second-half goals to bring the Villains back from 5-1 down at Tottenham, earning a vital point. In April there were creditable wins against high-flying Burnley and Arsenal, but also cringeworthy defeats against fellow strugglers Northampton Town and Sheffield Wednesday. As Villa fans prepared to man the lifeboats, they could only pray that their team's superior goal average would help them escape a clutch of ten similarly underwhelming sides. They were annihilated 6-1 at Old Trafford but then won 2-1 at Stamford Bridge the following week to finish as one of four teams on 36 points – one more than Fulham and just three better than relegated Northampton. Blackburn were long sunk.

Escapee: Tottenham Hotspur
Category: Sleepwalkers
Season: 1974–75

Having had a great start to the seventies under canny manager Bill Nicholson – two League Cups and the UEFA Cup to add to the five other major trophies he'd brought to the Lane – the 1974–75 season proved a shocker. Spurs were in need of a root-and-branch rebuild; trouble was, Bill and the board had fallen out big time over Nicholson's tapping up of Danny Blanchflower as his successor and Johnny Giles as player-coach. Chairman Sidney Wale was furious that he hadn't been consulted and Nicholson, whose side had lost their first four games, departed unceremoniously with a £10,000 pay-off. The board controversially appointed former Arsenal player Terry Neill as manager but the anticipated sea change in performances never happened. At the start of 1975, Spurs embarked on a disastrous run of eight defeats in nine games, and Neill didn't help the fans' mood by complaining to the *Daily Mirror* that he'd been pilloried for wanting the players to enjoy themselves. 'The trouble is,' he said, 'people surmise that if you are not winning then your method must be wrong; if you are winning then your method is perfect. But the game is just not like that.'

True, but the odd win would have been nice. Spurs had been in the top flight since 1950 and there was a suspicion that a sense of entitlement had permeated the camp. Neill's young side did finally wake up, posting a brace of big April wins against relegation rivals Chelsea and Luton. But they still needed to beat Leeds, a team heading for the European Cup final, in their last game of the season to survive and send Luton down with Chelsea. They managed it, thrashing the Whites 4-1, and by the final whistle the fans were chanting Neill's name.

Escapees: Coventry City and Bristol City
Category: Usual Suspects
Season: 1976–77

Two Great Escapes from the same fixture was always going to make nail-chomping drama. But the way Coventry City and

Bristol City managed to manipulate drop avoidance in their showdown at Highfield Road caused arguably the greatest last-day relegation controversy in the history of English professional football. It all hinged on the so-called 'No Score Draw' between these sides on 19 May 1977. Neither was in any sort of form – Coventry hadn't managed a win in their last four and their PPG had actually fallen from 0.85 prior to 1 April to 0.71. Bristol's comparable PPG had risen slightly from 0.75 to 0.92, but they had struggled all season and a surprise win over Liverpool three days earlier hadn't been enough to ease nerves. With Spurs already down, and Stoke effectively down, the Sky Blues needed a win to avoid joining them, although a draw would suffice if Sunderland, the third team in relegation jeopardy, lost at Everton. Bristol would be safe with a draw whatever happened at Goodison.

Then came the twist. Some 10,000 Bristolians had made the trip from the West Country and the A444 (now renamed Jimmy Hill Way) was gridlocked. Referee Ron Challis delayed kick-off by five minutes – a decision which would prove crucial – to allow fans more time to take their seats. By half-time Coventry were 1-0 up through a Tommy Hutchison goal and he doubled their lead in the 52nd minute, apparently confirming the view of local sages that if the Titanic had been painted sky blue it would never have gone down. Robins fans hung their heads until goals from Gerry Gow and Donnie Gillies brought them level and gave Coventry the heebie-jeebies. With five minutes left news came through that Everton had beaten Sunderland 2-0. Coventry chairman Jimmy Hill wasted no time getting that result out on the PA system and the players responded with what commentators later described as 'a good-natured kickabout'. Coventry retreated to their own half, making no attempt to gain possession, while the visitors languidly passed the ball around their defence. It finished 2-2; Sunderland, despite their protests, were dispatched to Division Two and both Bristol and Coventry retained top-flight status.

Escapee: Coventry City
Category: Usual Suspects
Season: 1984–85

Many Sky Blues fans regard this season as their Greatest Escape, some accolade considering there are so many to choose from. The previous year's stay of execution – a last-ditch 2-1 win over Norwich – doesn't even make our Hall of Fame, and compared to this one is barely noteworthy. The Sky Blues had improved their PPG in April and May and ground out a massive 1-0 win away at relegation rivals Stoke. But they still needed victory in their final match to be sure of survival, and that just happened to be against runaway league champions and European Cup Winners' Cup-holders Everton, who had lost only once since Christmas. Still, Coventry had reasons to be cheerful. A bout of flu in the camp over Easter had delayed their fixture programme, so this game kicked off on 26 May, after an FA Cup final which Everton had lost to Manchester United. Toffees players were still on a downer: they had nothing to prove in the league and the summer hols beckoned. An 11.30am Sunday start to avoid clashing with the Scotland-England international was about as welcome as cold haggis for breakfast, and four key players – Peter Reid, Gary Stevens, Derek Mountfield and Andy Gray – didn't even travel. Coventry won 4-1, inflicting Everton's heaviest defeat since the opening day of the season. That sent Norwich down with Sunderland and

Stoke. Canaries' complaints about Howard Kendall fielding a weakened side were voices in the wilderness.

Escapee: Oldham Athletic
Category: Miracle Workers
Season: 1992–93

'Rather a blowy day,' Barry Davies informed *MOTD* viewers from his commentary position at Boundary Park, where the Latics faced a do-or-die last day meeting with Southampton. As if to illustrate Barry's words, full-back Neil Pointon opened Oldham's account direct from a corner – his high ball curling on the wind into the top angle of Southampton keeper Tim Flowers' goal. It was exactly the fillip Athletic fans needed to convince themselves that survival was meant to be. Bottom in February after losing seven of their first ten games in 1993, they had found some form in March and April and went into their 9 May encounter with the Saints on the back of consecutive wins against two top-six clubs, Aston Villa and Liverpool. But Joe Royle's side still needed to beat Southampton and pray Crystal Palace lost at Arsenal. They managed the former despite a late scare which saw their lead cut from 4-1 to 4-3, the result of a Matthew Le Tissier hat-trick, while Arsenal obliged with a 3-0 win to send Palace down with Middlesbrough and Nottingham Forest.

Escapee: Everton
Category: Sleepwalkers
Season: 1993–94

A season which saw Everton in full sleepwalk mode. Here was a big-name club with an unbroken 40-year record in the top flight. Yet they were playing as though membership was a given. On 31 October 1993 they were 11th in the Premier League, just a point behind Liverpool, but then drifted serenely down the table. Replacing Howard Kendall with Norwich boss Mike Walker produced a brief new-manager bounce, but by the end of April the journey south had led them inexorably into the bottom three. On 7 May, as the final round of matches kicked off, two out of five clubs – Southampton, Sheffield United, Ipswich, Oldham and Everton – faced relegation. Four were well used to live-and-let-die survival battles. Could Everton be street fighters too?

The signs weren't good. Stories emerged that no one wanted to be designated penalty-taker, and the task had fallen to Graham Stuart by default. He predicted in advance that he would have to score one, and 'I'll be terrified.' Not as horror-struck as the home support though, who had to witness a performance against Wimbledon which was more clown school than street fight. First Anders Limpar punched away a harmless cross to concede a penalty, then Dave Watson and David Unsworth collided with each other, allowing Gary Ablett to bumble a clearance into his own net. At 2-0 down all seemed lost. But then Stuart conquered his demons to convert only the second penalty of his career; Barry Horne, who had not scored all season, unleashed a 30-yard worldie; and Stuart secured the win with a scuffed shot which bobbled past Hans Segers and sent Sheffield United and Oldham down with Swindon. Ludicrously, that third Everton goal fuelled rumours that Wimbledon had 'thrown the match', proving that no conspiracy theory is a conspiracy too far for fans of a relegated football club.

Escapee: Coventry City
Category: Usual Suspects
Season: 1996–97

Another relegation drama, another starring role for Coventry City, and another delayed kick-off. On ten occasions during their previous 30 years in the top flight the Sky Blues needed something from the last day to stay up. This time it was Tottenham Hotspur playing best supporting actor. After a dreadful start to the season (one win in 13) Coventry came into the 11 May fixture on the back of a good April which saw victories over Liverpool and Chelsea and draws against Arsenal and Southampton. But a 2-1 home defeat to Derby in their penultimate match meant they began round 38 second-from-bottom. Middlesbrough were above them on goal difference, while Sunderland lay one place and two points clear of the drop zone. If either of the north-east clubs won, nothing Coventry did against Spurs would matter. Two of the three were going down, unless a freakish set of results sucked in Southampton.

That afternoon an accident on the M1 delayed thousands of fans travelling from the West Midlands, and the kick-off at White Hart Lane was put back 15 minutes. This proved both a blessing and a curse to City. Having maintained their 2-1 half-time advantage comfortably until the 75th minute, they learned that Sunderland had lost away at Wimbledon and Middlesbrough had drawn away at Leeds. Now they needed only to maintain their lead to survive. Cue collective anxiety and panic. From controlling the game they suddenly looked like pub-side hoofers, and when the final whistle blew several players dissolved in tears. It would be four more years before

Coventry's top-flight status was finally ceded. As for Boro fans, they were left pondering their club's three-point deduction earlier in the season – the punishment for missing a league game at Blackburn. They did have the FA Cup final the following weekend to look forward to, but unfortunately they lost that to complete a rare League and FA Cup Losing Double.

Escapee: Bradford City
Category: Miracle Workers
Season: 1999–00

Bradford City qualify as miracle workers because their final-day win at Valley Parade against Liverpool seemed so unlikely. Liverpool knew that three points would hand them the third, precious, Champions League place, provided Leeds failed to win at West Ham. Bradford knew they had to better Wimbledon's result at Southampton to retain Premier League status. Of the two strugglers, the Bantams had upped their form in late April after losing six on the bounce, while the Dons had managed just one point from eight. But Wimbledon's slight goal difference advantage, coupled with a fixture that mattered little to Southampton, made them narrow favourites. Until, that is, David Wetherall's 12th minute booming header put Bradford one up. Liverpool responded in the second half with Steven Gerrard, Michael Owen and Emile Heskey orchestrating a game of attack v defence. But Bradford held out. Wimbledon's 2-0 defeat meant they went down with Sheffield Wednesday and Watford, ending their 14 successive seasons in the top flight, while Liverpool were left rueing what might have been. Had they beaten Bradford, as the world and his dog expected, they would have qualified for the Champions League because Leeds could only draw at West Ham.

Escapee: West Bromwich Albion
Category: Usual Suspects
Season: 2004–05

For last-day drop dramas it doesn't get any better for the neutral than Survival Sunday, 15 May 2005. Going into the final round of matches, four clubs were scrambling to avoid the three relegation places: Norwich, 17th on 33 points; Southampton, 18th on 32; Crystal Palace, 19th on 32; and West Brom, 20th on 31. Bryan Robson's Baggies looked doomed, but they were at least home to an unremarkable Pompey side and knew only a win and a prayer (the prayer was for none of the others to nab three points) would do. The clubs above Albion also had to push for wins, so tight were their respective goal differences, although in each case a draw might have been OK. In the *MOTD* editing suite it proved a frantic afternoon. 'It was arguably the hardest programme we ever had to make,' recalls then *MOTD* editor Paul Armstrong. 'We had to produce one long intercut edit of all the bottom four surviving and then being relegated "as it stands" at various points through a mad afternoon.' Hard, but not as grim as the mental torture inflicted during the closing minutes at the Hawthorns. Albion fans knew Norwich could not boost their points total because they were in the process of being thrashed 6-0 by Fulham. Southampton were 2-1 down at home to Manchester United and therefore needed to score twice. But Albion's 2-0 lead through Geoff Horsfield and Kieran Richardson was still not enough because, with five minutes left, Palace were 2-1 up at Charlton. Then Jonathan Fortune equalised at the Valley and West Brom instantly jumped three places to become the first Premier League club to survive after being bottom at Christmas.

Escapee: Portsmouth
Category: Miracle Workers
Season: 2005–06

The season Portsmouth's prodigal son Harry Redknapp returned
to Pompey in their hour of need to win forgiveness, mostly,
after his dalliance with the Dark Side (aka Southampton FC).
Redknapp's managerial to-ing and fro-ing between these great
derby rivals was a mixture of soap opera gold and pantomime
baddie – guess who played the baddie – and demanded
considerable mental strength from 'Arry amid vituperative
comments from fans. Brought back from the Dell by Portsmouth
chairman Milan Mandarić in December 2005, his brief was to
steer Pompey clear of relegation. But despite a promising start
they remained seven points from safety in early March, having
scored just 18 goals. Then, like the fairy godmother in *Cinderella*,
Harry chucked some magic dust around the dressing room
and his side became almost unrecognisable. A memorable 2-1
victory at home to Manchester City began a run of six wins and
two draws in nine games, ending with a 2-1 victory at Wigan to
secure survival. 'I knew when I came back from Southampton, I
would never win over everybody', said Redknapp afterwards, 'but
I took Pompey into the Premiership and kept them there twice.
People talk about great escapes but this has got to be one of the
all-time great ones.'

Escapee: West Ham United
Category: Miracle workers
Season: 2006–07

On 17 March 2007, as they prepared to play Blackburn, West
Ham's position was sub-dire. Ten points from safety with nine

games left, not even the dodgy acquisition of Carlos Tevez from Brazilian side Corinthians (short story: the deal broke Premier League rules because Tevez's registration was held by a third party rather than his club) had shifted the dial. Then Alan Curbishley, who had replaced Alan Pardew as manager in December, took the club on a sensational joyride of seven wins in nine, including a crucial 1-0 triumph at Old Trafford on the last day. Carlos Tevez scored that winner against a Manchester United side missing Cristiano Ronaldo, Ryan Giggs, Paul Scholes and Rio Ferdinand – all rested ahead of the FA Cup final. That inspired a conspiracy theory, fuelled by Sheffield United manager Neil Warnock, who felt Sir Alex Ferguson had done his old pal Curbishley a solid by fielding a weakened team – thus relegating the Blades instead of the Hammers. Since the Red Devils had battered Robert Green's goal with 25 shots, and Sheffield had only to avoid defeat against ten-man Wigan at home to secure survival, the theory was flaky to say the least. However, the Blades pointed out that Tevez's goals had kept West Ham up, despite the failure to observe registration rules. West Ham seemed to agree. They later paid the Blades a reported £20 million in compensation.

Escapee: Wigan Athletic
Category: Usual Suspects and Miracle Workers
Season: 2010–11

Wigan qualify under two categories. They certainly were among the usual suspects, having managed only one top-half finish (10th) since winning promotion to the Premier League in 2005. Yet from sitting bottom on 17 March, Roberto Martínez's side put together seven wins in nine, including the scalps of both Manchester United and Arsenal. In the context of top-flight football that's a miracle by any standards, and it spirited the Latics into 19th place, knowing a final-day victory away at Stoke City would probably be enough to stay up. But only probably. A single point separated five teams, two of which would be joining West Ham in the Championship. Wolves (16th) were playing a six-pointer against Blackburn (15th) at Molineux, while Birmingham City (17th) were away at Spurs and Blackpool (18th) faced perhaps the toughest challenge at Old Trafford. It briefly looked as though Blackpool, 2-1 up on the hour, might pull it off, until United blew them away with three in 19 minutes. Meanwhile, in the other games, late goals saw three of the four remaining strugglers bobbing in and out of the drop zone. The intricacies are too long to read but – keep up at the back – Wigan's 1-0 win at Stoke turned out to be more than enough and Wolves survived, despite losing 3-2 to Blackburn, because Steve Hunt's 87th minute strike for the Old Gold meant Birmingham City needed to find a late winner at White Hart Lane to avoid going down on goal difference. Instead, the Blues lost 2-1 through Roman Pavlyuchenko's rifled last-kick strike.

Escapee: Wigan Athletic
Category: Usual Suspects and Miracle Workers
Season: 2011–12

It makes you wonder whether Roberto Martínez used to tell his team not to worry too much about winning until the clocks go forward. How else do you explain yet another extraordinary turnaround, which saw Wigan triumph in only four games up until 23 March, when they were joint bottom, after which they produced a run of seven wins in nine, including a 2-1 win at Anfield, and successive April victories at home to top-of-the-table Manchester United and away to third-placed Arsenal? They did lose away at Chelsea but only because both of the Blues' goals were highly controversial or, as Latics fans would say, offside. This was first-class form, so what on earth had Wigan been doing bumbling around in steerage for months? Their 1-0 away win at Blackburn on 7 May secured another season in the Premier League, as if there was ever any doubt.

Escapee: Leicester City
Category: Miracle Workers
Season: 2014–15

The greatest of all Great Escapes began when the Foxes, marooned seven points from safety at the start of April, beat West Ham United through a late Andy King goal. That ended a run of eight winless games and was only the fifth victory in 30 attempts. Six points banked from matches against West Brom and Swansea helped build confidence, but the moment City fans finally began to believe came at Turf Moor in one of those bizarre sliding-doors moments. Fellow strugglers Burnley had won a penalty and Matty Taylor, who hadn't taken one for five years, stepped up to the spot. He hit the post and 59 seconds later Jamie Vardy sprinted up the other end to score. It was a smash-and-grab 1-0 win, but it gave Leicester a fighting chance to save themselves which they did in some style, collecting ten points from their final five games and scoring 11 times in the process. Alongside Vardy and strike partner Leonardo Ulloa, the versatile Esteban Cambiasso was pivotal, playing in almost every midfield and defensive position over the course of the season. No other side has remained in the top flight with fewer than 20 points from 29 games and without this remarkable recovery there would have been no run to the title the following year. But it still didn't save manager Nigel Pearson from being sacked to make room for Claudio Ranieri.

Escapee: Aston Villa
Category: Sleepwalkers
Season: 2019–20

Aston Villa's return to the top flight was heavily bankrolled by the club's billionaire owners, Wes Edens and Nassef Sawiris, who spent a cool £140 million on acquiring stars such as Tyrone Mings, Douglas Luiz and Brazilian striker Wesley. But this array of talent didn't prevent Villa nodding off for ten games either side of the 2020 Covid lockdown. They collected just two points during that run to leave themselves seven from safety with four matches left. Somehow Dean Smith's side roused themselves, and home wins against Crystal Palace and Arsenal, combined with a final-day 1-1 draw away at West Ham, saw them survive at the expense of Bournemouth. Smith called it a 'magnificent achievement', although Cherries fans recalled how Villa had salvaged a point the previous month after a goal-line technology failure denied Sheffield United a clear goal. Without that point, Villa would have been relegated on a marginally inferior goal difference.

MAY:
THE TITLE AND
THE TROPHY

The May climax to a domestic season rarely disappoints. Last-day deciders can mess even with the heads of neutrals, who will have picked the club they're backing on the basis of old rivalries, dislike of a particular player/manager, or that tenner they slapped on in December at decent odds. As for die-hard supporters, it's an experience close to Dante's Seventh Circle of Hell. Agonised expressions, pleading glances at fellow sufferers, eyes flicking between action on the pitch and phone app goal flashes, ears clamped to radios for match commentaries – it all looks, and is, painful. In the tightest title races, *Match of the Day* distils this drama into a highlights package which switches between games in 'real time', showing how goals scored or conceded change the destiny of the trophy and alter on-field tactics as coaches and fans respond to news emerging elsewhere. But title-defining games don't have to be last-day affairs. Sometimes an unlikely mid-season win leads to a momentum shift, a sense of belief, a cementing of team spirit which takes fans on the long ride to glory. There's also the elephant in the room – luck – a factor managers don't like to mention but which often transcends all the modern game's data analysis. In this chapter we look at some of the greatest title-defining games, along with six decades worth of classic FA Cup finals, the ultimate test of a team's tournament pedigree.

THE TITLE DEFINERS

Manchester City 1967–68:
Newcastle United 3-4 Manchester City, 11 May 1968

Dubbed 'The Goal Average Title' ahead of this season's final round of games – spoiler alert: it wasn't – leaders Manchester City needed only to equal any points gathered by Manchester United to become champions. That's because although both clubs were tied at the top on 56 points, City had a bulletproof goal average of 2.05 compared to United's 1.66. Goal average – goal difference's predecessor as a tiebreaker – works by dividing the number of goals scored by the number conceded; goal difference, which wasn't introduced in England until 1975, relies on subtracting goals conceded from goals scored. Having to do sums to decide the title caused a great deal of excitement in the press, but it turned out to be unnecessary. United were surprisingly defeated 2-1 at Old Trafford by struggling Sunderland while City won a 4-3 thriller at Newcastle with goals from players who would be pivotal to their following season's FA Cup success: Neil Young, who nabbed two, Mike Summerbee and Francis Lee. United took consolation from beating Benfica to win the European Cup 16 days later.

Arsenal 1970–71:
Tottenham Hotspur 0-1 Arsenal, 3 May 1971

Now this one really was a goal average title in the sense that a draw might, or might not, have been enough. Not that Arsenal fans gave two hoots about how they won it – nothing could be sweeter than being declared champions at the home of their bitterest rivals on the last day of the season. However, when teenager Ray Kennedy scored in the 87th minute to put them one up it counterintuitively increased tension for the visitors rather than eased it. That's because Leeds United, who had already completed their fixtures, were a point clear at the top with a goal average of 2.40 (72/30). Arsenal's goal average was 2.41 (70/29). So a 0-0 draw at White Hart Lane was fine for the Gunners but a scoring draw of any kind would make Leeds champions. Spurs had every incentive to equalise because the last thing they wanted was for Arsenal to emulate their historic Double of ten years earlier by winning the FA Cup final. 'That was the longest three minutes I have ever known,' Kennedy said later. 'As Tottenham came back I remember thinking that perhaps it might have been better had my header not gone in.' Five days later Bertie Mee's side secured their Double courtesy of Charlie George's iconic extra-time Wembley winner.

Nottingham Forest 1977–78:
Manchester United 0-4 Nottingham Forest,
17 December 1977

It may seem unfeasibly early to label a pre-Christmas game as a championship definer. But the manner in which 'unfashionable' Forest dispatched their hallowed opponents was the moment everyone realised they really were contenders.

As *MOTD's* Barry Davies observed, 'It's been a long time since United have looked so inept on their own ground – they've been made to look that way by a very good side.'

It helped of course that the visitors were led by Brian Clough, a man singularly unimpressed by reputation and who six years earlier had steered similarly unfashionable Derby County to the Division One title. On that occasion his team completed their fixtures a week before main rivals Leeds and Liverpool, both of whom still had a chance of glory. Rather than hang around Derby nibbling his fingernails, Clough took his team on holiday to Cala Millor, Majorca, where they learned they were champions in the bar of the beachside Castell de Mar hotel. For this Old Trafford encounter his Forest side, promoted only the previous season, had class to spare in players like Peter Shilton, Archie Gemmill, Peter Withe, John Robertson and Tony Woodcock. Their second goal, a sweeping seven-pass move started in their own half and finished by Woodcock, was a state-of-the-art team effort which gave fair warning of what was to come. As Davies noted, Forest were a team with 'the hallmark of its creator Brian Clough'. They remained unbeaten for the rest of the season, finishing seven points clear of defending champions Liverpool.

Liverpool 1981–82:
Southampton 2-3 Liverpool, 24 April 1982

This was manager Bob Paisley's penultimate season at Anfield, and with 11 major trophies already to his name, including four Division One titles and three European Cups, he'd developed a habit of winning. Even so, the 1981–82 championship was the toughest challenge of his reign. The

Reds had finished a dismal 5th the previous season, the team desperately needed a rebuild, stalwarts Ray Clemence, Jimmy Case and Ray Kennedy had either left or were leaving, and on Boxing Day Liverpool were in 12th place, having lost at home to Manchester City after a horrendous spill by new keeper Bruce Grobbelaar. By March Paisley made the decision to fully unleash his young lions, Ian Rush and Ronnie Whelan, with future *MOTD* pundit Mark Lawrenson and Craig Johnston also breaking through. It proved transformational. By the time Liverpool arrived at the Dell for this crackerjack of a game they had won nine on the spin and led the table, their rapid rise assisted by the new three-points-for-a-win rule. Rush supplied an opener from Dalglish's trademark flick-on but then Southampton striker Mick Channon completed a glorious team move to level. In the second half Whelan restored the lead with a cheeky chip over Saints keeper Ivan Katalinić, only for Anfield old boy Kevin Keegan to level from the spot. It wasn't until the 88th minute that Rush and Kenny Dalglish combined to present Whelan with his second goal, securing the win and establishing an ultimately insurmountable four-point lead over Ipswich at the top.

Arsenal 1988–89:
Liverpool 0-2 Arsenal, 26 May 1989

This was the greatest ever finish to a top-flight English league season, eclipsing even Sergio Agüero's last-gasp strike for Manchester City in 2013 (see below). The key difference was that these two remaining title contenders were playing each other on the last day. At Christmas, Arsenal sat top with a six-point cushion while Kenny Dalglish's team were wallowing in sixth place. But, following a depressing 3-1 New

Year's Day defeat to Manchester United, Liverpool dusted themselves down for an unbeaten run which saw them win 15 out of 17 – including five games played after the Hillsborough disaster while the entire city was still in shock. Crucially, the last of these was a 5-1 demolition of West Ham, which meant Liverpool could go into the Arsenal showdown three points clear with a goal difference advantage of four. To overtake them the Gunners, who had wobbled in previous matches, would need to win by two clear goals. No one had managed that at Anfield in three years and Arsenal hadn't managed any kind of win there in 14. But when Alan Smith's 52nd-minute header put the visitors ahead the Liverpool machine began creaking. As the clock ticked to 88 minutes, and with 20 million watching live on TV, Lee Dixon's hopeful ball forward was expertly controlled by the swivelling Smith to put Michael Thomas through. His attempted nudge past last-defender Steve Nicol rebounded into his path and suddenly the destiny of the trophy was at his feet. The 20 million watching live on TV held a collective breath as commentator Brian Moore shouted: 'It's up for grabs now!' Thomas grabbed it, tapping past Grobbelaar to break Liverpool hearts and see the Gunners home.

Manchester United 1992–93:
Manchester United 2-1 Sheffield Wednesday, 10 April 1993

Of all Premier League titles amassed during the Sir Alex Ferguson era – thirteen, count 'em – this one was arguably the most important. It replaced lingering doubt with rocket-fuelled belief, and propelled United into two decades of domination in which successive squads convinced themselves that, no matter how long was left on the clock, the battle was never lost. The 1999 Treble would provide ultimate proof of that, but as Ferguson's side entertained Sheffield Wednesday in April it felt as though his mission to end a title drought dating back to 1967 might once again elude him. Ferguson was in the sixth year of his tenure, his side had been pipped at the post by Leeds the previous season, and vultures were gathering. United had taken only six points from their previous five games and desperately needed a win to stay in touch with leaders Aston Villa. When John Sheridan's penalty put Wednesday ahead on 65 minutes things looked bad for Ferguson, and stayed bad until, out of nowhere, skipper Steve Bruce popped up to head an 85th minute equaliser. Then, in the sixth minute of injury time, Bruce nodded in another, putting United back in the mix and prompting assistant coach Brian Kidd to execute his famous knee slide on the pitch. The press labelled those extra six minutes 'Fergie-time', a reference to the Scot supposedly pressurising the referee (although the manager would insist there should have been *twelve* added minutes). Whatever, United went on to win all five of their remaining games to claim that coveted first Ferguson championship.

Blackburn Rovers 1994–95:
West Ham United 1-1 Manchester United, 14 May 1995

Between August 1994 and January 1995 Blackburn won 17 and lost just two of their 23 games. They stood six points clear of Manchester United and over the next three months were defeated only twice more. It seemed chairman Jack Walker, a steel tycoon worth around £600 million, had bankrolled an unstoppable force led by an astute manager in Kenny Dalglish and two of the League's deadliest goal-scorers in Alan Shearer and Chris Sutton. But then, like a tired racehorse trundling to the final fence, Rovers began to flag. Defeats by Manchester City and West Ham left Dalglish needing three points against his old club Liverpool on the last day to guarantee the title, while United would successfully defend their championship provided they won at West Ham and Blackburn slipped up. Racing enthusiast Alex Ferguson was not slow to play mind games, comparing his rivals to the 1956 Grand National runner Devon Loch, who fell at the last while leading. All started well for King Kenny as Shearer bagged his 37th of the season on 20 minutes and Michael Hughes put the Hammers ahead. Then, in the space of 12 agonising second-half minutes, the title rivals saw their fortunes flipped. Brian McClair equalised at Upton Park and John Barnes equalised at Anfield, leaving the Red Devils 38 minutes to find a winner. Only a string of outstanding saves by West Ham keeper Luděk Mikloško denied them, ensuring Jamie Redknapp's late winner for Liverpool was irrelevant. Sir Alex was left to rue Andrew Cole's missed chances, Blackburn took the title by two points and Dalglish took his players for supper at a Preston bistro.

Chelsea 2004–05:
Bolton Wanderers 0-2 Chelsea, 30 April 2005

'We have top players,' said the new manager, 'and, sorry if I'm arrogant, we have a top manager. Please don't call me arrogant but I'm European champion and I think I'm a special one.'

So began José Mourinho's first press conference at Chelsea after being headhunted from Porto by Roman Abramovich. By the time the Blues confirmed their first championship for half a century with this win at Bolton it was clear he was indeed special. His side ended the campaign with a bevy of what were then English records – highest number of points in a season (95); fewest goals conceded (15); most victories in a Premier League season (29); and most clean sheets in a Premier League season (25). True, Abramovich's deep pockets facilitated the signing of world-class players such as Didier Drogba, Arjan Robben, Ricardo Carvalho and Paulo Ferreira. But they still had to be gelled into a team and given tactical clarity – coaching skills Mourinho possessed in abundance. The Bolton match typified much of their season. With John Terry and Carvalho marshalling the back four, Claude Makélélé patrolling ruthlessly in front of them, and goalkeeper Petr Čech at the peak of his powers, Chelsea could defend for fun. Wanderers' waves of first-half attacks were absorbed and repelled before the visitors sealed the deal with two goals from a rampaging Frank Lampard. Mourinho's team went on to defend their crown the following season amid criticism that they played 'drab' football. Really? In those back-to-back league triumphs they outscored their opponents four goals to one, won 58 of their 76 games, and lost only six (two of which were after the 2005–06 title had already been won).

Manchester City 2011–12:
Manchester City 3-2 Queens Park Rangers, 13 May 2012

How to do justice to this? Like a finely structured whodunnit, the game moved into the final seconds of its jaw-dropping climax with no one having the faintest clue who *would* do it. City went in knowing a win would hand them the title on goal difference unless their only remaining rival, defending champions Manchester United, could somehow fashion a

minimum nine-goal winning margin away at Sunderland.
Queens Park Rangers also had plenty of skin in the game.
They needed three points to ensure Bolton stayed in the
drop zone – some task, as QPR had the worst away record
in the league and their hosts had dropped just two points at
home all season. At half-time everything was pretty much as
expected. City were one up through Pablo Zabaleta while at
the Stadium of Light Wayne Rooney had scored for United. But
Rangers were in no mood to shoulder arms and quietly shuffle
off to the Championship. At the start of the second half Djibril
Cissé ran clear to score and then, as City became gripped by
the collywobbles, Jamie Mackie's 66th minute header made
it 2-1. By now QPR were down to ten men, a consequence
of Joey Barton losing the plot with Carlos Tevez, but as five
minutes of injury time got underway the trophy looked bound
for the red half of Manchester. Then, in the 92nd minute,
Eden Džeko's leveller gave the home fans a smidgeon of
hope. A minute later the whistle blew at Sunderland with Sir
Alex Ferguson's side seconds from retaining their title. At the
Etihad, City manager Roberto Mancini was doing windmill
impressions to urge his players forward. QPR were now safe
by virtue of Bolton's draw (though didn't know it). As an entire
season coalesced on the edge of QPR's penalty area, Mario
Balotelli received Sergio Agüero's pass and toe-poked the ball
into space. There, ghosting past three defenders, was Agüero
again. Drop of the shoulder. One touch. Shot. Goal. Title.

Leicester City 2015–16:
Manchester City 1-3 Leicester City, 6 February 2016

Why a title definer? Because this was the game in which
Leicester City explained that they weren't joking. Having

watched them escape relegation the previous year, few people believed Claudio Ranieri's side could kick on and challenge for something, even though by the time they walked out at the Etihad they were top of the table with only two defeats, against Arsenal and Liverpool, against their name. Even Gary Lineker, a lifetime fan of the club where he began his professional career, convinced himself they couldn't win the league, tweeting in December that he would present *MOTD* in his underpants if they did (a promise he later fulfilled). The bookies had made the Foxes 5000/1 pre-season, but this was fine by Ranieri and his players who relished the underdog tag and seemed oblivious to pressure. With Wes Morgan and Robert Huth helming a formidable defence, N'Golo Kanté – there always seemed to be two of him buzzing around – imperious in midfield, Riyad Mahrez showing pace and trickery, and Jamie Vardy at his deadliest best, Leicester combined tactical nous and commitment with genuine class. They showcased all three in this game as Huth, who had previously amassed just 24 goals in 300 appearances, bagged a brace. But it was the Foxes' second goal against last year's runners-up, a side crammed with stars, that caught the eye. Put through by Kanté, Mahrez raced forward with only Martín Demichelis to beat. A step-over left the defender staring at fresh air, Mahrez found the net and, despite Agüero's late consolation, Leicester emerged five points clear of their second-place hosts. They took the title with two games to spare, an achievement widely recognised as one of the greatest in team sport. Some put it down to Thai chairman Vichai Srivaddhanaprabha persuading Buddhist monks to bless his players. Others suggested the discovery of King Richard III's body, and its reburial in Leicester Cathedral in

March 2015, had done the trick. The truth is more prosaic. Over the season, Leicester City were just too good.

SIX DECADES OF FA CUP FINAL CLASSICS

1964–65: Leeds United 1-2 Liverpool, 1 May 1965

A talented Leeds team came to Wembley as clear favourites and until the previous Monday, when their title challenge hit the buffers at bottom-of-the-table Birmingham City, they had still been pushing for the Double. Don Revie's side had finished a whopping 17 points ahead of Bill Shankly's Liverpool, who won only two of their last eight league games despite making the European Cup semis. In this final, a game low on quality for 90 minutes achieved classic status as it entered extra time, the first final to do so for 18 years. A low chip from left-back Gerry Byrne inside the penalty area was met by a stooping Roger Hunt to put the Reds ahead, only for Leeds to hit back seven minutes later through Billy Bremner's clinical half-volley. Then, inside the final ten minutes, Ian Callaghan's cross was met by Ian St John to give Liverpool their first FA Cup trophy. St John later described it as the 'most wonderful moment of my life', but the hero of the hour was Byrne who, it emerged afterwards, had played the entire 120 minutes with a broken collarbone.

1969–70: Chelsea 2-1 Leeds United, 29 April 1970 (FA Cup Final Replay)

This was a classic encounter in the sense that it delivered passion, determination and commitment in equal measure. But also, in the sense that it resembled gladiatorial combat in Ancient Rome. BBC Sport later described it as a 'meeting of pure malice' and 'the most brutal game in English football history', and although hyperbole is a thing in sport, that summary is about right. Despite a general perception that Chelsea's players were southern softies who hung around the King's Road quaffing champagne and nibbling canapés while Leeds comprised gritty, northern lads who drank in pubs with a spittoon in the corner, there was little difference between these sides in terms of physicality. The Wembley final, which ended 2-2 18 days earlier, was a red-blooded affair – literally in the case of players' shins – with hard men like Leeds' Norman 'Bites Yer Leg' Hunter and Chelsea's Ron 'Chopper' Harris redefining football as a contact sport. But it wasn't just them. Animosity stalked every corner of the Wembley turf: Johnny Giles v Eddie McCreadie; Billy Bremner v Peter Houseman; David Webb v Eddie Gray; and all this was carried enthusiastically into the Old Trafford replay. It took just two minutes for Leeds winger Gray to be welcomed by a both-feet-off-the-ground tackle from Webb, the defender he'd roasted for pace at Wembley. When in 1997 this game was 're-refereed' under a modern interpretation of the Laws, ref David Elleray said he would have dismissed six players. In 2020 Michael Oliver reckoned he would have sent off eleven. But on the day referee Eric Jennings put only one name in his book, prompting the great *Observer* sportswriter Hugh McIlvanney to report that 'at times, it appeared Mr Jennings would give a free kick only on production of a death certificate.' For the record, Leeds went ahead through Mick Jones' excellent solo effort, Peter Osgood equalised with a diving header and David Webb sealed the win for Chelsea off one of Ian Hutchinson's booming long throws.

1972–73: Leeds United 0-1 Sunderland 1, 5 May 1973

FA Cup shocks were hardly new. But this one was genuinely off-the-scale shocking. Not since West Bromwich Albion in 1931 had a team from the Second Division lifted the trophy and Sunderland, who hadn't even got close to promotion in the second tier, were handed the role of plucky underdogs destined to fail. The reality was rather different. While this young Sunderland team had some good fortune – not many sides got to see Leeds' Peter Lorimer having a bad day in front of goal and the Whites should have had a penalty when Billy Bremner was tripped – luck was not the Black Cats' greatest weapon. That turned out to be goalkeeper Jim Montgomery, whose extraordinary double reflex save from first Trevor Cherry, then Lorimer, ranks alongside the greatest ever seen in an FA Cup final. As for the goal, any top-flight striker would have been proud of Ian Porterfield's 32nd-minute strike – a flick up with his left foot and a venomous shot with his right. But as the final whistle blew, manager Bob Stokoe, clad incongruously in tracksuit, raincoat and trilby, made his first act of celebration a sprint onto the turf to embrace Montgomery.

1987–88: Liverpool 0-1 Wimbledon, 14 May 1988

It's hard to top John Motson's summing-up up of this one. 'The Crazy Gang have beaten the Culture Club,' he announced as the final whistle was blown.

> Wimbledon have destroyed Liverpool's dreams of
> the Double and all over the pitch their players are
> celebrating something which a few years ago would
> have been impossible ... Her Royal Highness [Princess

Diana] applauds one of the great Cup shocks of all
time ... Bobby Gould and Don Howe have earned their
moment of glory, [they are] real football people who
have been around.

It was rightful praise for Wimbledon manager Gould and
assistant Howe who, for all the fabled high jinks of their squad
off the pitch, and notorious tough tackling on it, had fashioned
the Dons into a successful top-flight side. Perceived in some
quarters as having a non-league Route One mentality – they
had been a Southern League club just ten years previously –
they were given little chance against Kenny Dalglish's runaway
champions. But once Lawrie Sanchez settled them with his
headed opener off a Dennis Wise free kick, there was only one
major scare. A wrongly adjudged penalty award on the hour
gave the Reds' John Aldridge the chance to level. But Dons'
keeper and captain Dave Beasant had done his homework,
dived the right way, and thirty minutes later was leading his
team up the Wembley steps to lift the Cup.

1989–90: Crystal Palace 3-3 Manchester United, 12 May 1990

This was the first final played at an all-seater Wembley,
although no one sat down for long. A frantic, fizzing
crackerjack of a game which pitched together opponents
desperate to win for subtly different reasons. United had
finished a dismal 13th in the league and manager Alex
Ferguson, still seeking silverware after three and a half years
in charge, feared defeat would spell the sack. Crystal Palace,
who had finished 15th on the same number of points, had
the chance to win a major trophy for the first time in their

history but went into the game with a problem. Talismanic striker Ian Wright had suffered two serious shin injuries and although he was on the bench he hadn't played for months. The Eagles struck first through a looping Gary O'Reilly header, Bryan Robson and Mark Hughes hit back for the Reds either side of half-time, and as the game entered its final 20 minutes it seemed United would close it out. Steve Coppell had little choice but to gamble with Wright, who that morning had told the BBC he was 'born for this day', and it was as though the striker had never been away. He first shimmied through a sleepy defence to score with virtually his first touch, then volleyed in a cross in the first period of added time to put Palace 3-2 up. It was left to United's leading scorer Mark Hughes to rescue a replay, United won that dour affair 1-0, Ferguson kept his job and Old Trafford's hegemony was underway.

2005–06: Liverpool 3-3 West Ham United, 13 May 2006

A topsy-turvy thriller, the last of five Cup finals staged at Cardiff's Millennium Stadium while Wembley was being rebuilt. It was dubbed the 'Steven Gerrard Final' on account of the Liverpool captain's outstanding midfield performance and dogged refusal to accept defeat. As his side reeled from a two-goal West Ham lead – the consequence of a Jamie Carragher own goal and Dean Ashton's pounce on goalkeeper Pepe Reina's handling error – Gerrard first played a teasing through ball for Djibril Cissé to volley home, then dispatched a thunderous volley of his own to level the scores. It felt like a momentum shift until, on the hour, the Hammers' Paul Konchesky floated a speculative cross over the head of a backpedalling Reina and into the net. The score remained at 3-2 until, with seconds remaining, a half-clearance from the Hammers' defence fell to Gerrard 35 yards out. A few moments earlier he had been prone on the turf crippled by cramp. Now he ran on to a bouncing ball to drill one of the great cup final goals into the bottom corner. Extra time couldn't separate the teams and the penalty shootout saw Liverpool win 3-1 with Gerrard, (who else?), stepping up to score and Reina shrugging off a poor personal performance to make three excellent saves.

2012–13: Manchester City 0-1 Wigan Athletic, 11 May 2013

Wigan arrived at Wembley still fighting for Premier League survival, though you wouldn't have guessed it from the intensity of their attacking play. Much of the credit went to young winger Callum McManaman who mercilessly roasted City's defence whenever the ball came his way. As for soon-to-be-sacked Roberto Mancini, his hot favourites produced a desperately disappointing performance duly reflected in the stony faces of the Etihad hierarchy up in the Royal Box. It didn't help to have Pablo Zabaleta sent off six minutes from time for a second bookable offence – only the third player to be dismissed in an FA Cup final – but by then Wigan had long looked the more likely winners. As the clock ticked into added time, substitute Ben Watson outjumped Jack Rodwell to nod the ball over a stranded Joe Hart and seal a deserved Latics victory. Sadly though, their triumph could not help them find some league form. Three days later they were thrashed 4-1 at Arsenal, becoming the first club to win the FA Cup and be relegated in the same season. By then Mancini had been replaced by Manuel Pellegrini and by month's end Wigan manager Roberto Martínez would be jumping ship to Everton.

JUNE:
COMING HOME?

In James Graham's 2023 hit play *Dear England*, newly appointed Gareth Southgate is asked to define his ambitions as England team manager. 'I suppose,' he replies, 'one of my main goals ... is to get people smiling again.' Graham portrays this as anathema to some players and coaches who see it as dangerous, touchy-feely talk when what's needed is more of a winning mentality, particularly when it comes to England's rubbish return from penalty shootouts. Southgate's own experience of shootout failure in the 1996 Euros semifinal becomes a metaphor for the culture of fear which stalks players amid a public insistence that they must not fail.

In three acts covering the 2018 World Cup, the 2020 Euros (confusingly played in 2021 due to Covid) and the 2022 World Cup, the plot unpicks Southgate's mission to reboot England's relationship with its national game by freeing players from psychological barriers, challenging lingering racism and tribalism and persuading supporters that, while everyone wants to win, winning isn't everything. Underpinning it all is the 'Dear England' open letter which the manager wrote to fans in 2021. In it he concludes:

> Of course, my players and I will be judged on winning matches. Only one team can win the Euros. We have never done it before and we are desperate to do it for the first time.
>
> *Believe me.*
>
> But, the reality is that the result is just a small part of it. When England play, there's much more at stake than that.
>
> It's about how we conduct ourselves on and off the pitch, how we bring people together, how we inspire and unite, how we create memories that last beyond the 90 minutes. That last beyond the summer. That last forever.

Anyone old enough to remember England's 1966 World Cup triumph knows all about lasting memories. It was self-evidently English football's greatest moment, and the players who delivered that 4-2 win against Germany at Wembley will long continue to be revered as sporting heroes. And yet the legacy of '66 was, in the eyes of many fans, an expectation that England would always be dining at the same table as world greats such as Brazil, Germany and Italy. To understand quite how unrealistic that turned out to be, you need only to glance at the table below showing England's performance in every major tournament over the *Match of the Day* years. You'll get used to the initialisms DNQ (Did Not Qualify) and LOP (Lost On Penalties). And don't be too enamoured by a third-place finish in the 1968 Euros, because only four countries entered that one.

Such has been the influence of the team's performance on the national psyche that it has on occasions shaped the political landscape. When they failed to defend their World Cup trophy at Mexico '70 (short story: manager Sir Alf Ramsey bizarrely substituted Bobby Charlton in the quarter-final with England two up against Germany, only to see his side lose 3-2) there were ramifications for Prime Minister Harold Wilson. Wilson's Chancellor Roy Jenkins was apparently nonplussed at an electioneering rally in Birmingham when, according to one colleague, 'no question concerned either trade figures or immigration but solely the football and whether Ramsey or Bonetti was the major culprit.' Defence secretary Denis Healey recalled how, two months prior to the tournament, the PM had asked 'whether the government would suffer if the England footballers were defeated on the eve of polling day'. He was right to worry. Four days after England's 14 June capitulation, Wilson suffered a surprise election defeat to Ted Heath's Conservative party. Local government minister Anthony Crosland later attributed this to 'a mix of party complacency and the disgruntled *Match of the Day* millions'.

ENGLAND'S POST-'66 WOES

Tournament (winners)	When eliminated
World Cup 1966 (England)	Champions
Euros 1968 (Italy)	Third out of four
WC 1970 (Mexico)	Quarter-final
Eur 1972 (Belgium)	DNQ
WC 1974 (West Germany)	DNQ
Eur 1976 (Yugoslavia)	DNQ
WC 1978 (Argentina)	DNQ
Eur 1980 (Italy)	Group stage
WC 1982 (Spain)	Second group stage
Eur 1984 (France)	DNQ
WC 1986 (Mexico)	Quarter-final
Eur 1988 (West Germany)	Group stage
WC 1990 (Italy)	Semi-final, fourth place, LOP
Eur 1992 (Sweden)	Group stage
WC 1994 (USA)	DNQ
Eur 1996 (England)	Semi-final, LOP
WC 1998 (France)	Round of 16, LOP
Eur 2000 (Belgium/The Netherlands)	Group stage
WC 2002 (South Korea/Japan)	Quarter-final
Eur 2004 (Portugal)	Quarter-final, LOP
WC 2006 (Germany)	Quarter-final, LOP
Eur 2008 (Austria/Switzerland)	DNQ
WC 2010 (South Africa)	Round of 16
Eur 2012 (Poland/Ukraine)	Quarter-final, LOP

Tournament (winners)	When eliminated
WC 2014 (Brazil)	Group Stage
Eur 2016 (France)	Round of 16
WC 2018 (Russia)	Semi-final, fourth place
Eur 2020 (UEFA countries)	Runners-up, LOP
WC 2022 (Qatar)	Quarter-finals
Eur 2024 (Germany)	Runners-up

As *MOTD* is a glass-half-full programme we're not going to set out details of the DNQs, Round-of-16 eliminations or the duller quarter-final exits. We will reference a few LOPs though, so prepare to relive those painful lasting memories.

England 1966: World Cup Champions

What else is there to say?

Oh, alright then. As hosts, England were among the favourites – after taking charge in 1963 Ramsey announced that 'we will win the World Cup' – yet the team's form was unconvincing. A drawn friendly with Brazil prompted *The Times* to declare that 'Ramsey's men slip even further from world class', while the new manager's first competitive match, the second leg of a 1964 European Championship qualifier, ended in a 5-2 victory for France and elimination. Then, with eight months to go before the start of the World Cup, England were booed off at the end of a 3-2 home defeat to Austria. Singing 'ee, ay, eddio, we're gonna win the Cup' was strictly for the delusional, and Ramsey rang the changes. His solution was the 'wingless wonders', a tactical formation which saw the irrepressible Alan Ball take a prominent midfield role with Nobby Stiles as ball-winner in front of the back four and Bobby Charlton given licence to attack. Flying full-backs George Cohen and Ray Wilson were tasked with providing wing service, a strategy common in today's game but unfamiliar in the early sixties, while Jimmy Greaves, Roger Hunt and Geoff Hurst competed to lead the line.

Against expectations it all seemed to work. After a laboured 0-0 draw with Uruguay, England produced confident 2-0 victories over Mexico and France but suffered a blow when Greaves was injured in the French game, ruling him out of the quarter-final against Argentina. That gave rookie striker Geoff Hurst his chance in a game the South Americans would dub *El robo del siglo* (the Heist of the Century), which quickly degenerated into a foul-fest. When Argentina's captain Antonio Rattín was sent off by German referee Rudolf Kreitlein on 33 minutes he refused to leave. An eight-minute delay while FIFA match officials held a touchline conflab with Argentina's coaches did little to calm tempers and three more *La Albiceleste* went into Kreitlein's book as England secured a 1-0 victory. Afterwards, Rattin claimed the referee 'played with an England shirt on', and seeing as the hosts committed 30 fouls to Argentina's 18, without a single booking, he may have had a point. The one saving grace was Hurst's winner – a flicked header which Bobby Charlton called 'the best England goal I ever saw in my time with the squad.' England went on to beat Portugal 2-1 in the semi-final, a game played with such exemplary conduct that it took almost an hour for the ref to award a foul. Which left the 30 July final and an appointment with West Germany. For the benefit of readers living as hermits in Tibetan caves for the last 58 years, it goes like this:

Greaves is fit but Hurst retains his place because Ramsey doesn't want to change a winning team. Helmut Haller opens the scoring for Germany, Hurst equalises with a header, Peters puts England back in front on 78 minutes then Wolfgang Weber equalises in the 90th. Eleven minutes into extra time, Hurst's fierce shot from eight yards cannons off the inside of the crossbar and, after consultations with Azerbaijani linesman Tofiq Bahramov, Swiss referee Gottfried Dienst awards the goal. Cue a further nineteen minutes of agony for fans of both sides before Hurst completes his hat-trick in the final minute to claim the Jules Rimet Trophy and give BBC commentator Kenneth Wolstenholme his immortal line, 'Some people are on the pitch ... they think it's all over ... it is now.'

Mexico 1970: World Cup Quarter-Final

Revenge is always a dish best served cold and West Germany made sure theirs was positively icy when they met England again in the Estadio Nou Camp, León, on 14 June 1970. For the first hour Ramsey's team enjoyed almost total control, with Alan Mullery and Peters both on the scoresheet. Then the nightmare unfolded. Goalkeeper Peter Bonetti, in for the sick Gordon Banks, allowed a speculative, long-range shot from Franz Beckenbauer to squirm beneath his body. It was a shocker, although Mullery's slow reaction to the German midfielder's run was at least partly to blame. Two minutes later Ramsey hooked the excellent Bobby Charlton, supposedly to 'save him for the semis', and sent on Colin Bell. Then with ten minutes left Martin Peters was pulled off for Norman Hunter, leaving England with a new-look midfield which had to adjust fast. It didn't. West Germany's captain Uwe Seeler equalised almost immediately and in extra time Gerd Müller, one of the greatest strikers ever to grace a football pitch, hit the winner. For England fans, the fondest memory of the tournament occurred during a group stage 1-0 defeat to Brazil which saw Banks make one of the truly memorable World Cup saves. Pelé's rocket downward header bounced up and appeared to have beaten the keeper. Yet, somehow, he arched backwards to deflect the ball over the crossbar. Although lauded for decades afterwards, his effort barely got a reaction from teammates. A pat on the head from Mullery and a passing slap on the backside from Moore was it. This was, after all, Gordon Banks. What did you expect?

Mexico 1986: World Cup Quarter-Final

Back we go to Mexico after sixteen years of epic under-performance. This was a tournament England steadily grew into, raising hopes that they had a genuine chance of making the final. But after a 1-0 defeat to Portugal in their opening Group F game, followed by a tedious 0-0 draw with Morocco, manager Bobby Robson was forced to make two key midfield changes. Talismanic captain Bryan Robson, who had courageously (some would say crazily) played the second of those games in a protective shoulder harness, was out of contention, while the usually cool-headed Ray Wilkins was on a red card ban after chucking the ball at the ref. The manager decided the balance of the team was now so altered that it needed a complete rehash. Winger Chris Waddle and striker Mark Hateley were dropped in favour of Peter Beardsley as Gary Lineker's strike partner while Peter Reid, Steve Hodge and Trevor Steven were brought in. This loose 4-4-2 formation worked a treat in the final must-win group game against a dangerous Poland. Lineker bagged a hat-trick – half his tournament total en route to taking the Golden Boot – and England kicked on to record another 3-0 victory in the Round of 16, this time against Paraguay. That meant a quarter-final against the competition's only unbeaten side, Argentina, a country with whom the UK had been at war only four years previously. Pressure on both sets of players was enormous, which perhaps explains why Argentina had included God – or at least the Hand of God – in their attack. Six minutes after half-time, with the score at 0-0, Hodge's ballooning back-pass into space on the edge of the six-yard box was met by the leaping Diego Maradona, who fisted the ball over an onrushing Peter Shilton into the goal. It was, Diego admitted later, 'a little with the head of Maradona and a little with the hand of God'. Who knew God had exemption from the handball rule? Clearly, Tunisian referee Ali Ben Nasser, because he summarily dismissed England's protests. Four minutes later Maradona showed he didn't need to cheat, collecting the ball in his own half and weaving for 68 yards past five defenders, including Shilton, before rolling the ball into an open net. Lineker's 73rd-minute close-range header wasn't enough to inspire a fightback and Argentina went on to beat Belgium 2-0 in the semis followed by West Germany 3-2 in the final. England were left to rue what might have been.

Italy 1990: World Cup Semi-Final (Penalties)

Until the Italia '90 semi-final against West Germany, England were a labouring side in a World Cup best remembered for Luciano Pavarotti's tear-jerking rendition of *Nessun dorma*. They progressed from the group stage with two goals – one in a drawn game against Jack Charlton's excellent Republic of Ireland side; the other in a narrow victory over Egypt. The third match, a 0-0 draw against the fancied Netherlands, did at least show some defensive nous and England carried that into their Round of 16 game against Belgium where, after 119 minutes of excitement-free football, they produced one of the goals of the tournament as David Platt allowed Paul Gascoigne's floated free kick to drop over his shoulder before swivelling to volley home. The win pitched them into a quarter-final against Cameroon, whose squad was split roughly 50:50 between amateur and professional footballers. The Africans had beaten Argentina, eventual competition winners, in a tasty 1-0 opener and seen off a dangerous Colombia in a game which saw Roger Milla famously celebrate his two goals with a snake-hipped corner flag dance. The Indomitable Lions were the best side England had played by a country mile – Barry Davies described them as 'unbelievably smooth in their movements' – but this didn't stop them being woefully underestimated. Platt's header put England ahead but then a penalty from Emmanuel Kundé and a strike from Eugène Ekéké meant the Africans led with seven minutes to go. Fortunately, the cavalry arrived in time: Lineker converted one penalty to take the game into extra time, then another to win it. Afterwards, manager Bobby Robson was characteristically honest, admitting, 'We pulled it out of the fire. And I don't really know how.'

No matter. It delivered a belter of a semi-final between two of Europe's great footballing rivals. The Germans got lucky with Andreas Brehme's opening goal, a deflection off Paul Parker which sailed agonisingly over Shilton, but then, with ten minutes left and naked tension in the air, Lineker showed his class, ghosting past three defenders to meet a bouncing ball with a left-foot drive for 1-1. Both teams might have sealed it in extra time as shots bounced off the woodwork and there was that heartbreaking moment when Gascoigne was booked, a card which meant he would miss the final if England progressed. Gazza's tears flowed and the abiding memory of the match was a pitch-side camera shot of Lineker grimacing at the bench and pointing to his eyes. The gesture said it all: You need to watch him. The inevitable penalties ensued, Stuart Pearce missed England's fourth, Olaf Thon obliged for the Germans and Chris Waddle had to score to keep the match alive. 'Would you want to be Chris Waddle now, or even Stuart Pearce?' asked John Motson. Waddle skied his kick, England were out and Germany went on to beat Argentina in the final. Brehme later described that game as 'horrible', claimed Argentina 'had a terrible World Cup but a lot of luck', and insisted that England's 'exceptional' squad would have been champions if they had won the semi-final shootout. Thanks for that Andreas, but it didn't help.

England 1996: Euros Semi-Final (Penalties)

It was the 'Cool Britannia' summer of '96. A worldwide boom in British culture and fashion, the Spice Girls leading the charge for girl power, a sport-mad nation hosting the Euros, and a terraces anthem written by two comedians which would ring out at every pub and fan-zone screening England matches:

> *Three Lions on a shirt,*
> *Jules Rimet still gleaming,*
> *Thirty years of hurt,*
> *Never stopped me dreaming.*

The song promised, 'Football's coming home', and for much of this tournament it seemed England really did have a chance of becoming European Champions for the first time. Until, that is, the Germans again spoiled the party from the penalty spot. But we're getting ahead of ourselves.

The opening match against Switzerland started well enough as Alan Shearer, who would go on to win the Golden Boot, put the hosts ahead on 23 minutes. But the Swiss, seen as the weakest team in the group, fought back in the second half to secure a 1-1 draw. That meant the next game, against 'Auld Enemy' Scotland, was a must-not-lose since the Scots had already held the Netherlands to a 0-0 draw. Shearer's second-half header calmed nerves but the game hinged on a 77th minute penalty which gave Gary McAllister the chance to equalise. In such moments sporting history is written. The ball, somehow, moved slightly as he began his run-up, David Seaman saved and within two minutes Gascoigne had conjured up one of the great Wembley international goals, running on to a hopeful Darren Anderton through ball, flicking it over the head of a befuddled Colin Hendry with his left foot before volleying past Andy Goram with his right. It was brilliant and Gazza knew it.

Waving his teammates over to a water bottle positioned on the touchline, he performed a pre-arranged 'dentist's chair' celebration, lying flat on his back while Shearer poured the contents of the bottle onto his face. This was a mischievous response to some awkward press coverage at England's pre-tournament get-together in Hong Kong a few weeks earlier. Players had been photographed at a nightclub participating in the bartenders' celebrated 'dentist's chair' method of serving drinks. This required customers to sit back, mouths gaping, as shots and spirits were poured down their throats – not exactly the kind of prep you'd expect from elite sportsmen. The *Sun* front page headline got straight to the point. 'Disgracefool', it screamed, above a sub-heading which read 'Look at Gazza ... a drunk oaf with no pride.' Whatever fans may have thought at the time, that goal – against Scotland of all teams – brought Gazza absolution. It gave England a huge boost to take into their last group game and they used it to full effect, demolishing the Netherlands 4-1 in what is still seen as one of the national team's greatest performances. The highlight was the third goal. Steve McManaman, Teddy Sheringham and Gascoigne combined to set Shearer free one-on-one with Dutch keeper Edwin van der Sar. In that scenario there was only ever going to be one outcome from a striker regarded by many as the best in the world.

Tournament success generally requires some luck, and in the quarter-final against Spain, England had it in spades. Spain had two decent penalty shouts turned down and two goals disallowed, including one from Julio Salinas which was clearly on-side. The game ended 0-0 after extra time but England banished the ghosts of Italia '90 by winning the penalty shootout 4-2, a moment to cherish for Pearce who stepped up to convert in the knowledge that failure in a second major tournament would have turned him into a pariah. Déjà vu beckoned. The Germans in the semis. Commentator Barry Davies later reflected that

> if somebody told me you are going up to heaven and
> you can take one game with you, I would take that

England [v Germany] game. I'd try to get the result
changed when I got up there though.

Him and Gareth Southgate both. Shearer opened the scoring
and although Stefan Kuntz equalised, momentum and an
impassioned Wembley crowd urged England on. Sheringham
saw a shot cleared off the line, Anderton hit the post and
in Golden Goal extra time, a transitory FIFA experiment in
which first team to score won, Gascoigne was an agonising
toe-poke away. But penalties it was, and after both teams had
exhausted their first-choice takers, and ten kicks had been
securely put away, it fell to Southgate to take the 11th. His
tame shot was saved and England fans embarked on their
biggest hangover for a generation.

1998–2016: World Cup and Euros

You might call this period the Wilderness Years but for the fact
that, aside from 1990 and 1996, England had already been
in the wilderness for quite a few years. After Glenn Hoddle
in 1998 they burned through five full-time managers – Kevin
Keegan, Sven-Göran Eriksson, Steve McClaren, Fabio Capello
and Roy Hodgson – none of whom managed to reach the
semi-finals of a major competition. During these 18 years
England did make two World Cup quarter-finals – South
Korea/Japan 2002 (beaten 2-1 by Brazil) and Germany 2006
(finished 0-0 v Portugal, LOP 3-1) – and also managed two
Euro quarter-finals – Portugal 2004 (finished 2-2 v Portugal,
LOP 6-5) and Poland/Ukraine 2012 (finished 0-0 v Italy, LOP
4-2). The Hodgson years included two of England's most
embarrassing tournament performances. Finishing bottom of
their group in Brazil's 2014 World Cup was bad enough, but

losing 2-1 to Iceland in the France 2016 Euros was the nadir, resulting in Hodgson's resignation at a post-match press conference. It wasn't until after Southgate's appointment as full-time senior team coach in November 2016 that the Three Lions once again began to show their teeth.

Russia 2018: World Cup Semi-Final

Southgate's style of management quickly endeared him to both players and fans. His respectful approach and astute game management forged a squad which felt a world away from the confused tactics and internal tensions which had so dogged England in 2016. Having qualified for Russia undefeated, they racked up eight goals in their first two group games and although Belgium emerged 1-0 victors in the third, both teams had secured entry to the knockout stage. Indeed, England looked to have an easier pathway to the final. Although they had to overcome the mercurial Colombians in the Round of 16, Belgium were now on the same side of the draw as Brazil and France. As it turned out, both European nations would make it through to the semi-finals and Southgate's side enjoyed the added morale boost of beating Colombia 4-3 on penalties – the first time an England side had won a World Cup penalty shootout. They went on to beat Sweden comfortably in the quarters, leaving only Croatia barring the way to their first final in five decades.

For 45 minutes, it seemed they would do it. The Croatians looked jaded after two extra-time wins over Denmark and Russia and Kieran Trippier's perfectly flighted free kick for a 1-0 half-time lead was scant credit for England's superiority. But, never more dangerous than when wounded, Croatia struck back through Ivan Perišić and Mario Mandžukić and somehow tapped reservoirs of mental and physical resilience to see out the win. For England it was hard to take. Yet this team had restored national pride, won the hearts of millions back home and shown what could be achieved. They finished fourth overall after losing to Belgium (again) in the third-place play-off while Croatia went down 4-2 to France in the final. As for Trippier, there was some personal consolation in becoming the unlikely third member of an exclusive club. The only other Englishmen to have scored in a World Cup semi-final were *MOTD*'s own Gary Lineker and the incomparable Bobby Charlton.

Europe 2020: Euros Final (Penalties)

Staged in 11 European countries as part of UEFA's 60th anniversary celebrations, the 2020 Euros were in fact played in 2021 – a casualty of the Covid pandemic. With both the semi-finals and finals due to be staged at Wembley this presented England with a great chance of securing their first major tournament win since 1966, provided they could navigate the early stages successfully. This they did, finishing top of their group with 1-0 wins over both Croatia and the Czech Republic and a 0-0 draw with Scotland. A tricky path to the final then lay ahead but the Three Lions produced a great run of form, beating Germany 2-0 – their first knockout tie victory over the Germans since the glory days of '66 – Ukraine 4-0 and Denmark 2-1 (aet). Goalkeeper Jordan Pickford had a superb tournament, setting a new record for largest number of minutes without conceding (725, five more than Gordon Banks between May and July 1966), while Harry Kane, Raheem Sterling and Harry Maguire were stand-out performers.

England were thrust into the final against an Italian side who had only just scraped through games against Austria and Belgium and who needed penalties to see off Spain. But Italy, past masters of tournament football, were on a 33-match unbeaten run. They recovered from Luke Shaw's second-minute goal to draw level through Leonardo Bonucci in the 67th, then took the game into extra time and penalties. Once again, England were found wanting in the shootout as Marcus Rashford hit a post and both Jadon Sancho and Bukayo Saka saw shots saved. In the end, Roberto Mancini's Italy were worthy winners.

Qatar 2022: World Cup Quarter-Finals

Another World Cup which began with considerable promise and ended in a penalty, though not, this time, a penalty shootout. England finished top of their group, beating Iran 6-2 and Wales 3-0 either side of a mind-numbing 0-0 draw with the USA. They coasted through the Round of 16 with a 3-0 win over Senegal, and in their quarter-final against France they played the better football overall. Aurélien Tchouaméni's opener for Les Bleus was cancelled out by Kane's penalty, equalling Wayne Rooney's record of 53 successful international goals, only for veteran campaigner Olivier Giroud to restore the French lead with 12 minutes to go. Then Mason Mount was fouled in the box, Kane stepped up to take the game into extra time and, to the dismay of English fans at the Al Bayt Stadium, uncharacteristically blazed his kick over the bar. It was agonising for the England captain, a player who prided himself on leading from the front – but whereas Southgate had felt publicly isolated after his miss in 1996, the manager's ethos of team support and unity now shone through.

Nineteen-year-old Jude Bellingham was first to comfort him, showing a maturity beyond his years, while at the final whistle Jordan Henderson, who had been substituted, was at his side, saying nothing but making clear there was no blame. Southgate simply embraced his striker in a gesture which spoke volumes: we win together; we lose together.

Germany – Euros 2024 – final

Ahead of the tournament England were made favourites by some bookies. Their three June performances in Group C – dubbed the 'Group of Dearth' by football writers - soon put paid to that. Nonetheless, a net total of two goals and dreary draws against Denmark and Slovenia saw Southgate's men qualify as group winners. This ensured they avoided hosts Germany in the Round of 16 and instead faced underdogs Slovakia in a game which, but for a sumptuous bicycle kick from Bellingham in the 95th minute, would have sent the Three Lions home with a whimper. As it was, Kane's header in the first minute of extra time proved enough to secure a 2-1 victory and a quarter-final against the Swiss. This Great Escape theme continued over the next two matches. First, courtesy of Saka's superb 80th minute equaliser against Switzerland and five 'perfect penalties' in the subsequent shootout; next through substitute Ollie Watkins stunning 90th-minute semi-final winner against The Netherlands. For a few precious moments, England fans even dared to think their team's name was on the trophy as another super-sub, Cole Palmer, slotted home a 73rd minute equaliser against Spain in the final. Then, with four minutes left, Mikel Oyarzabal, brought on for the tiring Spanish captain Alvaro Morata, poked home Marc Cucurella's cross. True, it was the tightest of calls – Oyarzabal was onside only by virtue of John Stones' kneecap – and England almost managed an unlikely second equaliser as Marc Guéhi's header was cleared off the line. But it was not to be and Spain, Euro 24's stand-out team, thoroughly deserved to be crowned champions. Gareth Southgate, mercilessly criticised over tactics and at one point showered with plastic drinks glasses by a small group of fans, was left to ponder his future and await the inevitable inquest. A message from the King sweetened the pill; 'Although victory may have eluded you this evening, nevertheless my wife and I join all my family in urging you and your support team to hold your heads high'. Many would have echoed those sentiments because the commitment of Southgate's group was never in doubt. And while critics may justifiably argue that he failed to fully tap the potential of his younger players, that surely cannot be the abiding judgement of his tenure. Over eight years, Southgate reforged the link between team and country, developed a culture of decency among his players, made watching England a pleasure (mostly) and embraced the crucial role of mental health in sport. In terms of major tournament results – the only sensible way to judge him – he is the most successful manager since Sir Alf. None of his predecessors reached a final abroad or guided their team to back-to-back finals in a major competition. And while Southgate's side had to qualify for, and play in, seven games at Euro '24, Ramsey's qualified automatically as hosts in 1966 and needed only six games to become world champions. Within hours of losing to Spain such comparisons became the remit of football historians. After consulting his wife, Alison, Southgate resigned. 'As a proud Englishman, it has been the honour of my life to play for England and to manage England,' he wrote in a personal statement. 'It has meant everything to me, and I have given it my all. But it's time for change, and for a new chapter.'

Small Nations – Great Goals

For the nations of Scotland, Wales and Northern Ireland, comparatively small player pools means that even qualifying for a major tournament is an achievement. Northern Ireland's best performance came in the 1982 World Cup when a historic 1-0 victory over Spain saw them emerge from their group with only France standing in the way of a semi-final. Sadly it was not to be, and against a French side orchestrated by Michel Platini they crashed out 4-1. Scotland, while never reaching the knockout stages of a major tournament, can also point to pulling off one of the great upsets. Needing to beat the Dutch by three clear goals to qualify for the Round of 16 at Argentina '78, their midfield general Archie Gemmill put his team 3-1 ahead with a goal still seen as one of the greatest in World Cup history. Gemmill beat four Dutch defenders with four touches before lifting the ball over goalkeeper Jan Jongbloed. The 3-2 final score wasn't quite enough for Ally MacLeod's side to progress, but Gemmill's hero status among 'Ally's Army' of fans was secured. As for Wales, they have recently established themselves as one of international football's most dangerous small nations – reaching the Euros Round of 16 in 2020 and the group stage of the 2022 World Cup. But it was at the 2016 Euros that they punched way above their weight, beating Belgium 3-1 in a quarter-final which saw Hal Robson-Kanu score a goal worthy of any Euros Hall of Fame. After finding space in the Belgian penalty area he executed a 'see-you-later' Cruyff Turn, putting three defenders out of the game, before finishing to Thibaut Courtois' right.

JULY: THE LIONESSES' ROAR

There was no thinking about it. At precisely 7.32pm on Sunday, 31 July 2022, the final whistle blew against Germany and it really was all over. In that moment, the *Match of the Day* camera zoomed in on substitute Chloe Kelly, whose instinctive, toe-poked, poacher's goal with ten minutes of extra time remaining had secured the 2-1 victory which made England Champions of Europe. Now Kelly was sitting on the pitch, hand over her mouth, unsure what to do. Her expression switched briefly between bewilderment and disbelief before settling on unrestrained delight. As predicted in that ubiquitous Three Lions song written to spur on another English team, football had finally come home. But the journey for the Lionesses – and the women's game in general – is far from over.

It seems incredible now, but for half the twentieth century there was an FA ban on women playing at the grounds of affiliated football clubs **(see below)**. It wasn't until 1972 that England Women kicked off their first official game – against Scotland in Greenock – where they recovered from 2-0 down to win 3-2. The scorer of England's opening goal was Sylvia Gore, a pioneer of the modern game, who went on to become a top coach and manager. Her endeavours persuaded the FA to appoint its Northern Regional Director of Coaching, Ted Copeland, as part-time national team manager, and in 1995 he guided England to their first World Cup final qualification.

Copeland was succeeded in 1998 by England's first full-time coach, Hope Powell, an iconic figure in the women's game with 35 goals in 66 appearances. Yet for all her experience (Powell was just 19 when she began studying for a coaching qualification and was the first woman to obtain a UEFA Pro Licence), success continued to elude England. They failed to get out of their Euros group in 2001 and, as hosts, in 2005, evidence that those long years in the wilderness had left a legacy of under-achievement. Other European nations, notably Sweden, Norway, Germany and the Netherlands, had cracked on with developing their women's teams, and it wasn't until Finland's 2009 World Cup that England made their first breakthrough under Powell. They beat the Netherlands 2-1 in the semis courtesy of an extra-time goal from midfield dynamo Jill Scott, who would make the last of her 161 England appearances in extra time at that 2022 Euros final. Although Scott's 2009 team lost 6-2 in the final to a dominant Germany, they had given everyone a glimpse of what was possible. Two years later they reached the last eight of the Germany World Cup, having beaten eventual winners Japan in the group stage. Scott, playing alongside another Euro 2022 hero, Ellen White, and future *MOTD* presenter Alex Scott, scored the opener in a quarter-final

1-1 draw with France. The resulting penalty shoot-out, which England lost 4-3, triggered a very public post-match inquest.

Three of the five penalty-takers were back-four players and one, left-back Claire Rafferty, had only just made her debut after coming on as a sub late in the game. She missed her spot kick, as did central defender and captain Faye White. The reluctance of other players to volunteer for kicks infuriated Powell who, in the highly-charged aftermath of defeat, accused them of cowardice. 'Three times I had to ask [for volunteers] before anyone stepped forward,' Powell told the *Guardian*.

> "Where are you?" I was thinking, and then a young kid [Rafferty] is the first to put her hand up. And Kelly Smith was dying on her feet but she stepped up and took one. You've got to want to take a penalty, but other players should have come forward and they didn't. That's weak, it's cowardice.

Others were more circumspect. 'When Hope asked who'd be prepared to take a penalty no hands went up,' said Casey Stoney, White's centre-back partner.

> But then Claire Rafferty volunteered and after one of our most inexperienced youngsters had stepped forward I felt it was my responsibility as a senior player to do the same. I was surprised and a bit disappointed that more players didn't volunteer. Kelly couldn't even walk but she stepped up, took our first kick and smashed it in – that was inspirational.

Stoney later played down Powell's 'cowardice' comment. 'I don't think any of the players are cowards to be honest,' she told BBC Radio 5 Live.

> That's not the impression I got from Hope. She said
> we should all be proud and keep our heads high so
> I'm not sure where that [comment] came from ...
> it's a situation we'd not been in before and I don't
> think anybody really wanted to take a penalty. But five
> people did.

BBC Sport's online match report of that France match
confirmed Stoney's view, quoting Powell as heralding 'a
gallant effort' from players who had endured tough games
and were 'dead on their feet'. Interestingly, it also referred to
the team as 'England Ladies'. This was the official name for
England Women at the time and was still widely used. But it
was painfully uncool. How was the women's game ever going
to market itself properly when its name seemed synonymous
with well-spoken, well-off types taking tea on the lawn with the
vicar? Things had to change.

There was never a single moment at which England Women
became Lionesses. Rather, it was a slow burn, a nickname
occasionally used in copy by the odd journalist or staff
member working with the team. But a revolution was coming.
On 17 June 2012 England had a crucial Euros fixture against
the Netherlands as they sought automatic qualification for
Sweden 2013. The FA couldn't find a suitable, dedicated
football ground so the game was played at the Salford
Community Stadium, home of rugby union's Sale Sharks
and rugby league's Salford Red Devils. To the tiny team of FA
employees working with the women, it felt like Hope Powell's
side was an afterthought. England Men were playing in the
Poland-Ukraine 2012 European Championships that week and
had cornered most of the publicity. It could be argued this was

fair enough – the men were, after all, playing in the finals – but why shouldn't the women get more attention?

Ahead of the Netherlands game, which England won 1-0 through a cheeky Rachel Yankey free kick, FA marketing staff started using the hashtag #Lionesses on Twitter/X. Every member of the squad and backroom staff were encouraged to join in, and soon #Lionesses was trending fourth in the UK. For the first time, the FA was officially describing England Women as Lionesses. It would prove transformational but, like all new brands, it would take time to cut through. And of course, the Lionesses still had to produce the goods on the pitch. England went into Sweden 2013 as the fourth-ranked team, attracting a million viewers for each of their group games. But they crashed and burned. Defeats to France and Spain saw them finish bottom of the group and only an extra-time goal from Toni Duggan in a 1-1 draw with rank outsiders Russia saved them from a three-match whitewash. Two months later, Powell was sacked. Alex Horne, the FA's general secretary, paid tribute to her 'commitment to developing the national teams over such a long period', but stated, 'After the disappointment of the recent tournament in Sweden, the Club England board believe the time is right to make a change and for a fresh outlook.'

That fresh outlook was Welshman Mark Sampson who would justify his appointment by steering the Lionesses to their first World Cup semi-final. At Canada 2015 England took on holders Japan, only to be denied a place in the final in the cruellest of circumstances. After each side scored from poor penalty decisions, Japan won through a freak own goal in the second minute of injury time as Laura Bassett's block ballooned over keeper Karen Bardsley, struck the crossbar and bounced inside the goal line. It was hard on an England side which had created the best chances and looked favourites to go on and win. They finished the tournament as bronze medallists, beating Germany 1-0 in the third-place play-offs, but any disappointment was soon tempered by the reaction of millions of fans back home. As the FA's director of women's football Kelly Simmons put it, England had 'fallen in love with the Lionesses'. It was great momentum for Sampson's squad to take into the Netherlands 2017 and they did not disappoint – running deep into the expanded 16-nation Euros with three group stage wins over Scotland, Spain and Portugal, and a 1-0 quarter-final victory over France which saw Jodie Taylor's angled strike give England their first win against Les Bleues in 43 years. It meant Sampson had become the first England manager since Sir Alf Ramsey to reach the semi-finals of two consecutive major tournaments, and there was a belief that they could go the distance. But it was not to be. Despite their status as the competition's highest-ranked team, the Lionesses were beaten 3-0 by a technically superior host nation who took full advantage of defensive errors. The Dutch, coached by a certain Sarina Wiegman, went on to win the tournament in a pulsating 4-2 final against Denmark, while England returned home to prepare for the 2019 World Cup in France. But there was trouble ahead.

Sampson believed he had put aside safeguarding allegations relating to his time at Bristol Academy, where he'd worked in the centre of excellence and become senior first team coach. Indeed, after these surfaced in March 2014, the FA's safeguarding and investigations team deemed he was fit to continue as England manager. When, in 2016, Sampson was accused of bullying and discrimination by England and Chelsea forward Eniola Aluko, he was again cleared by FA investigators. But a whistleblower prompted the governing body's chief executive Martin Glenn, who had joined a year after the Bristol inquiry, to read the full 2014 report alleging inappropriate relationships between the Welshman and female players. As England prepared to face Russia in the first of their France 2019 qualifiers on 19 September, the media was alive with rumours about Sampson's future, although none of this chimed with his squad. After scoring the first of their six goals against Russia at Birkenhead's Prenton Park, all eleven players – including goalkeeper Siobhan Chamberlain – sprinted to the dugout to embrace him. It was a powerful show of support, but neither Glenn nor FA chairman Greg Clarke was swayed, and Sampson was sacked the following day.

Sampson's replacement was Phil Neville, a distinguished professional who had played 59 times for England Men and posted 505 league appearances for Manchester United and Everton. Neville had no frontline managerial experience, but held respect, credibility, a UEFA Pro Licence and a reputation for working collaboratively. He took over on 23 January 2018 with the aim of leading the Lionesses into the 2019 World Cup and the home Euros in 2021. In-between these tournaments he was nailed on to manage Team GB at the 2020 Tokyo Olympics. He could not have known that the Covid pandemic would shred the later part of that timetable, with Tokyo pushed back to 2021 and the Euros to 2022, nor the effect it would have on his team's development. But results over his first eighteen months in charge were excellent. In the 2018 SheBelieves Cup, an annual four-nation invitational staged in the US, the Lionesses beat France 4-1, drew 2-2 with Germany and lost only narrowly to the United States. After qualifying undefeated for France 2019, they returned to the US to win the 2019 SheBelieves, beating Brazil 2-1, drawing with the United States and seeing off Japan 3-0.

On this kind of form, England were serious contenders for the World Cup and in the early stages of the tournament they were on fire, finishing top of their group, beating Cameroon 3-0 in the Round of 16 and then Norway with an identical result in the quarter-finals. The stage was set for a semi-final against the United States which would mark one of the Lionesses' finest performances. Ellen White's first-half strike had kept them in the game and when she found the net a second time it seemed they had the momentum. But VAR disallowed her goal for an offside toe, United States keeper Alyssa Naeher saved a Steph Houghton penalty, Millie Bright was sent off for a second bookable offence and the reigning world champions closed out a 2-1 win. They would go on to retain their crown. Nonetheless, this was the high point of Neville's tenure. His players had produced the second-highest pass completion rate – 79.9% – of any team at France 2019 having posted the second-lowest – 59.8% – at Canada 2015. They had proved themselves world-class and left nothing on the pitch. Sadly, it was about to unravel.

In March 2020 England returned from a disappointing SheBelieves Cup to a country on the cusp of a lockdown. Within weeks, both the Olympics and the Euros were put back a year, leaving the Lionesses with no meaningful matches. As host country for the 2022 Euros they had automatic qualification, and few international sides were interested in friendlies with the pandemic raging. Their form had also dipped badly: since that disappointing semi-final against the United States they had lost seven out of eleven games, their worst run of defeats for 17 years. On 22 April, Neville announced he would not be renewing his contract when it expired in July 2021. In the event, he left on 18 January 2021 and Norwegian coach Hege Riise was appointed caretaker until Sarina Wiegman could take over as new Lionesses manager eight months later.

Wiegman's record ahead of England's home Euros was impressive. Her team was victorious in all ten of their 2023 World Cup qualifiers, scoring 80 goals and conceding none, and won the invitational Arnold Clark Cup by beating Germany 3-1 in the final round of games. In the Euros they cruised to the quarter-finals, but then had to rely on a Georgia Stanway extra-time winner to overcome a formidable Spain side. The semis were comfortable by comparison – England thrashed the fancied Swedes 4-0 to set up that climactic showdown with Germany and cement their place on the world stage as European Champions – a title they would seek to defend at the 2025 Euros in Switzerland. Yet, while their triumph initially ramped up public expectations for Sydney 2023, there was a tacit acknowledgement among fans and players that a tough World Cup lay ahead.

In truth, the Lionesses would overperform in their run to the final. Their warm-up matches suggested variable form while three of Wiegman's starting XI in 2022 – Beth Mead, Leah Williamson and Fran Kirby – were absent through long-term injury. Add to that Ellen White's retirement and Rachel Daly's conversion from left-back to striker, and it was clear England would need a leg-up from the footballing gods. That they came so close is itself a tribute although few would deny that, on the day, Spain were worthy champions. As Wiegman put it afterwards: 'Most of all I feel disappointment because when you play a final you want to win it ... Spain played a little better than we did. The opponent was very strong.' Disappointment at the result, yes. But disappointment at this transformative, inspirational group of players? Never. The memories will be all about that July day at Wembley: England players rushing to embrace Jill Scott and Ellen White, veterans who had waited so long to win a major trophy; captain Leah Williamson consoling Germany's Lena Oberdorf; Chloe Kelly abandoning a BBC interview to join her team and an entire stadium singing a chorus of 'Sweet Caroline'; and, afterwards, players (led by their irrepressible keeper Mary Earps) gatecrashing Wiegman's press conference for an impromptu jig of joy.

It was a celebration at least a century overdue. For decades, women have fought an establishment view that they shouldn't be playing football. Although during the First World War they had performed complex and dangerous work in chemical and munitions factories, provided labour for heavy industry and on occasions died on active service, the thought of a woman getting a kick in the shins was, for some, too dreadful to contemplate. Fortunately, the establishment was largely ignored. There had been a boom in women's football during the war years and many thousands of pounds was raised through charity matches in aid of the war wounded. In 1917 a works team at Preston ammunitions factory Dick, Kerr & Co. started playing tea-break kickabouts against their apprentices and, under the management of back-office clerk Alfred Frankland, challenged and defeated the factory's men. A report in the *Lancashire Daily Post* described the Dick, Kerr Ladies as having 'a better all-round understanding of the game' than their opponents, and praised their attacking play as 'often surprisingly good, one or two of the ladies showing quite admirable ball control.' That Christmas, Dick, Kerr Ladies beat Arundel Coulthard Factory 4-0 in a match at Preston North End's Deepdale Stadium watched by a 10,000-strong crowd. Three years later they played an international series against a French team before taking on St Helens in a much-hyped Boxing Day encounter at Goodison. On 27 December 1920 the *Lancashire Evening Post* reported that

> The most remarkable 'gate' of the holiday ... was at Goodison Park yesterday morning where the Dick, Kerr Ladies beat St Helens Ladies 4–0 in a match on behalf of the unemployed and disabled ex-service men. The attendance was estimated at 53,000 and the receipts were over £3,000 exclusive of tickets [equivalent to around £110,000 in 2024].

Far from celebrating the expansion of the game, the blazer brigade at the FA, along with establishment politicians, looked on in horror. In her book *A Woman's Game: The Rise, Fall and Rise Again of Women's Football*, Suzanne Wrack points out that the FA also feared a conflict of interest with the men's game. In 1920 they had expanded men's leagues, doubling the number of clubs, with a Division Three North and South. Those clubs needed decent gate money to survive. But if they were competing against women's matches pulling huge crowds, how could they? In response to the Goodison game, the FA's Consultative Committee issued a ruling designed to halt the bandwagon.

> Complaints having been made as to football being played by women, Council felt impelled to express

the strong opinion that the game of football is quite unsuitable for females and should not be encouraged. Complaints have also been made as to the conditions under which some of the matches have been arranged and played, and the appropriation of receipts to other than charitable objects. The Council are further of the opinion that an excessive proportion of the receipts are absorbed in expenses and an inadequate percentage devoted to charitable objects. For these reasons the Council requests the Clubs belonging to the Association refuse the use of their grounds for such matches.

When that didn't go well the FA tried other tricksy ways to make it difficult for clubs to let women use their grounds. Teams had to seek FA permission, and were required to provide accounts after every game to show where profits had gone. When that too failed, the FA hit the panic button. It couldn't take the women's balls away, so it opted for the next best thing – hijacking their pitches. On 5 December 1921 the FA Council banned women from playing on all grounds belonging to its member clubs.

Wrack's research reveals a mixed reaction. At that historic Council meeting a statement was read from a Major Cecil Kent of Liverpool, former honorary secretary of Old Westminsters FC, who claimed the women's game had raised £100,000 for charity in two years. 'I have heard nothing but praise for the good work the girls are doing and the high standard of their play,' he wrote.

The only thing I now hear from the man in the street is: Why has the FA got their knife into girls' football?

> What have the girls done except to raise large sums
> for charity and to play the game? Are their feet heavier
> on the turf than the men's feet?

Dick, Kerr Ladies captain Alice Kell was also bewildered. 'We girls play football in a proper spirit. We do not retaliate if we are bowled over, and we show no fits of temper,' she told the press.

> We are all simply amazed at the action of the
> authorities in placing a ban upon the sport we love
> with all our heart. Surely to goodness we have the
> right to play any game we think fit without interference
> from the Football Association. We are all working girls,
> dependent upon our weekly wages and living with our
> parents and others partly dependent upon us.

Some newspapers, though, enthusiastically backed the ban. The *Hull Daily Mail*'s op-ed in support struck a tone of pompous relief:

> It is to be feared that some, at least among the crowd,
> went in order to see the women 'make exhibitions of
> themselves.' It does not follow that the women did so,
> but it is far more certain that medical opinion, on the
> whole, is against the practice. Hockey is as vigorous a
> game as our girls and women should go in for.

No wonder the road to that 2022 Euros triumph was long. But the Lionesses have left a legacy worth every step. *MOTD* presenter Gabby Logan's closing line from Wembley – 'They think it's all over? It's only just begun' – was one for the ages. It envisages a future in which the women's game takes its rightful place in grassroots and elite sport. And it hints at the formidable barriers ahead. Let's start with the optimism.

Firstly, the Lionesses' success ignited a love affair with England's sporting public. People recognised how hard this team worked to gain respect and credibility, their steel and footballing technique, their sense of teamwork and togetherness and the general joie de vivre with which they played. Maybe it won't always be so; maybe these are still their salad days. But even if that's true, the players have already grasped the nettle as standard-bearers for women's football. Hours after winning the Euros, as they headed to Trafalgar Square on a bus to celebrate with fans, defender Lotte Wubben-Moy persuaded all 23 members of the squad to sign a letter to both prime-ministerial candidates urging them to give girls equal access to school football. It would have been a brave or foolish candidate who denied a busload of national treasures that request, yet it wasn't immediately embraced. Behind the scenes, team members had to cajole and lobby in private meetings with politicians and advisers to ensure everyone understood this was no idle whim. Not until 8 March 2023, International Women's Day, did the UK government finally confirm that schools would deliver a minimum of two hours physical education per week with girls having equal access to all school sport, including football. Long-term, this was a victory bigger than anything achieved on Wembley's hallowed turf.

Secondly, there's a been a proven upsurge of interest in the women's game. The 2023 World Cup final between England and Spain attracted a peak audience of 12 million viewers on BBC1, with a further 3.9 million viewing on BBC iPlayer and the BBC Sport website. Compare that with the 11.3 million audience for the men's Wimbledon final between Novak Djokovic and Carlos Alcaraz the same year. At club level, attendances are also hitting record highs. The opening game of the 2023 Women's Super League saw 54,115 fans inside Emirates Stadium to watch Arsenal's 1-0 defeat to Liverpool, 7,000 more than the previous WSL record.

Then there's the prospect of two upcoming international tournaments which could give the Lionesses, and women's football generally, a further leg-up. Assuming they qualify for the 2025 Euros – and at the time of writing that's not a given – England will defend their European Champions title in Switzerland before embarking on the road to Brazil's 2027 World Cup, a tournament certain to rank among the biggest sporting events of the year. By then, girls who watched their heroes beat Germany at Wembley will themselves be professional footballers in a women's game hitting new performance levels, by virtue of the sheer numbers involved at grassroots level. If 2022 was a breakthrough year, 2027 holds the promise of growth on a once unimaginable scale.

And yet, and yet. Professional football remains largely locked in a world where men pull the levers of change, and big business dictates when that happens. Take wage structures. While England men and women have earned the same £2,000 international match fee since 2020, at club level there's a pay chasm. During the 2021–22 season Lionesses captain Leah Williamson reportedly earned around £200,000 – almost eight times the average UK salary, but still less than her male counterpart Harry Kane earned in a single week. And Kane was not even the highest-paid footballer in the English game. That accolade went to Manchester United's Cristiano Ronaldo, who pocketed £400,000 a week. According to a BBC analysis at the time, the average WSL player earned £47,000 per year,

a figure based on published financial reports from 7 of the
12 WSL clubs, while best estimates of the average Premier
League salary by management consultants Deloitte put the
male equivalent at 100 times more. This astonishing disparity
is partly created by our old friends Profit and Sustainability –
rules restricting how much clubs are allowed to pay players
– and the respective profits generated by the men's and
women's game. In the 2020–21 season, Manchester City's
title-winning men's team reported a turnover of £571 million.
They spent £354 million on players' wages, which works out at
£11.8 million per player across the 30-man squad. By contrast,
City's WSL operations turned over £2.9 million that season,
averaging out at around £75,000 per head when distributed
among a 44-strong squad and staff.

Following the filthy lucre is one thing. But it's only one aspect
of the yawning equality gap. When Spain's all-time top scorer
Jenni Hermoso stepped on to the podium with her 2023
World Cup-winning teammates, she was forcibly kissed full
on the lips by Spanish Federation chief Luis Rubiales. He later
resigned after admitting it was 'completely wrong'. But the
damage had been done and icons of the women's game, such
as US star Megan Rapinoe, wasted no time highlighting a
culture in which women were 'playing two games at the same
time'. As Rapinoe put it: 'One, we're playing all against each
other. And then the other one, we're all playing together to win
equality and progress and what we deserve.'

It is an injustice evident in comments at the very highest
level of the football establishment. Ahead of the 2023 World
Cip, FIFA president Gianni Infantino gave a news conference
in which he appeared to tell 'all the women' that it was up

to them to bring about change. 'Pick the right battles,' he advised, 'pick the right fights. You have the power to change. You have the power to convince us men what we have to do and what we don't have to do. You do it. Just do it. With men, with FIFA, you will find open doors. Just push the doors.'

Oh dear. One leading UK newspaper columnist called this diatribe 'patronising women beyond belief', *MOTD*'s own Gabby Logan described it as 'ridiculous and reductive', while commentator Jacqui Oatley called it simply 'nonsense'. Players were equally scathing. Norway forward Ada Hegerberg posted on social media that she was 'working on a little presentation to convince men.'

What's clear is that investment in women's football needs to be more ambitious and far-reaching, with the richest clubs particularly stepping up. Within the UK the Lionesses have a major advantage, courtesy of England's population size, its pool of players and the preponderance of professional teams. The three other women's national football teams have seen huge strides in recent years, but it remains hard for them to compete on the world stage. Scotland made debut appearances at the 2017 Euros and 2019 World Cup but were eliminated at the group stage in both tournaments. Wales came as close as they had ever come to World Cup qualification in 2022 but lost 2-1 in a play-off game against Switzerland, thanks to a last-minute extra-time winner. And although Northern Ireland made it to their first major tournament, the 2022 Euros, they failed to get out of their group. The potential for all three of these nations is obvious. The financial backing, not so much.

AND FINALLY ... FOOTBALL'S FUTURE

Equality gap aside, the big calls facing professional football are common to both the men's and women's game. On the pitch, refereeing will inevitably become increasingly influenced by evolving technology and the demand for correct decisions in games where vast fortunes are at stake. With the rise of artificial intelligence software, will we even need a human VAR or on-field human ref, and could a robot actually improve the much vaunted 'fan experience'? Anyone who has seen the sci-fi fantasy film *Robocop* might be tempted to think so, as they watch gesticulating players aggressively surrounding a referee to complain about perceived failings (with a Robocop Ref, modelled on the film's ruthless eponym, that might not end well). AI can already improve, or at least speed up, objective decisions such as handball or offside, but subjective calls – say, push-and-shove in the penalty area, or the difference between a yellow and red card tackle – are harder. But not impossible. Things move fast in the world of big tech, and Germany's 2024 Euros were the most cutting edge yet. They deployed semi-automated offside technology (SAOT) using ten specialised cameras to track 29 body points on every player. This worked alongside AI software which pinpointed those players' positions on the pitch through every game and connected ball technology (CBT), which did the same with the football. The upshot was that a VAR could immediately identify point-of-ball-contact for offences such as offside and handball. Meanwhile, an upgraded version of GLT (goal line technology) produced images generated by seven cameras per goalmouth to track a ball's movement. These are impressive innovations although you can't help but wonder whether Arsène Wenger, a senior member of FIFA's Football and Technical Advisory Panel, has a simpler solution – at least where offside is concerned. He wants a new interpretation of the rule, such that there must be clear daylight, not a toenail or a nipple's-worth of player, between attacker and last defender. In other words, a clear and obvious offence. There would need to be a few caveats – a player wouldn't, for instance, be able to thrust a trailing arm back 'onside' when receiving the ball in an offside position – but overall, the clear daylight interpretation would make life easier for the VAR, speed up decision-making and give a slight advantage to attacking players. Over many games this should produce more goals which is, after all, the point.

Wenger's plan is a common-sense tweak rather than a major shift in the refereeing of games. But there are some far-reaching proposals on the radar of the International FA Board, which oversees the rules of the game, such as the Premier League's request to approve temporary 'ten-minute' substitutes for players needing a head injury assessment. Few would argue with this precaution – already established in rugby – because the dangers of concussion are well known. However, there are also controversial ideas in the mix. These include a blue card which refs would brandish as punishment for dissent, resulting in players being 'sin-binned' for ten minutes, and cooling-off periods (COPs) to be triggered if teams collectively lose their tempers and start a free-for-all. COPs could see players sent to their own penalty areas to have a word with themselves, although you wonder how fans, already frustrated by VAR delays, would react to watching 22 highly paid pros milling about for ten minutes while feigning victimhood. As for blue cards, Infantino made clear in 2024 that 'there will not be any blue cards used at elite level. This is a topic that is non-existent for us. FIFA is completely opposed to blue cards.'

Off the field, the big challenges facing clubs revolve around governance and, inevitably, money. Many do a great job as community stalwarts, encouraging grassroots football and acting as a cohesive force for fans. But most smaller clubs struggle without a robust business plan, and even those that find one have to peddle hard to stay still. The received wisdom baked into the football economy ever since *Match of the Day* took its first steps into broadcasting history is that well-run clubs increase turnover, allowing them to buy better players, who bring success. which further increases turnover, and so on until they become a 'big club'. Would that it were so simple. In fact, big clubs stay big because they have the resources and fan base to generate cash. Smaller rivals, however well run, are eventually destined to be also-rans. Leicester and Blackburn achieved incredible things by becoming Premier League Champions, but they're exceptions that prove the rule. Neither obtained a permanent place at the top table, and both were relegated as their best players sought bigger rewards elsewhere. You can't blame the players for that. But neither can you claim current league structures are fair.

Which brings us to Manchester City and its legal action, launched in June 2024, to end the Premier League's policy on Associated Party Transactions. This, remember, is a different dispute to the one in which the Premier League charged Manchester City with 115 breaches of Profit and Sustainability Rules. But the two are inextricably linked and they surely herald further club-v-league spats. We touched on the principles of PSR – essentially, that clubs can spend only what they can afford – on **page 190**. APT rules, meanwhile, state that clubs mustn't inflate commercial deals struck with companies linked to their owners, or player transfer fees between clubs from the same 'ownership group'. The incentive to boost such transactions is, of course, to show more profit and therefore be allowed to spend more on players within the confines of PSR. Manchester City's argument is that APT restrictions are unlawful under the Competition Act 1998 and have been drummed up by fellow league members to curb City's success on the pitch, a tactic they have reportedly described in skeleton legal arguments as the 'tyranny of the majority'. As this book goes to print, both the PSR and APT independent arbitrations remain ongoing.

Ongoing. A word you'll often hear when football goes to war with itself. Even when you think a bust-up has been settled it somehow rises up again like that scary, indestructible band of skeleton warriors in *Jason and the Argonauts*. Take the 2021 Super League fiasco, in which the supposed 'Big Six' – Manchester City, Manchester United, Arsenal, Chelsea, Liverpool and Tottenham Hotspur – tried to create a new competition in partnership with 'big clubs' in Europe, fronted by the Spanish sports consultancy A22. As public relations train crashes go, this one was right up there with the most cringeworthy in the history of football. It collapsed inside 48 hours. The 15 founder clubs, who ludicrously planned to make themselves immune from relegation, faced an outpouring of fan fury in the UK and warnings from UEFA and FIFA that any participating club would face sanctions. The UK government said its proposed independent regulator for English football would 'stop clubs from joining any similar breakaway competitions in the future', while the Premier League announced a 35-point penalty for any member club which tried to do the same in future. Game over, surely, you might think.

And you'd be wrong. In football politics the game's never over if money is in play. On 21 December 2023 the European Court of Justice handed down a ruling stating that while new football competitions should be authorised by UEFA and FIFA, 'there is a basis for the possible abuse of their dominant position by the governing bodies.' It continued:

> The FIFA and UEFA rules making any new inter-club football project subject to their prior approval, such as the Super League, and prohibiting clubs and players from playing in those competitions, are unlawful. There is no framework for the FIFA and UEFA rules ensuring that they are transparent, objective, non-discriminatory and proportionate.

Companies behind the doomed 2021 Super League plan, who brought the case, immediately claimed victory and within an hour A22 announced a revised plan for a 64-team competition structured in three leagues – Star (16 teams), Gold (16 teams) and Blue (32 teams) – with annual promotion and relegation and an end-of-season knockout to determine league champions. This would effectively replace the Champions League and fulfil the ambitions of rebels led by Real Madrid and Barcelona, who want more money-spinning fixtures as a way of narrowing the financial gulf between the Premier League and the rest of Europe. Yet, while the ECJ judgement was binding within the EU, it created little certainty. Post-Brexit, the UK is not obliged to follow ECJ rulings, and UEFA pointed out that, in any case, the court had not validated or endorsed a Super League. Rebel clubs who joined it would still need approval if they wished to remain in the existing system. As for the six English clubs, they all pledged allegiance to UEFA (to varying degrees), and without them a Super League, albeit one including Real Madrid and Barcelona, would be barely worth the name. UEFA insisted it had already changed its 2021 rules to comply with European law, while president Aleksander Čeferin was scathing about the reworked A22 proposal. 'They can create whatever they want,' he said. 'I hope they start their fantastic competition as soon as possible, with two clubs. I hope they know what they are doing but I am not so sure about that.' His scepticism may be justified. It's also likely that English clubs will find it much harder to walk away if an independent football regulator is established. The legislation to set this up ran out of parliamentary time following the announcement of the UK's July 2024 general election, but both main parties remain committed to the principle.

Fans must sometimes wonder how it's come to this. The simple game – the beautiful game – shouldn't be ruled by politicians, entrepreneurs, technocrats and lawyers. Football is loved for its action, goals, skills, drama, passion and a little banter among friends. Fortunately, there's a fans' refuge where these are still the only things that count. It's been there ever since Phil Chisnall kicked off at Anfield back on 22 August 1964. It's *Match of the Day*. Here's to the next 60 years.

INDEX

Page numbers in **bold** refer to tables.

ACKNOWLEDGEMENTS

Sincere thanks to former MOTD editor and author Paul Armstrong for his invaluable comments and input. To Sam Finkelstein for his forensic fact-checking and text-editing. And finally, to Phoebe Lindsley, my editor at Penguin Random House, for her unswerving support and encouragement.